REPORTING YORKSHIRE

250 years of the Yorkshire Post

Written and edited by Michael Hickling

Designed by Robin Turton

YORKSHIRE POST

The story of the newspaper

Features

God's own country   10

The creative spirit   40

Coastal views   62

Cricket heroes   98

Special reports   122

A Yorkshire Post publication
in association with
Great Northern Books
PO Box 213, Ilkley, LS29 9WS

Copyright © Yorkshire Post 2004

ISBN: 1 905080 00 X

Printed by
The Amadeus Press, Cleckheaton

British Cataloguing in Publication Data
A catalogue for this book is available from the British Library

Introduction

The *Yorkshire Post* is known and respected throughout the world and we are proud to celebrate 250 years of commitment and service to our region. This book, published on our anniversary, reveals how the newspaper became woven into the fabric of Yorkshire life. It's a colourful and absorbing story.

The world was a very different place in 1754 when our predecessor, the *Leedes Intelligencer,* first appeared. Its style was quite different from what we expect today. That changed with the times, but the reputation for integrity and honest reporting endured. This is the bedrock on which the newspaper's authority has been built and the reason why its voice is heard by the powerful beyond the bounds of Yorkshire. We will continue to build on this unique heritage as we look forward to serving the people of Yorkshire in the centuries to come.

Chris Green,
Managing Director, Yorkshire Post Newspapers

Certainly this is a record of the *Leedes Intelligencer*-cum-*Yorkshire Post*, but it is much more – a veritable panorama of a lot of Yorkshire and some of Britain over the period. It is the story of a remarkable newspaper, as remarkable, I contended, as any in the world and one which has punched much more than might have been perceived its weight in national and international affairs. The book revealingly tracks the progress of the printed word and the explosion in the role of the media through three millennia. It is a robust presentation of Yorkshire, its glorious acres, its coastline, its distinctive people and their achievements, of events that have cheered and those that have disturbed.

Sir Gordon Linacre
President, Yorkshire Post Newspapers

1 A newspaper is born

In the beginning was a wedding. Mary Bridges married Robert Benson at St Peter's church in Leeds in the summer of 1754. She was *"an agreeable young lady with every charm to make the married state happy,"* reported the *Leedes Intelligencer* in issue Number One.

The start of a newspaper is a rare event. These days, months of intensive market research, detailed planning, editorial visions and marketing revisions precede a paper's launch around which a carefully orchestrated publicity campaign plays at maximum volume.

The *Intelligencer* arrived matter-of-factly into a quieter world. It had been set up in Leeds and would sell weekly in places like Bradford, Halifax, Huddersfield, Elland, Ripponden, Otley and Wakefield which then as now must have seethed with potential news among the daily gossip about bad beer,

illicit sex and the price of fish. Local stories and local people are the lifeblood of a paper, in the modern jargon, its unique selling point.

If the first purchasers of *Intelligencer* Number One picked it up hoping to read more about what was happening on the patch beyond Mary Bridges, then bad luck. This four line paragraph was the sole local news item.

With no illustration of the happy couple available, the writer editorialised about Mary Bridges's charms (it became a standard formula in the paper) when in all likelihood he knew nothing about her. The editor put the wedding under a bold 2nd July date-line – the Tuesday his new paper hit the streets – even though it had taken place the previous Thursday. The presentation suggests that from the outset, Griffith Wright possessed the newspaperman's instinct for polishing up thin stories on a slow day.

A printing shop with a wooden press

All days were slow in 1754: no phones, faxes, internet, radio or laptops delivered the torrent of information which almost engulfs today's newsrooms. There was no prompting from a television in the corner permanently switched on to rolling Sky News. Griffith Wright, a beginner in the newspaper business, was relying almost entirely on news-despatches from London. He had to take only a few steps from his printing premises in the narrow Lower Headrow into the broad thoroughfare of Briggate to meet the mails as they galloped into town and drew into the yard of the Old King's Arms.

Griffith Wright had decided on Tuesday, 2nd July for the start of his new enterprise, market day. It was when people – especially the cloth merchants – had money to spread about on high-priced items like a newspaper. As his first publication date neared, the mails rolled into Leeds on the 25th, 27th and 29th June. It was touch-and-go whether they arrived safe and on time. Leeds was off the main north-south route; the local roads were wretched and infested with highwaymen and footpads.

The news out of London wending its way to the West Riding was weeks old but Griffith Wright was prepared to print it wholesale. The result does not read comfortably today. A glance at his first front page (or at any paper of the time) is enough. Eye-strainingly dense columns of print, each column running to 700 words, march up and down the page. Using what looks to us like the letter "f" for an "s" does not make it any easier for modern eyes (18th century readers also complained from time to time about the size of the type).

Modern journalism requires crispness and concision. Griffith Wright's style was the opposite. His page one preface, addressed to "gentlemen – and others" sets out his stall in a windy 1,300 words.

The first issue's story selection suggests an extraordinary Yorkshire appetite for news from abroad. The front page stories are all foreign: one from Poland, three from Germany and two from France. The only passing British interest on the front page comes from a report from the Hague where the Earl of Cardigan and Lord Brudenel have reportedly arrived. Griffith Wright missed a trick here. These two aristocrats had local Leeds connections. Today, an alert newsdesk

The *Leedes Intelligencer* No.1, Tuesday 2nd July 1754

would expect to pick out that sort of significant detail in foreign agency copy and flesh out the bare-bones of the information into a more rounded story.

Turning the page on Issue Number One, *Intelligencer* readers would discover that in Leghorn, tagged in brackets *"a town in Italy"* the "Malcontents" had taken Bastia. In St Petersburg, *(the capital of Russia)* Catherine the Great was forbidding the export of timber. From Rome *(a city in Italy)* the hot news concerned the Pope who had instructed a gentleman of his bedchamber to inquire after the health of the Chevalier de St George. Below this item, a finger symbol points to the next line in italics, *"Yesterday it was reported that the Chevalier is dead."* It is hard to believe anyone was waiting breathlessly for this in Leeds. But reporting portentously on the death of an "important" figure to readers who never knew he was alive in the first place is an old newspaper trick.

The writing is flat but the difficulty and cost of delivering these despatches to Yorkshire lent them lustre and significance. The foreign emphasis would flatter readers, implying they were sufficiently cosmopolitan to appreciate the fine detail of Vatican politics – although the need to add, in brackets, *(a city in Italy)* to the copy from Rome rather gives that game away.

Nationally, 1754 wasn't the newsiest time to start a paper. Not a lot had happened since the excitement nine years before when the soldiers of Bonnie Prince Charlie marched south for the Stuart cause and reached Derby while 16,000 of the King's troops with foreign mercenaries camped for a couple of nights in Leeds ready for battle. Many in the town had fled in alarm. Now George II's realm was quiet, even if the outward placidity was deceptive.

The pages of the *Intelligencer* are a stark contrast to the visual drama essential for modern newspapers. The organising principle Griffith Wright followed seems crude now: he just stitched together the news as it arrived in date sequence and laid it out, carpet-like, across his four pages. A reader had to look for the latest stories at the back of the newspaper since they had come in the last despatches. Almost buried in the thicket of type are occasional disreputable stories about the lower orders which make better reading than the continental itinerary of toffs. The choicest is from Scotland where a minister, *"has run off with a young woman...and left behind a wife and small family to bewail his unreasonable amour and elopement."*

Today's reader would expect a fuller treatment: the minister's pleading for forgiveness, the wife's chagrin, the mistress's defiance. A reporter would be assigned to doorstep the main players, get the quotes and ask on the readers' behalf the who, what, where and why.

Readers now open their paper expecting it to reflect opinion, provide editorials, report on events and meetings, interview celebs, advise about sex and chilblains; where to eat, how to stay fit, what to drink and the car to drive. Above all, they demand immediacy.

Given these omissions, the bleak monotony of the pages, the lack of headlines and typographical emphasis, how did Griffith Wright's infant survive? Because the expectations of newspaper readers in 1754 were different.

A mid-18th century reader who waited all week for his newspaper to arrive had the time and the inclination to read every word and make up his or her own mind where the emphasis should be.

They accepted that newspaper stories would be fragmentary. Reporters who could pull them together had yet to emerge as a distinct breed. To us, it may appear that Griffith Wright filled his first issue with old stuff. But distant news was a scarce and expensive commodity. A foreign story was still fresh if a publisher put it into the customer's hand and said, "You read it here first". Readers enjoyed the world being delivered to their breakfast tables and having their horizons widened.

Just bringing out a newspaper of any sort required commitment in the face of huge obstacles. What look like stylistic shortcomings to us were not failings then since Griffith Wright did not have to catch the eye of a public sated by news and shout, "Look at this!" to attract attention in a crowded market.

A new paper in Leeds would naturally cause a stir. It wasn't unique but it was certainly novel. The town's other paper, the *Leeds Mercury*, was on the rocks and sank within the year – so the *Intelligencer* did not have to strain for further novelty.

4

HOW THEY GOT THE NEWS FROM THERE TO HERE IN 1754

Daniel Defoe took a swing through Yorkshire in the 1720s and described Leeds as "a large, wealthy and populous town" – which meant a good sprinkling of literate doctors, lawyers, merchants, schoolmasters and clergymen interested in buying a newspaper and with the means to do so.

Defoe was probably less impressed by his route to Leeds. The town's approach roads did not match its status and in 1754 the London stage-coaches ran only to York, Barnsley, Wakefield, Sheffield and Doncaster. To reach Leeds, the London despatches and mails had to traverse roads that were often no more than a narrow strip of stone flags across a common, deeply rutted either side. The 25 mile journey from York to Leeds took eight hours by coach, so it was probably quicker to walk.

Pity poor Griffith Wright. He had to wait another four years after starting his newspaper for the first regular London stagecoach service. Yet unless they arrived on time with the latest from the capital, he didn't have a paper.

In 1760 the stagecoaches were advertised ambitiously in the *Intelligencer* as "Flying machines on steel springs" – and reckoned to make the trip in three days. On both counts the claims were far from the truth. There was always a tendency to romanticize this form of travel with Charles Dickens the guilty party here in *Martin Chuzzlewit*: "*It was a charming evening: mild and bright. The four greys skimmed along as if they liked it; the bugle was in as high spirits...*" In real life the stage-coach journey was typically dirty, tedious and limb-wrenching.

It is exhausting just to follow on the page the creaking progress of the London stagecoach to Yorkshire as chronicled by one of our Victorian reporters, Tom Bradley. When the fare to Leeds of two pounds five shillings* was paid (outside passengers and children in the lap half price), the coach set off at five in the morning. It stopped for breakfast at the Angel in St Albans, for dinner at the White

Horse at Hockly and then did another leg before the dusty passengers were able to fall into bed at the Red Lion in Northampton.

They were up next day at the crack of dawn; they breakfasted at the Three Crowns in Market Harborough, dined at the Bull's Head in Loughborough, then pressed on to Nottingham where they spent the night at the Crown Inn.

> *"It is exhausting just to follow on the page the creaking progress of the London stagecoach to Yorkshire..."*

They had a three o'clock start the following morning. Dinner was at the Falcon in Chesterfield and the third night was at the Angel in Sheffield.

Day four (there were only supposed to be three according to the advertisements) was also gruelling. Breakfast was at the White Bear in Barnsley and the final dinner of the journey was eaten at the Coach and Horses in Wakefield before the worn-out travellers finally made their Leeds destination late in the evening.

Demand grew as roads got better. By 1838, about 130 coaches were coming in and out of Leeds every day. They would rattle into the main street, Briggate, rousing the shattered passengers by

toots on a bugle and heralding news from elsewhere. In the early days, the noise and bustle was a welcome change of routine on the street and was one of the big diversions of the day for bystanders. The destination of the first coaches was probably the Old King's Arms where Griffith Wright would be biting his nails. He would probably know the landlord, Richard Cooke, since the town's official business was often conducted here. There would be no time to chat. Griffith Wright had to get the London despatches back to his office. Once his next issue was complete, it would be rushed round the corner into Briggate where trestles were set out at six on Tuesday mornings.

The Market Bell was rung. "In a few minutes, without hurry, noise or the least disorder, the whole market is filled with cloth," noted Defoe. It was said £10,000-£20,000-worth of business was conducted in a morning. At the top end of the street were stalls for general wares, vegetables and fish.

The *Intelligencer* would be just the thing to divert market-goers when they stopped for a break to eat a Brig End Shot. This was unique to Leeds, an 18th century version of the lunchtime special offer – "a noggin o'porage and a trencher of either boiled or roasted meat" to go with a pot of ale. All for twopence, probably the same price as the *Intelligencer*. No cover price was printed. Reading a paper was accepted as a sociable event where the not-so-well off, and poor or non-readers, might gather to listen-in to someone reading theirs aloud at an inn or barber's shop.

* See page 152 for note on pre-decimal currency

2 The power of print

Human curiosity is inexhaustible. This is a threat to holders of absolute power who must keep a grip on what people are allowed to know and the ideas that are put into their heads.

That was tricky enough when communication was limited to word of mouth or handwritten despatch. The possibilities opened up by the printing press could only be viewed with unease by autocrats who punished or executed printers who they felt stepped out of line. The fears of the powerful were well-founded. Only a tiny elite could understand what came off the early presses but they released the freedom genie from the bottle. Ultimately, people's demand to know could not be denied and that meant a calling to account of the people who governed them.

Trade grew in the medieval cities of Europe and with it a flow of vital information which translated into money for merchants and power for politicians. Informal private letters, passed from hand to hand, in time expanded into a system of documents delivered by couriers known as "intelligencers". In Britain, booksellers extended the meaning of intelligencer to cover the scribes employed to hand-write news sheets.

The seed of our mass communications was sown in the 1550s by Wynkyn de Word, a Dutchman, who spotted fertile ground around St Bride's church in London at the bottom end of what is now Fleet Street. He reckoned that where there were clergymen there had to be a demand for books, so he moved his press there from the other side of town.

A compatriot, Frederick Freez, styled a "buke prynter" settled in York. The details of his career are sketchy. He seems to have set up the first press in the North and was made a Freeman of the city in 1479. In the York of those days printed words could be inflammatory things. Frederick's son Valentine was burnt at the stake on the Knavesmire for heresy.

The first printed news sheets in Britain were reports on the defeat of the Scots at Flodden in 1513. It was over a century, in 1620, before the first newspapers in English were printed. They came from Amsterdam and despite the best efforts of the authorities to suppress them, they started to circulate in London.

Journalists escaped the tight leash when the world turned upside down during the ferment of the Civil War. Radical news sheets sprouted, some carrying war stories. The poet John Milton, Latin secretary to the State Council, believed passionately that licensing printers meant state control of thought and said so in an essay, *Areopagitica*, in 1644.

But the freedom to express opinions and to report ended once the country was back in good order and the monarchy restored. Charles II turned the screw with a Printing Act in 1660 and brought back licensing. Damned up by the censors, news, often scurrilous, still found its way around the official restrictions in torrents. Pamphlets and satirical street ballads, lampooning the powerful did a roaring trade. By 1695 the government conceded its licensing system was a mockery. It shrewdly decided it could ease the ineffective controls but discourage newspaper publishers by hitting them in the pocket instead.

Publishers would have to pay duty on the blank paper they used and on the advertisements they ran. A further duty had to be paid on each copy of their newspaper sold, bearing an official stamp on the front page to say so.

The Stamp Acts in 1712, 1725 and 1757 – damned by the publishers as taxes on knowledge – did a better job than a censor. Price kept newspapers out of the hands of the majority of the population. The sole supplier of stamped paper was the London Warehouse of the Commissioner for Stamps in Serle Court, Lincoln's Inn. For a newspaper publisher based around St Bride's that was no problem. The stamped sheets were printed in batches of 25 and it was a short stroll for a man with a handcart to go each week to purchase a fresh supply,

The arrangement was hopeless for a publisher 200 miles away in Leeds. The length and difficulty of the journey to London required investing in larger consignments of paper, a big outlay which played havoc with the cash flow. To claim a rebate on the stamps on unsold copies of a newspaper, they had to be carted all the way back to Serle Court. Balancing supply against probable demand for a newspaper has never been an exact science and in the 18th century there were too many links in the supply chain that could fail.

On 8th January 1740, a hapless James Lister, the publisher of the *Leeds Mercury*, which had started in 1718, confessed to his readers of "being disappointed of a parcel of stamped paper for the news, which should have come to hand by Samuel Fenton, the London carrier on Saturday 29th past." Lister had gone ahead and printed the *Mercury* on unstamped paper. Since it was illegal to sell it unstamped, he had to give the paper away.

It was all a huge waste of time, energy and money and deeply demoralising to publishers. That's exactly what the authorities wanted: maximum discouragement. To add to the practical obstacles, there was a chronic shortage of paper. No endless rolls of machine-made newsprint were available. All paper was hand-made in single sheets from cotton and linen rag – and there was never enough rag available because English clothing was mostly wool.

Then, as now, politicians played a double game. They were flattered by coverage of their activities so long as it was favourable but irritated at attempts by the evolving newspapers to cover their parliamentary debates.

Banned from covering the proceedings officially, the newspapers got round the restrictions by reporting the debates as fiction or changed the names of the speakers. A 1771 debate on press freedom concluded a reporting ban on debates served no purpose although nothing much changed until the 1780s. From these beginnings, newspapers became the leaven in the bread of our political process. They rose together.

Any direct criticism of the government in newspapers was usually interpreted by judges as sedition and newspapermen as a breed were distrusted. Some like Thomas Gent were harassed and intimidated. Gent was a chancer, an Irishman who ran away from his apprenticeship in Dublin and arrived in York by way of London in 1714 as a journeyman printer. Gent fell in love with a young woman servant, Alice Guy, but lost her to a rival, Charles Bourne, owner of the *York Mercury*. Gent returned heartbroken to London. Ten years later when Bourne died, Gent came back to York, married the widow Alice and took joint control of the *York Mercury*.

During the middle part of his career in London, Gent went to bed one night suffering from a fever and was woken between one and two in the morning by heavy knocking at his front door. In Gent's account he recalled: "I asked who was there, and what would they have? They answered they must and would come in; and without assigning any other reason, they violently burst open the door. Being undrest, and all over in a sweat...

"I looked in a woeful condition; when Mr Crawford, one of the King's Messengers, took hold of my hands...but the insolence of Kent, his companion I could scarce bear, when helping on my clothes, he went to search my pockets for what written papers he could find therein..."

Gent was thrown into Newgate prison and released when the trumped-up charges didn't stick. It was a common device. The printer regained his freedom but was seriously out of pocket from lost work. If the authorities kept trying it on, they knew they could bring any printer to his knees.

The men who peopled the infant trade of journalism were not all unblemished defenders of free speech. The term hack had yet to be invented but the doings of some who plied that trade were already attracting the scorn of London playwrights. One referred to them as men, "who will write you a battle in any part of Europe at an hour's notice and yet never set foot outside a tavern."

Then there were the inhabitants of Grub Street, described by Samuel Johnson, who had been one of them, as "fittest for the common sink". These poorly paid literary drudges lived in desperate circumstances and scraped a living by offering their services as "colour" writers to London newspapers.

Why would a young Leeds businessman like Griffith Wright, from an impeccable Christian home, want to associate himself with characters like that?

All newspapers had to carry the official stamp as proof of duty paid

7

LEEDS 1754

"Last Monday at a bull-baiting at Quarry Hill, near this town one John Westerman had his thigh terribly gored by the bull of which wound he languished 'till Saturday and then expired..."

Griffith Wright's Leeds showed a roistering face. The gentry organised horse-racing with a bit of cock-fighting on the side. Spectators risked life-and-limb at bear baitings and the ale-houses were full of gamblers.

Outside the town, travellers faced hazards on lonely roads, as the *Intelligencer* reported on 12th November 1754.

"On Tuesday last, between the hours of five and six, as one Craven a cloth maker who lives in Horbury, was returning from Leeds market, he was stopped on Rothwell-Hague by two men on horseback, one of which brandishing a sword before his face and demanding his money, took from him two guineas in gold and two shillings and sixpence in silver.

About an hour and a half after, Jno Briggs, a gardener of Wakefield, was attacked upon the same common by the above two persons; and about two o'clock on the same day, Mr Pyeman, a farmer at Lofthouse and Cheeseman, a shoemaker of Oswald Green, were attacked by the same two persons, who took from Mr Pyeman his watch and a sum of money and from the shoemaker five shillings in silver. The day following, Jaques Saggarson, a French fencing master, was taken up on suspicion and committed to York Castle by Smith Esquire."

There were other hazards. Bulls, when being tortured for entertainment, sometimes turned the tables on the watchers. The *Intelligencer* reported in September 1755:

"Last Monday se'nnight [seven nights ago], at a bull-baiting at Quarry Hill, near this town one John Westerman, a labouring man in the Shambles had his thigh terribly gored by the bull of which wound he languished 'till Saturday and then expired."

By 1757, the Leeds Magistrates were attempting to reign-in the worst of the gambling excesses and threatened: *"Publicans permitting journeymen, labourers, servants, or apprentices to play cards, dice, draughts, shuffle-board, Mississippi, billiard tables, skittles, ninepins or any other implement of gaming in their houses, alehouses, or grounds shall forfeit 40/- for the first offence, for every subsequent offence £10 to be levied by distress and sale, a quarter to the informer, the rest to the poor."*

The gamblers were not deterred. In May that year they were invited to a cockfight. *"To be fought at the Rose and Crown the Back of the Shambles, Leeds, a main of cocks, betwixt gentlemen of Leeds and the gentlemen of West Riding, for four guineas a battle. To weigh on Saturday...and fight 30th, 31st and 1st June. Signed Abraham Ferrar for Leeds and William Beeston for West Riding."* The Talbot Hotel was also renowned for its cock-pit.

In May the next year, a mixed day of racing and fighting was advertised, *"Leeds races on Chapeltown Moor, 14th June, £50 in specie [in money], by five and six year olds. A main of cocks will be fought during the race week betwixt Lord Viscount Donne and Jno Stanhope Esq for ten guineas a battle."*

The town did show a more civilised face as well. It had a theatre of some repute which became a nursery for the London stage and a serious music scene. An *Intelligencer* advert on 6th November 1757 offers:

"Concert of music, vocal and instrumental at the Assembly Rooms with works by Corelli...and a concerto by Mr Crompton. A ball to follow. Tickets 2/6d."

Map of Leeds circa 1725. The original premises of the *Leedes Intelligencer* were located on Lower Headrow

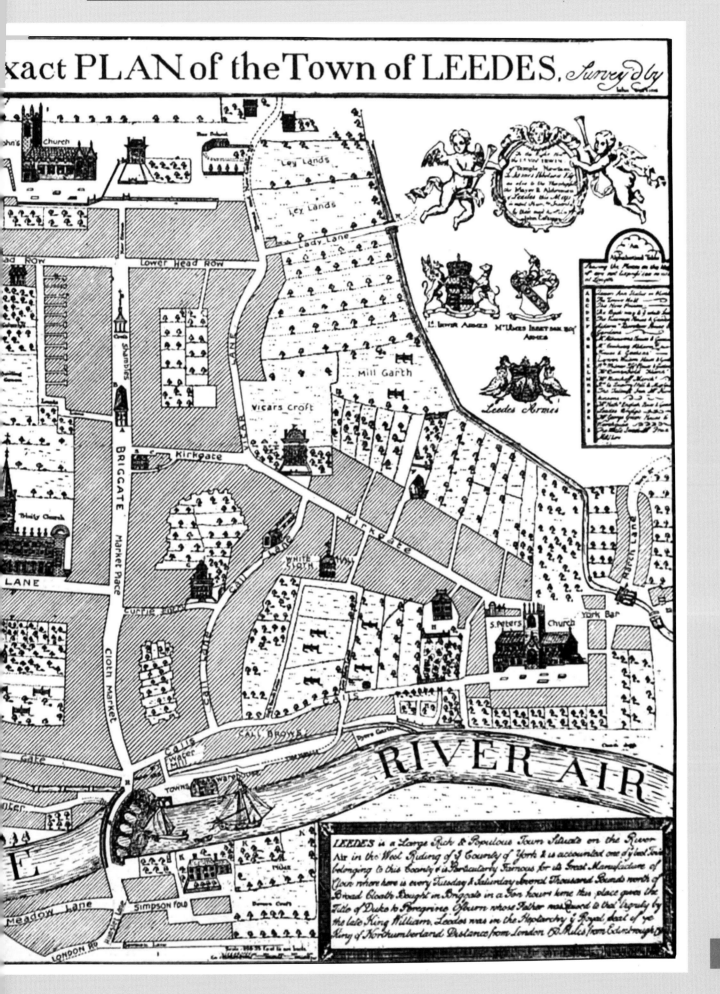

God's own country
AND ITS PEOPLE

"Joshua Horton, gentleman near Ripponden in the parish of Halifax, did, several times last year in a haughty, insolent and unmannerly way come hunting into the lands of John Dyson Esq..."

In 1754, there was hunting out in the dales and the Tempest family, who still live at Broughton Hall near Skipton, were among the first to keep a pack of harriers.

Yorkshire was overwhelmingly rural, but that did not mean people saw eye-to-eye about pursuing animals for sport. It led to bitter disputes between neighbours, revealed in a notice in the 2nd September 1755 edition of the *Leeds Intelligencer*. *"Whereas Joshua Horton, gentleman near Ripponden in the parish of Halifax, did, several times last year in a haughty, insolent and unmannerly way come hunting into the lands of John Dyson Esq at Westwood and also into the lands of the tenants...These are to give notice that if the said Joshua Horton, or any others along with him, do for the future come into the lands of the said John Dyson, he and they will certainly be prosecuted..."*

On Tuesday 2nd December 1777, another complainant was more temperate. *"Whereas the gardens, pleasure grounds, plantations and woods of Gledhow have, at various times, been very much trespassed upon and materially injured by hare-hounds and persons attending them; it is hoped that gentlemen who follow the diversion of hunting in this neighbourhood will see the impropriety of such conduct."*

An angry objection on Tuesday, 14th January 1791 from a sleepless "correspondent" addressed to the Master of the Hunt suggests it might have come from the *Intelligencer's* editor himself. *"A correspondent has for several whole nights during the last week been much disturbed by a number a Leeds hounds bellowing in the streets...it is not, he says, either*

comfortable or agreeable, at midnight to hear a pack of hounds in full cry."

A less contentious rural pursuit was running horses for cups and sweepstakes on improvised race courses by the gentry of lower

Mike Cowling

Reeth Brass Band on the village green at an open air church service on St Bartholomew's Day

Wensleydale and Swaledale. Besides these activities were village sports days, rooted in religious festivals that were held on the Saints' Days of the village church. Their modern successors continue in places like Reeth.

Where work was concerned, out in the fields of the East Riding, women did the reaping or shearing of corn with sickles. They got two shillings a day (plus ale) for cutting a quarter of an acre each. Scythes, quicker but more wasteful, were mainly kept for barley and oats. A good mower could

scythe an acre a day and following behind every six to ten mowers was a man binding and stooking.

A ploughman, William Marshall, said of his job on the Yorkshire Wolds in 1788, "The hours of work are long. In spring seed time the plow teams will sometimes stay out from six to six; the plowman having their dinner carried out to them in the field; the horses remaining all day without a bait, and with only a small allowance of corn when they reach the stable."

Although these work rhythms continued as they had done time out of mind, social organisation was being turned upside down. Many villagers found themselves dispossessed and semi-destitute as the enclosure of common land speeded up. Increased demand for wool accelerated the pressure

Opposite: Rainbow in Gunnerside, January 2004
Bruce Rollinson

The limestone pavement above Malham Cove

Bruce Rollinson

technologies. The impulse led to HS Thompson, heir to an East Riding estate, calling for a dinner with like-minded friends. A celebrated meeting followed in October 1837 at the old Black Swan Hotel, in Coney Street in York, and the Yorkshire Agricultural Society was born. Their first Yorkshire Show in Fulford, on the southern fringe of York, was staged the following year. It was held annually in 30 towns until they decided to build a permanent showground in 1949. Harrogate was chosen for the site, much to York's disgust. The Great Yorkshire Show now attracts 130,000 visitors over three days in July with 8,000 animals in competition.

to convert arable land to sheep pasture. In the 20 years from 1760, 78 villages in the East Riding enclosed their fields.

The positive side of the farming revolution was a dramatic improvement in yields. Farmers could drain the land, rotate crops and introduce turnips, potatoes and clover to over-winter livestock. They could feed bigger flocks and herds and develop scientific breeding for which Yorkshire became a major centre.

The urge towards self-improvement gathered pace and a showcase was needed to make farmers aware of the newest methods and

Beautiful Yorkshire

PUBLISHED BY " THE YORKSHIRE POST "

Caught in time –
pictures from the 1930s
(clockwise from left):

Harvesting near
Roseberry Topping
in Cleveland

Sheep farming in
Swaledale

The lighthouse at
Flamborough Head

Kilnsey Show

The changing seasons

Bruce Greer

Mike Cowling

Chris Lawton

14

James Hardisty

Dan Oxtoby

Clockwise from opposite page, top left:

Brian Thornborrow tends to his sheep at the head of Swaledale

The Bramham Moor Hunt, around Bilbrough, near Tadcaster

Dandelions near Bramham Park mark the gateway to summer

Filming *One Man and His Dog* at Castle Howard, July 2003

Mist rolls in on the remains of Roche Abbey in South Yorkshire

The show must go on

Roger Cross searched for the key to Yorkshire's rural character and went to see the hill-folk at play at the Nidderdale Show.

Prince Charles shares a joke at the 2003 Nidderdale Show   Gerard Binks

There's trouble in them there hills beyond commuter land, where the winters are tough and the bank managers are getting tougher.

Appalling wet weather this summer has created havoc, with many hay crops flat and dejected in the fields well above sea level, and some are destined to stay that way. Hill farmers in the Yorkshire Dales traditionally rely on their summer crops to feed their livestock, particularly their sheep, throughout the winter. Not for them the comfortable cushions named "EEC subsidy" slipped under their envied and often rich arable-producer counterparts in the flatlands, down where the yards are full of Mercedes and BMWs rather than Datsuns and Toyotas.

The first Monday after the first Sunday after September 17, as legend has it, was planned as a day to forget such things for a few hours, to escape the vagaries and ramifications of our perverse climate. The Nidderdale Agricultural Society's annual show in the idyllic valley-bottom setting on the banks of the Nidd at Pateley Bridge, is the last show of the summer, and one of the most eagerly awaited.

Hill farmers travel from strange and distant lands such as Swaledale and Wharfedale to join their brothers and sisters in toil for a final knees-up before the winter is reluctantly acknowledged as being at hand. For some, whose families have known each other for generations stretching back well over 100 years it is virtually the only time they get together each year to swap their news.

The roads over the tops were thick with vehicles yesterday, and guess what the main topic of conversation was after they had queued for an hour to get into the showground? With rain cascading from leaden skies, the peat-brown Nidd rushing by almost unnoticed, the question was not had they got their hay in, but would they get it in?

The townies who had braved the weather were easily distinguishable, and not simply because they were not wearing dark green, waterproof jackets and/or green wellies. They were the ones sheepishly (no pun intended) hidden under umbrellas as Beverly Park was transformed into a First World War battlefield of mud and spinning rear wheels in just a few short hours.

Yet the lads and lassies down from the hills did not seem to bother. It was, after all, the first Monday after the first Sunday after September 17 and nothing, not even the weather, was going to spoil it. Ironically, the very element which had created so much heartache in terms of lost crops, was simply ignored.

> **"Hill farmers travel from strange and distant lands such as Swaledale and Wharfedale to join their brothers and sisters in toil for a final knees-up before the winter is reluctantly acknowledged as being at hand"**

In steadily falling rain the menfolk stood resolutely outside the beer tent and got wet when they could easily have stepped inside. The showjumpers carried on jumping and the dry-stone wallers carried on building probably their wettest-ever wall.

The determination to enjoy themselves among the hill folk was infectious. Townies in slip-on shoes and white socks shrugged their shoulders and plunged through the mud, and on the cricket pitch which is part of the showground, play continued unabated. Not a light-meter to be seen.

Unlike the Great Yorkshire Show and its spectacularly appointed facilities at Harrogate, and which have as much a feel of the country about them to some as the Blackpool illuminations, the Nidderdale is close to an ideal. Soaring green hills in all directions, a pretty Dales town across the river, the show secretary's office in a glorified garden shed and hardly a country Sloane supping champagne and bleating (no pun intended).

The Nidderdale does have some intrusive elements, such as a mini-fairground, pop music and all, a stall endlessly auctioning towels

The shows in pictures

Gary Longbottom

("not £1, not even 90p etc") and a seafood stall offering ubiquitous ocean sticks. And as for the gents toilet...corrugated metal sheets behind which one communes directly with the grass were heard to be described, by one of the lads from Swaledale (where they apparently talk with more of a "twang", than, say, Wharfedale, which is considered quite sophisticated) as "daft".

Trying to force opinions from these hillmen about the weather, the EEC, or the Government's attitude to their plight, proved more difficult. As one show committee man put it: "They are a bit inward-looking even when things are going well but when they are struggling they won't want to bother with a nosy bugger from Leeds."

Show chairman Frank Dawson, being from Norwood near Harrogate, and a wool-broker as well as a farmer, was more diplomatic. He said that many farmers would be lucky to be left with £9,000 a year, and some as little as £5,000, after expenses had been met.

The overriding message from the last of the summer shows yesterday was simple: "If the outside world really does want to know, then tell them the hill farmers will survive, as they always have."

And one farmer's wife, bareheaded, soaked to the skin and the wrong side of 70, ate her sandwiches and contemplated the cricketers as they slid about in the pouring rain. She glanced at leaden skies and asked: "What do you think Ernest, is it going to spoil itself?" with the sort of twang you only find in Swaledale.

Clockwise from above:

The main ring at the Great Yorkshire Show, 1996

The gates to the Yorkshire Agricultural Society

Farmers watch the judging of Ayrshire Cattle, 2003

The *Yorkshire Post's* guide to the 1994 Show

James Hardisty

Simon Hulme

Finding the lady of the hills

Our North Riding correspondent Alec Donaldson came across Hannah Hauxwell's isolated farm where she was contentedly making £3 a week. It was a life-changing moment for her. Since this article appeared television documentaries, books and worldwide fame have followed.

Could you live on £170 a year – and be happy? It can't be done, you say? It can, you know, though for proof you would have to explore one of the most northerly parts of the Yorkshire Pennines.

You would have to find Miss Hannah Hauxwell, very feminine in her masculine workaday clothes, who has a little farm deep in the quiet confines of Baldersdale.

She's content enough, far removed from the down-country world she rarely visits, on her £170 a year.

Her detachment is remarkable. Out of deference to my calling, no doubt, she asked me at one time: "That Mr Anthony Gray, the Reuters gentleman, was he ever released by the Chinese?"

Nothing could have emphasised so much the loneliness of Miss Hauxwell in the remote world of her dale. The owner of Low Birk Hat Farm did not know what the rest of the world had known these many months.

She sees newspapers only when they are left occasionally by her few friends. Her radio set does not work. Neighbours are few in those desolate parts, and far away. All the same she has about £170 a year and she is content.

Low Birk Hat, about 1,000ft above sea level, sits on the edge of ground which falls sharply to the upper reaches of Blackton reservoir, the middle one of three man-made lakes in a dale which strikes west at Cotherstone in Teesdale into the Pennines.

Its limited acres make up a little world of last year's spent grasses, powdered snow, and a cold wind which soughs or shrieks according to mood. Its house stands four-square, exposed but unyielding in a winter scene. The land covers about 80 acres. Thirty-seven of them Miss Hauxwell describes as meadows; the remaining 43 or so are much rougher.

She came to Low Birk Hat when she was three, though the family have had it for more than a hundred years. She is deeply attached to it.

"I have no other home, I like this countryside, I like the privacy and I like the freedom," she says. So there she is: with a farmhouse, 80 acres of farm land and £170 a year. And she's content.

Her mother died 12 years ago; her uncle, who had lived with mother and daughter, died nine years ago. At 34 or so she was left alone with Low Birk Hat and its sour acres.

Though for most of her life she had worked out of doors, she knew that she alone could not farm Low Birk Hat as it had been farmed. So she sold off the 30 or so dairy cattle, and let the allotment land to neighbours for sheep grazing, and the in-bye land for summer-feeding cattle. This land-letting provides the main source of her very limited income.

Hannah Hauxwell is 43. Her life has been hard, yet she has a smooth pink and white face. Her hair is greying, her work-grimed hands are fine and sensitive.

She has a curious but-not-of-this-century grace and courtesy in speech and manner. She shows a woman's concern for the ritual of tea-making and serving, despite her old Harris tweed jacket, her breeches and gum boots.

Water has to be drawn from a stream some distance away. In winter, when the upland country around her home is so filled with snow that the contours are rounded off, she has to dig down to the stream. There is no electricity or gas. Lamps are used for winter lighting; coal and wood for firing.

In summer it is different. Miss Hauxwell, on the day of bitter cold when I visited her, spoke wistfully and hopefully of summer. "Ah, then it is really beautiful. One could not wish to have a better place when the days are long and the air is warm."

Then she can make hay for her own stock of three or four head of cattle which she winters indoors. She can go around the farm repairing stone walls, putting in stakes where they are needed, and spreading muck.

Then this lonely, independent woman who has no brothers or sisters or other near relatives can look forward to visitors other than the postman and her other few callers.

Low Birk Hat stands hard on the Pennine Way, and by May she can expect its very attenuated traffic to start. She looks forward to that, and is patently flattered when people greet her with a, "We saw you last year and wondered how you were getting along."

Oh, yes, when May comes the grip of loneliness on Low Birk Hat is eased – reluctantly and almost imperceptibly.

Her wants are few, which is just as well for she must budget carefully. Coal – a heavy item – is delivered to her home by the gated grass-track from Clove Lodge a mile or so away on the other side of the valley.

She has to walk three fields to a gate to collect her bread where it is left. She walks more fields to High Birk Hat ("I have good neighbours there") where her groceries are delivered.

She regards herself as "not good at cooking and baking because so much of my life has been spent out of doors," but does some sewing to save on personal and domestic wants.

Is this life enough or satisfactory, even though far from financially rewarding? Is there enough work, in housekeeping and about the place, to keep her occupied?

"Well. I have more to do than I can get done," she says. "I know I am not one of the quickest or ablest of women, but I'm kept going so much that I could really do with more time."

Does she ever get away from Low Birk Hat, perhaps to the auction mart at Barnard Castle when she has a beast to sell?

"No, I don't reckon I'm a business woman, and that is taken care of for me. I was out of the dale only five times last year. Four times I had to go to Barnard Castle on business, and once I visited a half cousin at Mickleton, a few miles away."

She talks animatedly about the time, two years ago, she spent in a Northallerton hospital. She had

become "rather poorly" and the staff and other patients were "very, very kind". Her eyes lit up with the recollection of that intimate contact with other humans in a close community.

Is her life one to be recommended to others?

She ponders and thinks, just as she does over every question. Then with a politeness which is unexpected because it is so unusual, replies: "I think perhaps it is not to be recommended. It is too extreme. My income is very little, and I try hard to keep outgoings to £150. It is not adequate and barely provides for the necessities of life."

This is not by way of complaint or criticism of her own curiously remote place in society. It is merely comment in response to an inquiry.

Miss Hauxwell continues: "I suppose there is a happy medium. It would, I think, be nicer to see rather more people and hear something of what is going on in the world.

"Yes, I have sometimes thought about leaving, and I suppose as I get older I shall have to consider this more and more. But for the moment this is my home. I have known no other."

She has a few pleasures besides her work. Reading is one, although this is becoming a restricted pleasure because of eye pains.

She loves the birds around her home; the swans, geese and ducks on the reservoir below, the curlews which bubble on the high land around her, and the owls which screech about the house.

She enjoys the pleasure, which most country folk know, of sticking, or collecting kindling and bigger wood for her fire. And she enjoys playing the harmonium ("I play simple things for my own entertainment") which has a prominent place in her living kitchen.

You may wish to salute, as I do, the Lonely Lady of Low Birk Hat...remote and independent but quietly content in her upland place far from a world she tends to ignore.

"I have no other home, I like this countryside, I like the privacy and I like the freedom"

Above: Hannah working the land in winter
Far left: Hannah in later years

It happened to a vet

The warmth of James Herriot's Yorkshire characters captured hearts everywhere. Roger Cross went to Thirsk to meet the real-life Herriot, Alfred Wight, then aged 69 and the most famous vet in the world.

The ritual is enduring and unchanging, a simple act of homage the like of which can be witnessed at the Lourdes, Knock and Fatima shrines daily.

Queues are orderly outside the ivy-draped house at 23 Kirkgate, just off the North Yorkshire market town's traffic-choked square. Worshippers are cordially asked to arrive between 2.45pm and 3.30pm on Wednesdays or Fridays.

Some days there are as many as 150 genuflectors, mostly Americans, mainly women whose first bloom of youth is on the retreat, and, yes, they do say, "Can I touch you?"

Alfred Wight's hazel eyes cloud almost imperceptibly as he contemplates the phenomenon. If it is a real problem being public property in such a tangible, typically trans-Atlantic way, he is not saying.

All he will admit is that the bombing of Libya ordered by President Reagan, inadvertently, had produced a brief respite in the pilgrimage to his red painted door. That and something about clouds and silver linings.

Alf Wight is now 69, still works as a vet in and around Thirsk, which for all time will be known as Herriot Country. As James Herriot he is, simply, one of the world's most famous authors.

He was 50 before rising to his wife's put-up-or-shut-up challenge about recording for posterity his anecdotes from his life as a country veterinary surgeon. A steady tapping at an old Olivetti for no more than an hour in front of the television each evening and his warm and unashamedly nostalgic tales were to touch hearts and minds around the world.

The television series and feature films, as well as a rare review for the first book in the *Chicago Herald Tribune*, cannily reproduced in the form of an advertisement by the then small-time publishers St Martin's Press in New York, brought a remarkable and unflagging reaction. Millions of sales were generated and an almost God-like, literary-folksy status was draped around his modest shoulders.

The yarns have earned many dollars but, even now, there is an air of bemusement about this Glasgow-born vet who arrived in Thirsk in 1939, and says: "It felt like heaven." The joy of Yorkshire, what he describes as a "miraculously-preserved place", has not receded.

The sitting room at the house in Kirkgate is now the waiting room. But on that first morning 47 years ago he stepped out of the French windows into the idyllic garden and vowed never to leave.

Literary success beyond the wildest dreams of every closet scribbler seems to have affected him little, if at all. A bungalow in the Hambleton Hills, a weekend cottage retreat near Middleham, are relatively modest signals of his financial prowess. Two Audi 80 Quattros, one cluttered with the debris of a vet's chores, one kept for social use, earned their keep during last winter's snow.

Promotional tours in this country and the USA were quickly abandoned, as were appearances on television talk shows and newspaper and television interviews. He surprised himself by relenting for the *Yorkshire Post*, offering a few minutes after his small animals surgery and when "The Americans" had departed.

But his devotees tend to linger, so it was into the scruffier Audi, out of Thirsk and into a field away from all prying eyes other than those of Bodie, a wilful border terrier.

He explains that he organised the twice-weekly audiences for his fans to try to bring some order to his life as Alfred Wight, vet, although it is James Herriot they all want to meet. His natural benignity wavers again as he disclosed that even that plan has been found to have its drawbacks. Magazine journalists sit in at the back of the room during the 45 minute sessions, saying nothing, and turning his mainly anodyne words to his fans, along with some judicious culling from the books, into yet one more definitive "interview" with the great but elusive man.

"It is one of the few things in life that really irritates me. These people are often making lots of money, literally by false pretences, but I don't suppose I can do much about it," he muses. He accepts the often gushing adulation of his fans with grace and not a little gratitude; any darker thoughts that may lurk are kept well hidden. "They are paying me a compliment, after all. They are all basically in Thirsk because they like me and what I represent. And as well as asking to touch me, some of those American matrons give me a hell of a cuddle as well," he says with a chuckle.

One American literary critic said that behind James Herriot's rustic veneer was a "shrewdie", and he admits that the wisest decision he took was to make his work episodic, just a year at a time. When the much-lamented television series (now into its eighth screening in the USA) finally ended on BBC, there was national grief.

Young James was setting off to war, his wife was waving forlornly from the bedroom window that still looks down on Kirkgate. "I must admit it was strange watching that very emotional bit in our lives on television, lumps in throats, and it really did seem the perfect place to end the series for good."

After a few moments deliberation, Alf Wight decides to reveal at this point in the conversation, the news that will cause breasts to beat faster on all continents. He has actually started writing material for a proposed new series for the BBC and they should be on the box by the end of next year.

"It's easier than writing a book, but the room still tends to close in on me after I have been tapping away for an hour. The new series will be about the 1950s, when the kids were growing up, and a revolutionary time for vets when we emerged from a witchcraft world. I just hopes it makes people happy."

He no longer needs the money, of course, and is even able to make a joke about the 83 per cent tax he paid under the Labour Government. His agents wanted him to join Jack Higgins in blessed tax-exile on Jersey and he spent ten days there looking around "Just to humour them, you see. Because I didn't start writing as a way of making money in the first place, it didn't seem important. And I could never leave Yorkshire."

One local farmer did once say the books were "all about nowt". A treasured if unintentional compliment.

His son (also a vet) and daughter (a doctor) work in Thirsk and the local bookshops, as they see the Americans staggering away towards Kirkgate on Wednesdays and Fridays with arms full of books to be signed, must say a prayer of thanks that Alfred Wight spotted Siegfried Farnon's advertisement for an assistant all those years ago.

Life in Herriot Country seems to go on forever, charmed and unchanging, almost like a work of fiction.

Christopher Timothy as James Herriot in the successful television adaptation of *All Creatures Great and Small*

EJF 467

21

Posing a question for the WI

The eleven ladies from Rylstone Women's Institute sent ripples around the world with their nude calendar. Michael Hickling found out how they coped with Tinseltown.

It was dark, it was deep, it was noisy. It was Hollywood, sure enough, but was this how glamorous film premiere parties were meant to be?

The bemused stars of *Calendar Girls* felt they'd been ushered into a basement night club. There was vodka or champagne to drink out of plastic cups and Thai food to eat with chopsticks out of envelopes. "There was all this headbanging music going on," says Lynda Logan. "Someone said to me, 'Feel my hair, I haven't washed it for eight years' and said to come for a hairdo tomorrow. We didn't go. We met a Geraldine, who was a Gerald – and lovely. That's the sort of

Terry Logan

Lynda Logan, wife of Terry, who took the photographs, poses for the calendar

person they were, a bit bizarre.

"I bumped into a woman who told me she was the organiser of the party. She told us Disney had given her a preview screening of *Calendar Girls* so she could get a feel for who to invite. I think she must have been to the wrong film." That's showbiz.

It's quite a step from frantic Hollywood to the calm of Lynda Logan's kitchen in Threshfield in West Yorkshire. On inspection it seems oddly familiar territory. Up on a shelf, a yellow jug catches the eye. Yes, it's the same one which did just enough to hide Chris Clancy's modesty as she poured tea in the buff and became recognised the world over as Miss September in their celebrated nude calendar. Here's the large scrubbed pine table around which the original calendar photoshoot was debated. The kitchen, initially the nerve centre of their project, is now the launch pad for their global success.

In the new feature film they take Hollywood by storm before the two main characters suffer a loss of nerve as they prepare to film a soap commercial. They anguish over whether they've diminished their noble cause of raising money for leukaemia research by selling out to commerce and chasing fame for its own sake.

In real life it didn't happen like that. The women had never been to Hollywood as a group. Disney, who made *Calendar Girls*, put that right when they arranged the premiere. Bring someone with you, they said, make a holiday of it.

Aren't the women all premiered-out? They've had three in England alone, including Leeds and Skipton.

The one at the Grosvenor House Hotel, which coincided with the 70th birthday of one of the group, Beryl Bamforth, was pure fantasy-land, they say. But Hollywood was a must. The excitement began when the tickets arrived at their homes with a Mickey Mouse on them and they were chauffeur-driven from their front doors to Manchester airport.

The Renaissance hotel in Beverly Hills ("with European style sophistication...guest rooms lavishly furnished, luxurious, and comfortable...with a flair of service reminiscent of a time gone by") had been used in their film. "It was wonderful, just as you imagine it," says Ros Fawcett, the original Miss November. "I've never seen such tall palm trees and brilliant blue skies. I was in this huge bedroom and it looked out on to the famous Hollywood sign."

For the night of the premiere they got the whole works – red carpet, lines of photographers, media folk calling for interviews. Posh and Becks eat your hearts out. "There were cheers and laughs and claps all through the film," says Lynda. "We tried not to forget what we were doing it for. We'd look round and think, 'There's a lot of money been spent there – that could go towards the charity.' But what can you do? It's a promotion. It's all being done to make more money for us."

Lynda is an artist who paints in oils and the germ of the original idea found root here. Her group of friends from the Rylstone WI used to go to the Turkish baths together. After one trip, they suggested to Lynda that she did a painting of the group in the nude before the effects of gravity

Terry Logan

became so advanced that no-one would want to look at it. Then one of their number, Angela Baker, lost her husband John to leukaemia and they discussed raising money for leukaemia research with coffee mornings. Lynda's husband Terry suggested that a nude calendar could be a surer way of raising cash. The women doubted their pulling power as pin-ups.

"Angela had lost John in July and really we just thought this would be something for her to do with all of us in the winter months," says Lynda. "As for the outside world, we thought, 'Who'd want to see us with no clothes on?' It's a bit flukey what happened after."

She reflects for a moment on that statement and then concedes she believes there was more to it than that. John Baker, she says, was a highly organised man. When the Logans went on holiday with the Bakers, they found they had nothing to do but sit back and watch the scenery: John had arranged every detail in the trip.

Lynda's home is a beautiful farmhouse built in 1643 – mullioned windows, vaulted cellar, atmospheric

kitchen, stone-flagged floors and oak beams. The Logans had rented it, never expecting to be in a position to buy. Just before John died, the house had come to them under the wishes of the owner.

The astonishing success of the Rylstone WI calendar required a picturesque domestic setting and meticulous pre-planning. Lynda believes some higher agency was at work in bringing such conditions about. "If there is such a thing as a life hereafter, John's up there organis- ing us," she says. "It's quite amazing the coincidences we've had and when one happens, we've said, 'It must be John again'."

The printer they'd approached at the start looked at their order for 1,000 calendars and shook his head. "Nay, I'm not switching on t'machine for that. It'll have to be 3,000." They prayed that if they could generate a bit of public interest through the local weekly paper or the *Yorkshire Post,* shifting that many might not be too ambitious.

In the event, their postman Roy had to deliver sacks of orders. Some arrived with requests to send a calen-

dar to a poorly aunt and for them to attach a note, "Hope you're feeling better". In one case they were asked to find a hankie and enclose that as well. The women sat round the table and cried as they read many of the letters insisting the calendar had given them new inspiration. They responded to every one, a task they refer to as "fulfilment". Angela Baker has kept the letters in suitcases.

They haven't counted the money they've raised for leukaemia research recently. It's estimated at £800,000 and that's before the big bucks start rolling in from the "very generous" royalty deal with Disney for *Calendar Girls.* The film opens in Europe in the New Year and in the Far East some time later.

When Ros Fawcett and her husband Chris got back to Heathrow from Hollywood the stewardess called out their names and explained they were to be met on landing and would be whisked through the airport's VIP entrance. Says Ros: "We were on a walkway, looking down on economy passengers below and I said to Chris, 'Look, that's us next week – down to earth again'."

APRIL 1998

Whistle-stop tours

For some, it's just a way of getting about. For others, there's nothing to match the romance of Yorkshire by rail. Stephen McClarence shared their pleasure.

The whistle shrieks, the train pulls away from the station and the men across the aisle start chuffing.

"Chuff Chuff," they chant in quiet unison. "Chuff chuff chuff." They tap their Ordnance Survey maps in time to the train's rhythm and their faces glow with contentment. Chuff chuff chuff.

There's something about a day-out by train that turns adults into children. It doesn't have to be steam, like this train on the North Yorkshire Moors Railway – inducing nostalgia for the days when seats were horsehair-hard (but comfy) and carriage lights were just dim enough to make reading impossible.

Any "Special Excursion" can do the trick and make chuffs of us all. For many people in these car-driven days, a rail journey of any sort, however ordinary, however Leeds-to-Wakefield, however Doncaster-to-Rotherham, is an event in itself, a little adventure.

"If my father ever goes on a plane or a train, he always takes a bottle of water with him," a young woman tells her friend on Grosmont station, at the northern end of the 18-mile line down to Pickering.

If he ever goes on a plane or a train? You remember trains, dad? Like planes without wings.

As a non-driver, I'm making what could turn out to be a very long day indeed. Getting to and from the North Yorkshire Moors Railway – which traces the route of the world's first railway excursions, back in 1839 – involves me in a tight jigsaw of public transport. Three buses, six trains, a nine-hour round trip and whiff of the stunt about it.

It takes me from the very bottom of Yorkshire – home in Sheffield – to the very top, and back again. One missed connection between Sheffield and York, York and Middlesbrough, and Middlesbrough and Grosmont, and I could be stuck for weeks in Potto or Boosbeck or Sexhow or any of the hundreds of Yorkshire villages that used to have stations.

They're all marked on the cream tile map of the London and North Eastern Railway on Middlesbrough Station – a cobweb of lines covering the whole of Yorkshire, with the Grosmont-Pickering line squiggling its way down the middle.

It was built by George Stephenson in the 1830s to link Whitby with the outside world. Another route was added – along the Esk Valley from Whitby through Grosmont to Middlesbrough – and, thanks to the campaigning enterprise of the Esk Valley Rail Partnership, that too survives.

It's a wonderful journey – all the more so because it's a working line, carrying schoolchildren and holiday-makers and men in tweed jackets going from this village to that village and back home again.

Like a pocket Settle-to-Carlisle, it trundles across russet moorland, through glades with the branches scuffing the windows, past pheasants and herons and stoic sheep. It stops at stone stations that look like hunting lodges, screeches round bends and crosses the odd trim viaduct.

Every so often, even on misty mornings, spectacular landscapes open out – long valleys, high hills and clustered pines on top of them.

On a normal day, I'd carry on to Whitby – twice up and down the Abbey Steps and fish and chips to follow – but this morning (no missed connections so far, incidentally), I get off at Grosmont, cross the platform and step back 40 years.

Dr Beeching, the axeman of access, closed the Grosmont-Pickering line in 1965, but it reopened in 1973 after an enthusiasts' campaign.

Twenty-five years on, it's one of the most successful of England's 97 preserved steam railways, pulling in 270,000 passengers last year – and it's generally "full to bursting" in July and August, says marketing manager Christine Hudson.

Some come for the evening dinners in the Pullman dining cars, some for the Thomas the Tank Engine Weekend, some for the Wartime Weekend.

"You step on the platform with *Goodnight Sweetheart* playing," says Christine Hudson. "There will be 400 personnel in army uniforms, a 1940s' dance and you might get a spiv who'll open his coat and say: 'Want any nylons?'" Er, a little later, perhaps. For the moment, the season's first passengers are photographing the engine and its glowing red firebox before climbing aboard.

Inside, the chuff-chuffing is about to start and an elderly couple are having the sort of conversation that suggests they've either just met, have been married for 40 years or are hoping for starring roles in a Samuel Beckett play.

"I didn't hear him blow his whistle.

"No. Dog collar's askew."

"I took the *News Chronicle* very briefly some years ago."

"Did you?"

"I'm thirsty."

The Captain Cook Pullman steams through the North York Moors

Tony Bartholomew

"Well, we've not brought anything to drink."

Clouds of cumulo-nimbus smoke drift past the window – particularly pretty from the loo windows, frosted glass with little peepholes to let you peer at the passing scene, or at any rate a slightly distorted version of it. The loos, with their citrus yellow washbasins, have alarm chains ('Penalty for Improper Use: 40/-'). Disappointingly, they come with soft toilet tissue, not rolls of stiffest Izal.

The smoke, the rhythm, the regular chuffing are all very lulling, but I'm getting out for an hour at the first stop, Goathland, a once-quiet moorland village now reputedly pulling in over a million visitors a year on the strength of its new role as a location for the *Heartbeat* TV series.

A coach party is up from Essex, heads down, collars and camcorders up, to nose over the Goathland Hotel ('Yes!' says the front of the bar meals menu. 'We are the Aidensfield Arms') and buy *Heartbeat* videos, model cars, books and signed posters from the Aidensfield Stores. "Some people think *Heartbeat* has been a good thing for the village," says assistant Val Tolhurst. "Some think it hasn't. Most are very glad of it."

They include the local trader who pointed out last year that, until *Heartbeat* came, the week's highlight was people meeting in the Post Office to draw their pensions. Now they have belly dancing classes in the Village Hall.

So, from a recreated 1960s village back to a 1960s train, trundling down Newtondale. It's bleak and brackeny in early spring, with the moors brooding all around. Summer, with heather and trees in full leaf, softens it.

At Pickering, according to the cream-tile LNER map, you could once get connections to Thirsk, Harrogate, York, Hull – even Withernsea, if you really wanted to.

These days, it's the end of the line and, with every connection on time and proving that public transport can work, I wait for the Yorkshire Coastliner bus down to York and the train home.

"You live in York?" the lad in front asks. "No," I say, "Sheffield."

"It's all right for some," he says.

This is not a common response. I ask him what he means.

"Brilliant clubs," he says. "I went down with my mates in the New Year. Got the eight o'clock train home."

"That was a short night," I say.

"Eight o'clock next morning," he says. And looks at me as though I've wandered in out of the chuffing 1960s.

25

The Glorious Twelfth

The world comes to the Yorkshire moors for the start of the grouse shooting season. Frederic Manby reported from Arkengarthdale.

Moorland advice: watch out for the Americans on the grouse moor. Unaccustomed to a grouse hurtling towards them at anything up to 80 miles an hour, they shoot too late, then commit the penultimate sin before the red card –

they take the follow through shot, risking death or serious injury to other shooters or beaters who are standing to the side.

These "beaters' tales" are part of the sport's baggage. No doubt not all Americans are duffers, but there was

a nod of accord as the story was told among a huddle of shooting men on East Arkengarthdale Estate yesterday, the ever so Glorious Twelfth of August.

While grouse shooting has a serious environmental importance ("take the wildlife out of the hills and you take the life out of the hills" as one sandy haired gunman put it in eloquent brevity) there is danger if it isn't done properly.

A helper was paid off with £5,000 cash after a mishap last year when a shooter (not an American, by the way) ignored the rule and swung his gun round in a level arc, chasing a fleeing grouse. Bam! The shot missed the helper's eye by a whisker.

"We have a saying in Sweden: 'You'll never regret the shot you didn't fire'," says Peter Ahlås, a Lloyds broker who was one of the guns enjoying a day's shooting on the 7,500-acre grouse moor. His message: if in doubt, don't pull the trigger.

He explains this is why he always picks a good loader – the person who loads his guns in the shooting butt. "I'll knock the gun up if I see something dangerous," confirms Peter's loader, Keith Hubbard, a retired computer technician from Durham. Like most loaders, he is also a shooting man.

In the butts – the stone or wood low-walled shooting positions – the action can be very fast and very furious. Adrian Thornton-Berry, land agent for this estate, and a serious shot, finds himself in such a shoot-up.

The red grouse, almost black against the sky, come on in waves. Bang! bang! "I pillowcased that one" (shot too close); gun rapidly handed

to Robert Crowther (day job, Huddersfield fireman). It's loaded in a trice, spare gun handed over in a split second. Bang! Bang! Two birds with the first shot, maybe another with the second, behind the butt; too frantic to count. "Gun," yells Adrian. "The ejector's jammed," shouts Robert, who reloads the other smoking gun. Flurry of hands. "Duck," snaps Adrian. So, duck I do. The barrel swings inches over my head. Boom! Another down. This goes on for several minutes, as wave after feathery wave comes on. Finally, there are no more. "That was fantastic," exhales Mr Thornton-Berry.

The beaters are now in view, an assorted band of holidaymakers' children, including a woman from the *Shooting Times*; John Baker, engineering graduate and son of the head keeper (sidelined with a back injury); stalwart chaps in shorts and boots. They wear yellow industrial protective glasses and flap away with flags made from coloured plastic sacks: these rustle like ship's sails in a light breeze.

The downed birds are laid out by the butts. Any still alive are quickly dispatched. They are placed with the others, their chests sighing one last time.

The day had started not long after dawn for Adrian Thornton-Berry, the third generation to live in a big square family house in Wensleydale. As well as being agent at East Arkengarthdale for a wealthy Swede, he is also a sporting agent. Among his clients, a party of eight Austrians who were also shooting yesterday. There had been a mix up when one of the guns had been "stuck" on a plane because of security. Now gun and the Austrian prince were united. All was well.

The Austrians are paying £120 for each pair of grouse shot. They are here for four days: total bag, possibly 100 brace a day. Maths: £12,000 a day multiplied by four equals £48,000.

What? You are going to invest in a grouse moor? Well, it sounds profitable but there are only so many birds available and everyone one talks to insists that the money is put back into the moor.

The Swedish-owned Arkengarthdale shoot yesterday was a treat for the owner's guests. The 7,500-acre moor costs about £100,000 a year to run. Adrian's calculation is that the 700,000 acres of grouse moors in England and Wales cost £80m a year to maintain.

Grouse moor owners tend to be wealthy people, who have the moor because they like shooting and they like moors. Among them is Simon Bostock, who has a moor in Nidderdale and is chairman of the Moorland Association, which is dedicated to promoting heather moor.

In doing so, the grouse thrive, as do other upland birds and insects and plants.

Certainly, the moor at Arkengarthdale is a picture, a pattern of heather in full bloom, the essential grasses and other plants that give the grouse a wholesome, year-round diet. They are not accidents of nature. It costs time, and money – much of it in grants to restrict the numbers of sheep.

"Paying guns are paying for our lapwings and curlews," says Adrian Thornton-Berry. Shooters find it infuriating that the anti-bloodsports campaigners can't see the synergy between grouse husbandry and the ecological spin-offs.

In much of Europe, there is not the same public outrage. "Shooting (in Britain) is portrayed as an elitist activity," says Peter Ahlås, a visitor to the moor since 1976. "In Sweden, the general support for shooting is considerably higher than it is here, and the public are better informed. To be allowed to shoot you have to pass a written and a practical test, which are quite demanding, and include conservation and wildlife management. It took me a week's tuition to pass it."

Only northern Britain has the red grouse and a moor like East Arkengarthdale will yield a bag of 1,400 brace. These wild birds feed on heather, bilberry, cotton grass and crowberry. Little surprise that their flavour is so prized. Some of yesterday's Arkengarthdale grouse will be on the table of London's fashionable restaurants tonight. From £5 unplucked off the moor, the price rises to £8 or £9 to the restaurateur, who will put it on the plate for £30. As the season progresses the prices fall. All shooting has usually ended well before the deadline of 10th December.

Then the gamekeeper will begin again, warding off predators, such as weasels and carrion crow, and always watching for the grouse's biggest killer after the gun, the intestinal "worm", which strikes cyclically, and often hardest when the grouse population is high.

Grouse shooting is full of apparent paradoxes. For example, the species would dwindle if it were not protected by the men who shoot them. And here's another. The way to restrict the advance of the worm is to shoot lots of grouse, therefore reducing the spread of the disease.

Among the loaders yesterday was Bryan Burrows, well-known for many years as a keeper for Earl Peel.

He says with feeling: "Everybody who lives in these dales is very proud of the grouse shooting. It would be a sad place without it, wouldn't it? The local community is so proud of it. I used to think I was not very important in life, that I didn't produce anything, like a bag of coal. Then I realised that I did, and that I could hold my head up."

The beautiful heather moors of Yorkshire are testimony to the work of men like Mr Burrows. A globule of lead shot on the side of his nose is testimony to the carelessness of some shooters. It has remained there for years, as a silent reminder.

Adrian Thornton-Berry with his dogs at Arkengarthdale

Simon Hulme

27

3 An eye for a story

As a newcomer to the newspaper game, Griffith Wright can be forgiven for playing it safe in the early days. For the *Intelligencer*'s second week it was the same foreign news as before, although it did come across something a bit more dramatic on the patch than a wedding. *"On Saturday last, in the evening, Mr Robert Bakehouse, an eminent farmer of Rothwell Haigh, was killed by a fall from his horse."*

The week after, an advertisement reveals the roads around Leeds had started to improve (the Leeds to York turnpike had just been completed) and suggested a novel idea to readers: a seaside holiday on the east coast.

"For the season a coach will set out every Wednesday from T Spinks's painter and undertaker, in Kirkgate, and take in passengers for Scarborough." The fare was 4/6d.

The English climate, particularly treacherous summer conditions, is always a favourite with newspapers and it rated this bald mention the next week, 30th July 1754. *"Some mowers last week found ice on their scythes early in the morning."*

At last, on 27th August, the *Intelligencer* got its first decent local story. It gave Griffith Wright the opportunity to find his editorial voice, speak out on a matter of general concern and inform his readers in no uncertain terms where he stood. It had religion, it had punch-ups. Even better, this was a story that would run and run, on and off, for three years.

The *Intelligencer* supported the religious establishment in Leeds and was deeply suspicious of the dissenters, especially because of their ability to attract enormous attendances to open-air meetings in the town.

In the summer of 1749, one of the most celebrated dissenters, George Whitefield, preached to a huge crowd in Leeds at five o'clock in the morning. John Wesley caused a riot and annoyed Griffith Wright so much he referred to him as "J—n We-sl-y, arch-preacher" ...whose aim was to "establish Methodism upon the ruin of good works and sound learning."

The long-running story was mired in church politics and began with the death of the vicar of Leeds, which was then a pivotal position in the town, the Reverend Joseph Cookson. Two rivals vied to be his successor at St Peter's Parish Church, the Reverend James Scott and the Reverend Samuel Kershaw. It was a bitter contest which went to court and dragged on for six years. Kershaw was elected in the end but the animosity it created continued to burn.

One of Kershaw's supporters was a Reverend Fawcett and his reward for backing the winning side in the dispute was the curacy of Holbeck, one of the largest villages adjoining Leeds. The locals however wouldn't stand for it.

The tale began in the *Intelligencer* on 27th August. *"On Sunday last, the Rev Fawcett attended with near 1,000 people from Leeds and all the constables of the borough 18 in number, made a second attempt to perform divine service at the chapel of Holbeck, to which he was deservedly nominated by the vicar of Leeds... but immediately upon his approaching the chapel, he was opposed by a furious, frantic and lawless rabble of Holbeckers, who assaulted him with dirt, stones and brickbats and whatever instrument of violence their fury could furnish...when a spotless, innocent character, abilities equal to the ablest of his brethren, and a function that should be held sacred can claim no respect; nay more cannot protect from personal injuries amidst a set of people who call themselves Christians; what may not be apprehended! Whose property is secure? or whose life is not in danger?"*

Three weeks later, 18 constables having proved insufficient to face down the mob, the army was recruited to try and strong-arm the controversial Mr Fawcett into the pulpit. *"On Wednesday last Mr Fawcett for the first time performed divine service in the chapel at Holbeck, but was escorted to and from the chapel by a party of dragoons who kept guard at the the doors during the service. Notwithstanding this precaution some evil-disposed people found means to break a window and*

George Whitefield preaching in Leeds

throw a brickbat at Mr Fawcett while he was at the reading desk."

The following weekend, the paper reported that things had settled down, except that: *"Some profane sacrilegious villains broke into the chapel and besmeared the seats with human excrement."*

Having tried the heavy mob, with limited success, the authorities clearly decided to think their way out of the crisis. The next Sunday, the newspaper said the "tumultuous part of the people" had been drawn away from Holbeck by the ruse of getting one of their favourite preachers to preach elsewhere in town, "So the Rev Mr Fawcett was behaved to with great decency."

It was only a temporary respite. The 20th October issue reports a further incident which seems to have been the last straw so far as the *Intelligencer*'s editor was concerned. Henceforward, the people of Holbeck were the enemy, their name so loathed they would appear in his columns in italics. *"In the night between the 16th and 17th...the windows of the chapel of Holbeck were broken again. No wonder when Holbeck contains such a nest of vermin whom neither the laws of God or man can confine within the boundaries of decency."*

Next month, a court case reported on 3rd December, provided some satisfaction for the editor. *"Last week were holden the sessions by adjournment for this borough when John Robinson, **an Holbecker** convicted of breaking the chapel windows at Holbeck was sentenced to be whipped and to pay a fine of £5."*

Just after the *Intelligencer*'s first anniversary the following summer, came an unsatisfactory twist in the Fawcett affair. The battle with the reviled Holbeckers had been lost. The paper announced a sermon preached at Holbeck would be published, *"Being the first time the author preached there after his admission to the curacy; together with a preface, giving some reasons why he chose to resign that curacy."*

So after all this time, the *Intelligencer*'s thundering hadn't actually achieved anything for Mr Fawcett. The horrible Holbeckers got their way. But getting the elbow at Holbeck did not mean the end of the Rev Fawcett's career.

On 30th August 1757, the *Intelligencer* reported the Rev Cookson, lecturer of the Parish Church had died. And it added, "In which place we hear he will be succeeded by Mr Fawcett, curate of the said church."

The *Intelligencer* had lost its first campaign, but perhaps helped Mr Fawcett win the war. Griffith Wright, journalist, really was in business.

29

4 Words and business

Before launching his new enterprise in 1754, it appears Griffith Wright already had a perfectly good business. His family must have wondered why he did not stick with the more ordered trades of jobbing printer and patent medicines retailer.

Starting a paper was a gamble requiring serious money. First there were the stocks of stamped paper to be bought: figures relating to another Yorkshire paper of the time indicate about £500 a year. The cost of "obtaining intelligence from London" was nearly £240. Ink, wages, other essentials, overheads and distribution were on top of that.

The reason why Griffith Wright chanced his arm may have had less to do with money and more to do with excitement. This is usually why people go into newspapers. They find the prospect of creating words, recording what is happening, spreading it around, intoxicating. There is also the small matter of being desperate to see your name in print.

The proud proprietor of the *Intelligencer* may have been able to carry initial losses from the newspaper because his stock-in-trade consisted of much more than words. In common with other printers of the time, he had plenty of things for sale.

Among the products on his shelves was Dr Daffy's Original Elixir. The *Intelligencer* advertisement in September 1755 explained that Griffith Wright had taken this product on when the previous supplier, the *Leeds Mercury* printing office, went out of business.

"Dr Daffy's Original Elixir
Sold above 30 years at the late J Lister's
printing office: removed from thence to
Griffith Wright's printing office in the
Lower Head Row.
Out of the said Griffith Wright may
also be had:
Stoughton's Elixir
Dr Benj Godfrey's cordial
Turlington's Grand Balsam
Greenough's Tincture for the Teeth
The Ladies Black Sticking Plaister
The celebrated volatile essence Eau de Luce
just imported from Paris
The famous worm-destroying sugar cake

JUST ARRIV'D,
At *G. WRIGHT*'s Printing - Office, at *New-Street-End,* LEEDES, A Large and Fresh Parcel of
Dr. DAFFY's Original ELIXIR, From the Great Wholesale Warehouse, *London*

THE good Sale that Dr. Daffy's Elixir hath met with in these Parts, and the many great Cures it hath done in most of the principal Towns in Great-Britain and Ireland, particularly in our NeighbouringCounties, has encouraged some ignorant People in counterfeiting the same, to the manifest Injury of their fellow Christians, and no Benefit to themselves. This may inform the Public, That a large and fresh Parcel of this Right Sort of ELIXIR, truly prepared at LONDON is arriv'd at LEEDES, and appointed to be sold at no other Place in the said Town, but

The famous Dutch Blacking Ball for boots and shoes, Anderson's Scots Pills etc etc"

Business must have been brisk: on 28th October 1755, this notice appeared. *"Griffith Wright, editor, gives notice of removal of offices to New Street End and thanks subscribers."* By January 1756, Griffith Wright was expanding his scope as all-purpose medicine man and now recommended: *"A most sovereign and never-failing remedy for all symptoms of the venereal disease: A Transcendent Restrictive Electuary. The only short and most infallible cure in the universe for the VD from the lightest infection to the most extreme and deplorable degree of it even when the blood and juice are thoroughly contaminated... Ask for a 5s pot of the Electuary and it will be delivered without any questions..."*

The *Intelligencer* was also starting to extend its reach, announcing on 26th October 1756, *"This paper may be seen every week at the Chapter Coffee House in Paternoster Row, London, where advertisements are taken in."*

As a jobbing printer, Griffith Wright must have been at the hub of Leeds life. Customers would want notices printed about events or sales that were of general interest. It's not entirely clear why he did not develop those as news stories. Time would have been one of his main snags. His newspaper was simply too slow to put out local information when the time-honoured face-to-face method was perfectly adequate. There was not much point in printing the latest prices at the cloth halls in Kirkgate or Mill Hill if the people who needed to know them had picked them up in conversation days earlier.

The same drawback applied to reporting the social flow in a town which was still small enough for people to know each other. Who was up, who was down, going bust or going to jail, would be part of the market gossip. To be in the know, locals did not need to buy a newspaper. Most could not read one.

For a modern reader the *Intelligencer* is scattered with tantalising fragments which cry out for a reporter to take them in hand, like this on 29th March 1757: *"Last Saturday se'nnight [seven nights ago] died in the parish of Tadcaster Jon Shephard in the 109th year of his age. He lived in a cave upon Bramham Moor for many years."*

And with extraordinary insouciance the newspaper noted that same day, *"We hear from York that yesterday Mary Ellah was burnt there for murdering her husband."*

Sometimes the faint echo of an individual voice is detectable in the writing of these sparse paragraphs such as this later in the same year on 29th November. *"Last week was married in our Parish Church Mr Jno Darnton of this town, cloth dresser and Mrs Story, a widow gentlewoman in the 84th year of her age, possessed of 1,500 charms."*

The random nature of the *Intelligencer's* local news gathering did not change all that much during the early years. Some stories suggest last minute desperation as press time approached.

The 6th May 1773, edition has a story that seems to have been brought by a likely lad on the staff after a heavy night. *"On Monday fe'nnight, a young man of this town (only 16 years of age) after eating one pound of cheese and three penny loaves to his drinking, undertook for a trifling wager to eat one pound of funeral biscuits in five minutes which he performed with great ease in four minutes and a quarter to the astonishment of the beholders!"*

The social contours and behaviour reflected in the early *Intelligencer's* pages seem at times reasonably familiar to modern eyes and at others quite alien. One Mary Bateman from Hunslet, known as the Yorkshire Witch, was hanged at York and her body brought back to the old Leeds Infirmary where spectators were charged threepence a look. It was said her skin was tanned for souvenirs and sold in pieces to the curious.

The *Intelligencer* warned the citizens who lived in Cross Parish not to clean their chimneys by sending up cats with firebrands tied to their tails. This was not out of concern for the animals' welfare. The cats tended to make neighbouring houses catch fire.

Modern sensibilities are jarred by another story to which no special significance is accorded, not even a headline. Thomas Hardy constructed a novel, *The Mayor of Casterbridge*, on the back of a tale about a West Country man who sold his wife. It happened in West Yorkshire too, but you needed good eyesight to spot the paragraph reporting it on 19th November 1776.

> Laſt Tueſday one John Knot, a labourer at Pontefract, ſold his wife for half a guinea, to Robert Rider, a ſtaymaker of the ſame place.—They had been married thirteen years, and have three children.—She was led from her huſband's houſe to the Market-Croſs, (which is near a quarter of a mile) in a halter, her three children following her, weeping, and was there delivered to her purchaſer amidſt the ſhouts and acclamations of the ſurrounding multitude.

Why did John Knot volunteer to bring such humiliation to his entire family? Was he cruel; was his wife (who does not even rate a first name), a scold and is that why the crowd yelled its approval? What did Robert Rider think of the bargain and what happened to the kids? Having stoked up anticipation, the *Intelligencer* moved briskly to the next item, a dull letter from New York.

Also worth further inquiry was a paragraph from Durham where James Harrington was find £20 (a stupendous sum for the time) for wearing hair powder without a licence.

Griffith Wright lived until he was 86. Through his newspaper and the dynasty he created, he must have been in the public eye. It is surprising then, how few personal details of him (and no pictures) survive. He was the son of the clerk of St John's church in Briggate and he probably went to the grammar school. He married Mary Pullan the year after he started the *Intelligencer*.

He was no more than 22 or 23 when he embarked on being a newspaper proprietor and editor and he ran the *Intelligencer* for 30 years, until handing it over to his son Thomas. When Thomas died in middle age, his grandson, Griffith Wright Junior, was put in charge. At the time of his death, the *Gentleman's Magazine* reckoned he was the oldest newspaper proprietor in the kingdom, maybe the world.

For newspaper production he relied on a simple flat bed wooden press worked by hand. Printing was demanding work, setting up small type in candlelight, with three or four men in the team. We can only guess at the number of men he employed, the length of their day or their wages. He must have been a reasonable employer since one of his men, Abraham Nichols, who joined the *Intelligencer* when it started, still seems to have been working there when he died in 1807 aged 79.

To get the *Intelligencer* out, Nichols and his colleagues had first to dampen the paper overnight. There was no paper especially for newspapers. It was all sized in its manufacture to give it a hard opaque surface to take a quill pen. Dampening the paper was required to give sharper definition in the press.

The ink was probably mixed from linseed oil and soot. When printing commenced the daubers – the "dab hands" – using pads of supple goatskins attached to handles would ink up the formes with the type set inside. The printed sheets would then be hung up to dry.

Griffith Wright probably planned the typesetting in batches as each stagecoach arrived with the "freshest advices", the news from London. He took his news from Lisbon, Vienna, Prague and St Petersburg because there was a well-established system for delivery which by the standards of the day were relatively quick.

News took four months to arrive from India where Robert Clive was beginning to make a name for himself with the East India Company. Agents in London provided this selection from the papers published in the capital and abroad and sent them out to provincial publishers like Griffith Wright.

Sometimes, as they do, stories fell into his lap. In the *Intelligencer* of 23rd December 1755, its readers were offered "an extract of a private letter from a gentleman at Lisbon to a merchant in this town, dated 20th November." It gives a first-person account of the effects of the devastating earthquake in Lisbon at the beginning of the previous month.

A young man starting a newspaper would have been aware that the authorities were suspicious of printers as spreaders of sedition. He would have been wary at first of expressing his own opinions in print. This was another advantage of using foreign news for him: it was safe. If the threat of prosecution did arise, Griffith Wright could fall back on the excuse he had only published verbatim what others had already printed. So, if anyone needed arresting, they were in London.

Distributing the newspaper were carters who took the parcels of papers from Leeds to outlying areas and doubled-up as salesmen, delivering *Dr Daffy's Elixir* or other goods from the shelves of the merchants who advertised in the newspaper.

Once these bundles arrived, all sorts of people then delivered them to the subscribers. The *Leeds Mercury* had a grocer in Otley, a clockmaker in Skipton and a barber in Halifax. The subscriber got to know the man who delivered his paper and the newsman would probably do other errands on the way.

The newspapers' arrangements were ahead of their time. The Post Office system was only reliable from London to the main centres. As early as 1718 the *York Mercury* was getting its editions out as far as Whitby, Scarborough, Malton, Northallerton, Darlington and Hull.

The Post Office complained that their monopoly was being undermined by these newspaper "runners" who "not only disperse a considerable quantity of newspapers, but carry also letters, which most materially injure the revenue contrary to the law."

5 Peace and war

Yorkshire has always loved its newspapers. For 20 years from 1700, an average of two newspapers a year appeared in England and outside London, York was one of the pace-setters. It produced six titles, some of which had already gone out of business by the time Griffith Wright got started. York was a competitive environment and sales ploys were tried which reveal there is nothing new in the realm of promotional wheezes. Anyone prepared to fork out a three month subscription for the *York Mercury* was promised a Monday morning delivery so they could read it before the paper was "cry'd about the streets by the hawkers".

In the preface to his first issue, Griffith Wright aimed his sales pitch specifically at gentlemen readers. Oddly, women were often the prime movers in the newspaper business in Yorkshire.

A York widow, Grace White, was one of the first to introduce them to this part of the world in 1718-19. She had taken over the *York Mercury* in Coffee Yard off Stonegate, when her husband died. Thomas Gent described Grace as of "comely stature, pretty features and generally good-conditioned; but of too great passions when put out of quiet temper. However her charity to the poor could wipe away a multitude of faults that way..."

Alice Guy, the York widow who later married Gent, helped carry the paper forward until it closed in 1740. A new title, the *York Courant*, was run from 1759 by Ann Ward. She seems to have been the Rupert Murdoch of her day, controlling one of the largest printing operations in the north of England for 30 years.

Ann Ward's *York Courant* tended to sell east and north of the *Intelligencer*'s patch. Griffith Wright clearly had concerns about it. When his only immediate competitor, the *Leeds Mercury*, folded he printed this on 24th June 1755: *"Last Tuesday died, after a tedious illness, the Leeds Mercury aged 1,816 weeks. He has left the goodwill of his circuit, which is considerable, to the York Courant."*

On 23rd September 1755, Wright was sufficiently concerned to make room to run some knocking copy about his competitor.

"The extraordinary piece of news in the York Courant of last week, relating to Colonel Dunbar's success against the French and the Indians, we find, was taken from the Newcastle Journal, and how little foundation it had in truth we are sorry to find by the following extract from a letter, dated September 18th, from a person at Whitehaven, to his friend in this town. 'We have no news from Virginia worthy of your notice, notwithstanding the specious letter in the Newcastle Journal...that I know to be utterly false and without the least foundation from this quarter.'"

The price of the *Leeds Intelligencer* (it dropped the extra "e" in issue number 603 on 8th October 1765) was raised to threepence ha'penny on 28th July 1789, to take account of stamp duty going up to twopence and sixpence being added to the duty on newspaper advertisements. The first issues of the *Intelligencer,* for which no cover price was printed, cannot have cost less than twopence. It was beyond the means of working people like spinners who made fourpence to sixpence a day. Fourpence could buy a pound of cheese, mutton or beef and pork. A pint of milk cost a halfpenny in summer, twice that in winter.

Griffith Wright wanted to put his paper in the hands of those with the income to buy the advertisers' goods and some merchants in Leeds were prodigiously wealthy thanks to the burgeoning woollen trade.

The old Moot Hall in Leeds

In the preface of his first issue Griffith Wright had made his appeal to those *"who have applied themselves with some degree of attention to any branch of science or business in the neighbourhood."* It was a shrewd sales pitch. During his long lifetime science and business would transform Britain and his native town in particular, creating wealth on a scale the rest of the world could only marvel at.

This process would sharpen the differences between the haves and the have-nots which were already in evidence when Griffith Wright started his newspaper. Turnpike trusts, financed by private capital to make improvements in roads which were beyond the means of local townships, stoked up anger. People had to pay to use the roads which led to rioting. In 1753 a mob gathered in Briggate to rescue rioters in custody. A troop of dragoons was ordered up who fired into the crowd, killing several of them.

It was the sort of incident to make people suspicious of soldiery in general. An advertisement in the *Intelligencer* offered half a crown a day for those willing to become troopers in the Royal Regiment of Horse Guards (The Blues), yet people were reluctant to march to this drum.

There were other sound reasons for ordinary people to be wary of the military. State abduction through the Press Gang was always a lurking possibility. A notice in the *Intelligencer* in 1757 on behalf of the Clerk of the Peace of the West Riding refers to a "Press for Soldiers" by the King and these were fairly frequent.

The army often had to search further afield for its cannon fodder as the *Intelligencer* reported in March 1757: *"Last Saturday arrived here under a guard of soldiers 270 pressed men from Scotland, several of whom are Highlanders and can't speak English. They are to be incorporated into the new battalion...quartered in this town."* Anyone who hung about Leeds bridge in a less than alert state might find themselves spirited away across the seas to fight for King and country as the *Intelligencer* revealed on 3rd July 1759. *"Last Thursday 35 volunteers and impressed seamen were put on board a vessel at our bridge in order to be conveyed to Hull."*

1805: DEATH OF A HERO

In 1805 came the decisive naval battle of the Napoleonic wars at Trafalgar. Napoleon's strategy had been to bring together the French fleets at Toulon and Brest with Spanish ships from Cartagena and Cádiz and create an Atlantic fleet.

Nelson sank that grand plan, gave Britain unquestioned superiority at sea and died in the process. That did not mean the *Intelligencer* would put it on the front page, although the death of Nelson did get a headline of sorts on 11th November 1805 with a report on the battle of Trafalgar whose source was the *London Gazette Extraordinary*, Admiralty-Office, of 6th November.

It said despatches had been received at the Admiralty at one o'clock that morning from Vice-Admiral Collingwood, Commander in Chief of His Majesty's ships and vessels off Cadiz.

"...As the mode of our attack had previously been determined on and communicated to the flag officers and captains, few signals were necessary and none were made, except to close order as the lines bore down.

The commander in chief in the Victory led the weather column, and the Royal Sovereign, which bore my flag, the lee.

The action began at twelve o'clock by the leading ships of the column breaking through the enemy's line, the commander in chief about the tenth ship from the van...the succeeding ships breaking through, in all parts, astern of their leaders, and engaging the enemy at the muzzles of their guns; the conflict was severe; the enemy's ships were sought with a gallantry highly honorable to their officers...about 3pm many of the enemy's ships having struck their colours, their line gave way...

A circumstance occurred during the action which so strongly marks the invincible spirit of British seamen...the Temeraire was boarded by accident or design by a French ship on one side, and a Spaniard on the other; the contest was vigorous, but, in the end, the combined ensigns were torn from the poop , and the British hoisted in their places.

Such a battle could not be fought without sustaining a great loss of men. I have not only to lament, in common with the British navy, and the British Nation, in the fall of the commander in chief, the loss of a hero, whose name will be immortal...but my heart is rent with the most poignant grief for the death of a friend, to whom by many years intimacy,

and a perfect knowledge of the virtues of his mind, which inspired ideas superior to the common race of men, I was bound by the strongest ties of affection; a grief to which even the glorious occasion to which he fell, does not bring the consolation which perhaps it ought; his Lordship received a musket bullet in his left breast, about the middle of the action, and sent an officer to me immediately with his last farewell; and soon after expired."

Beneath the despatches from the London Gazette, the Intelligencer carried this more personal and heartfelt addition with a poignant detail about Nelson's coffin. "To the above details we are enabled to add the following particulars...When Lord Nelson found that by his skilful manoeuvres he had placed the enemy in such a situation that they could not avoid an engagement, he displayed the most animation...he said to Captain Hardy and officers who surrounded him on the quarter deck, "Now they cannot escape us; I think we

shall at least make sure of 20 of them – I shall probably lose a leg, but that will be purchasing a victory cheaply."

His Lordship lived about an hour after he was wounded, during which he remained perfectly collected...A few minutes before he expired he ordered Captain Hardy to be called to him...turning to Captain Hardy, he said, "I know I am dying. I could have wished to survive to breathe my last upon British ground..." in a few moments he expired!!!

Thus fell one of the best and bravest men that ever graced the British annals. His Lordship was in the 48th year of his age; he had been engaged in upwards of 128 actions with the enemy...He lost one eye at Calvi, and one arm at Teneriffe...he had with him, it is understood, the coffin which Captain Hallowell of the Swiftsure, presented to his Lordship a short time after the glorious victory of the Nile, formed from the main mast of the L'Orient...In this his hallowed remains will be brought to England."

An excerpt from the *Leeds Intelligencer*'s report of Nelson's death

A recruiting sergeant for the 33rd Regiment of Foot in West Yorkshire

Efforts to set up a system of militia in Yorkshire met with initial disaster. On 30th August 1759 the *Intelligencer* reported, *"At a meeting at Pontefract 56,130 men were found to be able to serve in the militia (18-50 years) for the West Riding and 1,989 incapacitated."* The motive for the meeting left people suspicious and hostile.

On 19th September, there was a riot at Holmfirth. A mob of 1,000 had assembled, *"on account of constables taking down the names of persons liable to serve in the militia. They went to the constables' houses and vowed if they would not give them the lists they would pull down their houses and kill them and their families; in the end the lists were given up."*

The revolution in France and growing prospect of war altered the public's perceptions of the military. War, as always, was good for selling newspapers and by 1793 the impact of the struggle with France was starting to be felt in the columns of the *Intelligencer.*

Elizabeth Beecroft, incandescent at being accused of providing succour to the enemy (starvation was widespread in France) paid for this notice in the paper, headed, *"A vile and infamous report...Whereas some evil-minded person or persons have, very industriously for some time past propagated reports that I have exported butter and bacon to France which is totally unfounded and false. I therefore hereby give notice that*

whoever will give such information to me as will lead to the discovery and conviction of the propagator...that I will, on this, or on conviction, pay a reward of ten guineas... Elizabeth Beecroft, Kirkstall Forge."

Those who signed up to fight the French but then proved reluctant to do so, were hunted through *Intelligencer* advertisements. In July 1793 was offered, *"One guinea reward. Deserter from His Majesty's Coldstream regiment of foot from a party recruiting in Leeds. Thomas Cotton, aged 27 years, five feet eleven and a half inches high..short brown hair and complexion, round shouldered, stoops in his walk and he had on when he deserted a thickset coat and waistcoat, corduroy or leather breeches, and a rough round hat."*

Three young lads destined for the sea had also made off. *"Run away of Saturday last, from their master's service at Selby, George Harrison, born at Royson, near Wakefield; he is about 17, slender made, about five foot three inches high, yellow complexion and had light brown hair..."* (The advertisement also describes in detail the two others who have gone AWOL).

"The above boys are all apprenticed to sea service and had on sailors' dresses. If any person will apprehend either all of them or give notice to Mr Edward Wilkinson, constable, at Selby shall receive a very handsome reward; but if they will return to their servitude they will be kindly received."

6 Enter a talented rival

War may be good business for a newspaper but on the home front a rival had come to attack the *Intelligencer's* supremacy. He was called Edward Baines. Born near Preston, Baines was a young printer who had hiked over the Pennines in 1795 to complete his apprenticeship at the *Leeds Mercury*. The *Mercury* – which had folded the year after Griffith Wright launched the *Intelligencer* – had been re-started in 1765 without any great success. When Baines arrived to work there it was selling 700-800 copies a week. Within five years he was in a position to buy the paper, with the help of friends who shared his political outlook, for £1,552, paid for in three instalments. He brought out his first *Mercury* on Saturday 7th March 1801.

Baines's paper offered a voice to those excluded from the Tory-Anglican ascendancy which ran Leeds and as competition intensified between the *Mercury* and the *Intelligencer*, their respective political views polarised. The *Intelligencer,* which for 40 years had been fairly mild in its advocacy, sharpened its claws and ripped into the *Mercury's* Whig-Dissenter agenda.

The attacks grew more personal when Griffith Wright Junior took charge of the *Intelligencer* in 1805 on the death of his father Thomas who had run it since 1785. He trashed the *Mercury's* readers as *"confined to the disaffected and the illiterate, who are easily misled, deceived and cajoled by flattery..."* and he jeered at Edward Baines as *"an aspiring bloated frog".* He suggested that to get more readers the *Mercury* egged on the workers who were smashing up the machines they believed were taking their jobs.

The end of the war with France threw thousands onto the job market who were now semi-destitute. As industrialisation roared ahead they were left standing as the quality of life around them deteriorated. The new Leeds factories were making their presence felt on the landscape by 1806 when it was reported the westerly winds drove *"the columns of smoke which rise from our numerous manufactories to the eastern parts of the town...where from the lowness of the ground it is apt to make its lodgement".*

Griffith Wright Junior needed to expand to keep pace with opportunities as Leeds almost doubled in size from its 1754 status as the regional hub of a rural textile economy to an industrial power-house. It was all the doing of those men first targeted by his grandfather as *Intelligencer* readers – the wealth creators from the worlds of science and business.

In March 1811, Griffith Wright was confident enough to bring out a supplement. By July 1813 he had enough to retire his wooden press and buy an iron Earl Stanhope hand press for £50. Transport was improving and the competing stagecoach companies, locked into a price-war over fares, vied to advertise at the top of his front page. One of the advertisements, on Monday 10th April 1815, read: *"Reduced fares by the Royal Union Post Coach (carrying four insides only). Sets out every morning at half past eight o'clock from the Hotel, Leeds, by way of Ferrybridge, Doncaster, Newark, Grantham, Stamford to the Angel Inn, St Martin's-le-Grand, London where it arrives next day at noon. Fares from Leeds to London: Inside £3.13.6d. Outside £1.18.0d"*

Powerful Yorkshiremen had long been among the movers and shakers of London's business community and the *Intelligencer's* columns gave them a rallying point away from home. On 24th April 1815, the Yorkshire Society announced: *"The next annual dinner of the gentlemen connected with the county of York will be held in the London tavern, Bishopsgate Street, on Thursday, 11th of May. Earl of Harewood in the chair."*

The less powerful found it increasingly difficult to eat at all. As the price of wheat soared, average wages for many workers fell disastrously from 1800 onwards and working hours increased. Commenting on this explosive situation some years later, the *Intelligencer* conceded that this was a moment *"...when the revolutionary mania was advancing with rapid strides amongst us; and when the inhabitants of Leeds and surrounding districts were suffering under the pressure of severe distress."*

At the time however, the *Intelligencer* denied any distress existed among the poor and challenged anyone to find evidence of it. Editors who antagonised public opinion like this risked more than a sheaf of stinging readers' letters by way of response. In March 1817 an infuriated mob met outside the *Mercury* offices in Briggate, then marched to the *Intelligencer* looking for Griffith Wright Junior *"breathing the most outrageous threats against his person"*. He was not in but they knew where he lived. When the mob did not find Wright at home in Harehills, they vented their anger on a bystander and almost killed him.

People's suspicions of the authorities deepened even further three months later when they read a story by Edward Baines. It was the scoop of his career. Baines had received a tip-off and took a post chaise to Dewsbury where a character called William Oliver had been discovered organising a West Riding conspiracy against Lord Liverpool's government. Baines revealed the real Oliver: a bankrupt recently released from jail, he was an *agent provocateur* secretly employed by the Home Secretary Lord Sidmouth as an agent. Baines's story in the *Mercury* was read

COVERING THE PETERLOO MASSACRE, AUGUST 1819

"A scene of confusion and terror now existed which defies description..."

"REFORM MEETING AT MANCHESTER: It is our painful task to have this week to record, the fatal results of the proceedings of the Lancashire reformers, spirited on by the miscreant Hunt to a contempt of the laws and in open defiance of magisterial authority. We have endeavoured in the following narrative, to give a faithful and accurate account of the unhappy transactions during the past week having spared no pains to procure the most authentic intelligence, upon the spot, and by a comparison of the various reports...

Hunt was proceeding to make some indecent references to the magistrates when the Manchester and Salford Yeomanry Cavalry suddenly appeared on the ground ...Hunt said to the people, "stand firm my friends: you see they are in disorder already: give them three cheers," at the same time taking off his hat with a malicious grin, in token of defiance and waving it above his head. The cheers were

The *Intelligencer*'s first on-the-spot report: the Peterloo massacre

instantly returned by the cavalry and the whole of the peace officers, the former brandishing their swords while huzzaing.

Mr Trafford, a highly respectable Cheshire magistrate, headed the Manchester and Salford yeomanry and an order was given for the

whole to advance and take their prisoners...And when Hunt found them approaching near to the hustings the colour fled from his cheeks, the grin forsook his countenance and he appeared ready to sink into the earth.

The cavalry had not advanced many yards when they were assailed with volleys of stones...Till thus assailed no yeomanry-man used his sword, each man having confined himself to waving it above his head...Now the duty of self-preservation obliged them to strike, but in very few instances to cut.

Whilst they were in execution of their duty the soldiery were on every side attacked...many of the cavalry were struck to the ground and the reformers attempted to knock out their brains with large stones (previously provided)...

One gallant youth, Mr John Hulme, was struck in the face with a brick. It took away his senses, and he checked his horse so suddenly that

out in Parliament and *The Times* which followed it up put the headline on their version: *"Horrible Plot of Spies and Informers to Excite Insurrection."*

Baines's exclusive did not convince everyone and may not have been quite what it seemed. The *Intelligencer* argued that in these fraught times, a spy network was not necessarily a bad thing. William Cobbett was not impressed either and called Baines "The Great Liar of the North", a title which stuck.

Civil discord in the North came to a head in the second week of August 1819. The *Intelligencer* carried preliminary reports about a reform meeting that was to be held in St Peter's Fields in Manchester and for what seems to have been the first time, it engaged reporters to cover a big story (they also knew Baines's son Edward Junior would be there for the *Leeds Mercury*).

On Monday, 16th August 1819, a crowd of over 50,000 gathered where the Free Trade Hall now stands to hear a speech on parliamentary reform by the radical Henry Hunt. The local authorities panicked and sent in the cavalry who charged with sabres drawn. When the blood-letting was over, eleven people lay dead and about 400 had been injured.

---

both fell together. A man had also stabbed him in the back...A scene of confusion and terror now existed which defies description. The multitude pressed one another down and in many parts they lay in masses,

piled body upon body. The cries and mingled shouts, with the galloping of the horses was shocking...

It was scarcely to be anticipated that the number of the reformers would come to the meeting

prepared with offensive weapons...

The whole of the affray lasted but a few minutes...The military have had the greatest merit in their forbearance, as so little firing took place when compared with the circumstances under which they were called to duty. Strong bodies of cavalry and constables patrolled the streets and the town had every appearance of being in a state of complete insurrection..."

On the Friday, Hunt and others appeared in court.

"Hunt was placed at the Bar. He looked boldly round. The magistrates said he was being remanded on a charge of high treason.
Hunt: "I presume I am not allowed to say anything?
Bench: "No"
Hunt: "I beg to state one word. I am perfectly innocent of the charge and am ready to meet it."
Hunt then bowed to the bench and went down."

It was the *Intelligencer* readers' first opportunity to find out what a good reporter – alert to dramatic nuance, an eye for significant detail and a skilful pen – brings to the party.

The Peterloo Massacre

The creative spirit

Titus Salt had the imagination to challenge the assumption that manufacturing and squalor were necessarily linked. He quit dirty Bradford and in green fields built Salts Mill, creating around it the model community of Saltaire to give his working people the chance to live decently.

Salt was good at spotting an opportunity and according to legend he came across a cargo from Peru at Liverpool docks one day which no-one quite knew what to do with. It was alpaca, the fleece of the llama, and Salt used it with great commercial success. This creative combination of Yorkshire shrewdness and compassion came to the attention of Charles Dickens. Picking up on the Liverpool story, Dickens wrote admiringly in his magazine *Household Words*, "Our friend Salt took it [the alpaca] up, looked at it, felt it, pulled it about; in fact he did all but taste it and he would have done that if it had suited his purpose, for he was 'Yorkshire'."

After Titus, textiles and the world

moved on. By the mid-1980s, no-one quite knew what to do with Salts Mill. Its monumental proportions had been floated by a high tide of Victorian confidence, now receded. In 1986 it was a neglected hulk, high and dry, and was offered by its last textile company owners at a peppercorn rent to charities interested in preserving it. There were no takers.

The potential of Salts was not lost on Jonathan Silver, a local businessman who had been wheeling and dealing ever since he had been a pupil at Bradford Grammar School. Silver had bought his first empty textile mill, in the Colne Valley, in the summer of 1982. The following year, with his partner Sir Ernest Hall, he took on Dean Clough, the old Crossley carpet factory in Halifax with 1.25 million square feet of derelict space. Art was to be a key element in Dean Clough's revival.

Silver could be impulsive in other areas of life. Stunned by television reports of Khmer Rouge genocide in Cambodia he decided on a plan to raise cash for the victims. He turned up one Friday evening in the *Yorkshire*

Post newsroom asking for a reporter to go with him to write about what was happening in Cambodia, the stories to be sold to the highest bidder. Silver and reporter were on the plane to Bangkok the next morning. They crossed the border in northern Thailand, made contact with anti-Khmer Rouge Cambodian guerillas and secured interviews. The *Yorkshire Post* carried an exclusive and Silver elbowed his way into Fleet Street editors' offices to fix up lucrative payment for a feature article the proceeds of which went to charity.

In June 1987, he was convinced that art could also be an engine to drive Salts Mill into the 21st century. This time he was on his own when he bought the mill and 17 acres around it. A scheme to move the Victoria and Albert Museum's south Asia collection here from London foundered. But he fostered his friendship with David Hockney – begun years before when he had persuaded him to do an illustration for the school magazine – and the 1853 Gallery at the mill became the world's largest permanent exhibition of Hockney paintings and a

Mel Hulme

Mark Bickerdike

Top: Hockney's 1997 painting of Salts Mill. Left: Jonathan Silver and the mill, and (above) Titus Salt

magnet for art lovers.

The echoing stone-flagged spaces of the old production sheds became populated with technology businesses, shops and cafes. Ambitious artistic productions like Opera North's community version of *West Side Story* were staged here.

The 850 workers' dwellings and the rest of Titus Salt's model community which had sagged during the long years of textile's decline took on a new lease of life as the mill prospered, and Saltaire was designated a World Heritage Site. Prince Charles gave the seal of approval to the Salts method by launching here in 1996 the Regeneration Through Heritage programme. Silver died the following year of cancer.

41

A Hockney portrait

Reginald Brace talked to mothers about the success of their celebrated sons. Here he interviewed Laura Hockney, mother of David.

Whenever anyone asks Laura Hockney, the mother of David Hockney, how her son is going on she always replies "Which one?" David's achievements in art have made him a celebrity, but Mrs Hockney is ever mindful of the rest of the Hockney brood, which includes three other sons and a daughter.

Paul Hockney, 41, is a chartered accountant and Bradford City Councillor, Philip, 39, has his own engineering business in Australia, and John, 33, also works in Australia, as a representative. Margaret, 37, is a widely-travelled district nurse who has settled in Bedfordshire.

"David is famous, but all our children have done well in their own way," said Mrs Hockney. "We are proud of them all." She is a nice lady of 72, white haired, sympathetic, friendly and articulate – a benevolent Bradfordian of the old school.

Laura and her husband, Kenneth, a retired accountant aged 69, live in a stone terrace house in Eccleshill. Their friendly front room has a green moquette suite; wall lights, a gas fire in a teak surround and several etchings by David, including a view from a Parisian window inscribed "Paris for Mum and Dad with love from David." It was a Christmas gift in 1971 and it is Mrs Hockney's favourite. "I think it's lovely. The detail is so good you can almost see the curtains wafting about."

Mrs Hockney produced some of the earliest examples of David's work in a blue, hard-backed exercise book bearing the title "Log Book of the Panther Patrol." David was leader of the patrol in the 4th Bradford East

Laura Hockney

(Eccleshill Church) Troop of Boy Scouts, and the book contains descriptions and drawings of the 1951 Soap Box Derby at Scarborough and other troop occasions. Another book, written when he was ten, describes a visit to Keswick in 1948.

"David won a scholarship to Bradford Grammar School, but he didn't want to go at all. He wanted to go to art school. I went before a committee at the Town Hall to see if he could go to the Regional College of Art but they said that first he should have the all-round education which was not available at the Regional College at that time.

"So he went to the Grammar School. I don't think he liked it a bit. If he could go without wearing his blazer and cap, he did. He was there, but he resented it. All his school books were decorated with little doodles. The masters must have been absolutely at a loss with him.

"But he won the art prize every year. At speech days we couldn't understand the reaction of the other boys when David went up for his award. They stamped their feet, booed, clapped and shouted and made a terrific noise. We spoke to the head about it and he said it was because David was so amusing.

"He was certainly an unconventional boy, out of the usual rut. When he gave his mind to it he did reasonably well in other subjects besides art, but very often he didn't bother. He didn't like games a great deal apart from a bit of running and swimming. Once they asked him to write an essay on cricket – all he wrote was "Wet day, no play."

When the front door bell rang, Mrs Hockney left to answer its call, and returned carrying a handsome bouquet of red roses and carnations, encased in Cellophane.

"Belated birthday greetings, David," said the card. "Two days late, but he never forgets completely" said Mrs Hockney.

"As a boy he was gentle, kind and appreciative of the smallest thing you did for him. He was a happy child, never short of friends. Mind you, he didn't tell us everything. It wasn't until quite recently that I found out that in his early days at the Royal College he lived in a hut at the bottom of someone's garden.

"By the time he was ten it was obvious he had artistic talent. Many people in Eccleshill remember him going about pushing a pram containing his paints and easel. He would wheel the pram to the spot he wanted, set up his easel and paint. He didn't worry about what people might think.

"He did a painting of the inside of a fish and chip shop in Eccleshill. It used to hang in the shop, but the owner left and took it with him. David had an easel in the attic, and we still have a huge painting of a nude figure he painted up there. It's horrible.

"His first big sale was a picture of his father he did in the attic. It was oil on canvas and the year was 1955 when he was at Bradford Regional College of Art. He rang me up and said: 'Hello mum, I've sold my dad.' It was so funny the way he said it. He got £10, which was a fortune to him at the time. He was so proud.

"I don't know who David takes after. Kenneth does a bit of art, but nothing as intriguing as David. I was always good at art at school, but I didn't have time to do anything once I got married. My only creative outlet was sewing and embroidery, but I have lost that now because of arthritic wrists. In his ways, David reminds me of my father, who was a gentle man.

"David was an untidy boy, but he is not so untidy now because he has got his flat in Notting Hill and he likes it to look nice. He's got it lovely now. He made the kitchen into a library and he has a good, big studio. There is a huge dining room with a glass roof, and the bathroom has a round shower.

"He has lots of friends of both sexes. When you are at his flat, people are always calling, or the telephone is ringing. David is happy in his work, and with his friends. I don't think marriage matters to him, though one never knows. Anyone who

Hockney at Salts Mill in 2000   Bruce Rollinson

marries an artist has to have a special type of patience. David does just what he likes. He enjoys what he is doing, and he does it. If you are married you have to consider someone else. You can't just live as you like.

"I once asked David if he ever got depressed. He said: 'Maybe I do sometimes.' But with so many friends around he doesn't stay depressed for long. When he comes home, I don't see any change in him. He's just David. He often brings his friends – artists or actors. I wonder what to give them to eat, but they don't seem to mind my home cooking.

"He doesn't like Bradford. He thinks it is rather dull, and he is very much against pulling down lovely old buildings like Kirkgate Market. But as long as we are here he will carry on coming.

"He drives up in his sports car, and you never know what he is going to wear next. His shirts and ties are all kinds of colours, but always very good things. He wears odd socks, because he likes to. I thought it was terrible at first, but you get used to it – like his bleached hair.

"David's hair is really a beautiful chestnut. One night in America he was watching TV with a friend when an advert came on which said people with blond hair live longer. They both went out and had their hair bleached, and he's bleached it ever since. When I first saw him with his hair like that I walked straight past him because I didn't recognise him. It wouldn't be my choice.

"But neither the clothes nor the hair alter his personality. They may be 'arty' and he may look different, but he is the same loving, straightforward person he always was. And that's all that matters. If we were all as straightforward as David, the world wouldn't go far wrong.

"He's been lucky. We always pictured him having an ordinary job during the day and painting in an attic at night, but he was born in an era when artists are being recognised during their lifetime not after it. He has a style of his own and his work is appreciated. And he has worked hard."

Behind the fringe

Paul Vallely met Alan Bennett who had turned his back on the plays which made him famous to write about his native Yorkshire.

"I DON'T believe in the things that Yorkshire people vaunt themselves for. There used to be a terrible advert on the outskirts of Settle which said: 'In Yorkshire we know better'. That really sums up what I hated about it all...that collective self-assurance, the sense of we know best, we're going to go our own way."

Harsh words from Leeds-born Alan Bennett looking back at his home country from the distance of his Edwardian house in Camden Town. But his attitude is ambivalent and the words hide a deep affection for the county and its people.

"I live in London only because it is now where most of my friends live. But I enjoy going back to Yorkshire. There's something about the people, as individuals, which makes me feel at home. It makes my accent blossom." It is an affection which has caused a remarkable new development in his career as a writer.

The phone rang once in a prearranged signal. Across the road he was expected for tea. In the same road live many of his friends including the theatre director, Jonathan Miller. He did not go but instead served scones, seedcake and tea in enormous cups.

At 43, Alan Bennett still looks like the fresh-faced boyish Oxford graduate who took the theatre by storm in the early Sixties with *Beyond the Fringe*. The son of a Headingley butcher, he was educated at Leeds Modern School. Before university, where his theatre career began, he did National Service.

"I was put on the Russian course. I enjoyed that enormously. The discipline was lax and I was in a congenial group which included Michael Frayn and David Marquand. What most people get at university I had in the Army in a much more intensified form.

"I look back on that as the happiest time of my life. It seems absurd really to say that about the Army. But I actually didn't even mind the drill."

After that came a history degree at Exeter College, Oxford, followed by research into Richard II. It was only as a postgraduate he became involved by chance in student dramatics. The result was *Beyond the Fringe* with Peter Cook, Dudley Moore and Jonathan Miller which ran for years in the West End and toured in the United States.

"It was a runaway success. I've never had notices again like that. Afterwards I was lost for about two years. I wasn't confident of my ability to do anything by myself."

But Bennett consolidated his reputation after those fallow years by writing and appearing with Sir John Gielgud in *Forty Years On*, an affectionate and wistful satire on the old, dying English way of life. It was a theme of lament for bygone ways he continued in *Getting On* and *Habeas Corpus*. But it is now over four years since the last of those stage plays and in that time Alan Bennett's work has taken a most unusual turn.

"In 1974, my father died. That stopped me in my tracks for reasons which I can't put my finger on. It stopped me writing. It was quite hard to get over. Then I started a few television plays."

In these plays the stylish comic elegies have given way to a new type of work which is steeped in the county of his childhood and birth. Normally writers work out their auto-biographical preoccupations early in their career and then turn to broader subjects. With Alan Bennett, the reverse is true.

Since *Habeas Corpus*, Bennett has written eight television plays which record the passing of time in Yorkshire with a poignancy far more acute and moving that that of the much-lauded *Forty Years On*. The plays are in various stages of production. *A Day Out* is the story of a Halifax cycling club in 1911, a world of cobbled streets and common sense, bone-shaker bikes and unshakeable beliefs – all soon to be shattered and changed forever by the Great War. This play did for industrial Yorkshire, in an unashamedly nostalgic way, what his earlier work had done for the cricket pitches of old England's public schools.

Sunset Across the Bay showed an elderly couple retiring, as their Leeds home is torn down for redevelopment, to live in Morecambe where they find the water does not make a decent cup of tea. Like all his new Northern plays it displayed a sensitivity, economy of style, and verisimilitude lacking in so many of the "eebygum" style of television plays set in the North.

Ironically, Bennett feels that this work, in which he is much more attuned to his subject, is somehow less "worthy" than his earlier work. "I somehow feel the stage is much more serious and demanding. I regard it as 'literature' and television drama as 'non-literature' which I'm sure is not a good thing. A stage play, I feel, has to be as near the finished product as possible about six months before rehearsal starts. But with telly...we start rehearing one next week and it still isn't finished yet. The BBC thinks it is, of course, but I know it isn't."

That attitude stems from the days when the *Beyond the Fringe* team would write, rehearse and act material for the late-night television satires in less than one day. "I tend to think of it as somebody else who did all that, not me. It's part of another life."

It seems so. Alan Bennett describes his life now as like that of a bachelor uncle, dining out with married couples five nights a week. Despite his displays of wit in appearances on TV panel games, in private he is a shy and reticent man whose life is quiet, unassumingly and casually elegant, and private; he asked me not to write about this house in Camden Town – "I'd feel as if everyone who read it had been there."

It is mainly hours at the typewriter – "the thing about writing is that you don't have any spare time, it somehow spills over into all the time you've got" – seeing friends, and regular trips to Bristol, where his mother now lives with his brother. Occasionally he visits his parents' old cottage in the village of Clapham, near Settle, where he is president of the civic society and involved in the preservation of the town's old buildings.

HIs passion for conservation – he has described himself as politically Left-wing and socially Right-wing – is the practical expression of an emotion which runs through all his work, for television or for the stage: a rich sense of nostalgia and an awareness of the passing of people, things and time.

"I think it's something you're born with. I remember first coming to London for the Festival of Britain and then returning when I was in the Army and the festival site was derelict.

"I remember thinking how happy I'd been the first time I'd seen it. It's absurd to think that even at the age

"It's absurd to think that even at the age of 18 I actually thought I had already had the best part of my life. If you're born with that attitude you don't get rid of it"

of 18 I actually thought I had already had the best part of my life. If you're born with that attitude you don't get rid of it."

Bennett has never been afraid of sentiment, which is what keeps his nostalgia from slipping into the merely sentimental. He has always been able to balance that lyricism with outrageous humour. "People say that you can't make fun of something one minute and then be lyrical and poetic about it the next. I think you can.

"Serious plays are often only serious because they have had the jokes eliminated, sieved out. That seems to me the wrong sort of seriousness. You can actually be serious while keeping in the jokes in the same way that you can go to a funeral and feel moved and yet things can strike you as funny and you laugh without detracting from your sadness. Critics don't appreciate that very often; they like things in a box so they can label them. They don't like to be left with an unidentifiable feeling. Audiences appreciate it much more than they do."

Bennett's next play for the box is set in an old people's home in Leeds. *A Little Outing* is about a couple who

go to visit the wife's father and its setting, language and naturalism are typical of his latest work. "I think the Northern plays are more lyrical although they too are full of outrageous jokes. I'm very interested in exactitude of dialogue. You have to be. There are so many plays about the North on the telly which seem to miss what is special and touching and good about living in the North. It's partly because the dialogue doesn't represent the way people speak, it's often just a stereotype." To help him get this right, he keeps a series of notebooks in which he jots down things people say – his mother claims she gives him most of his dialogue.

Bennett has not turned his back completely on his old style. He has a fourth stage play with which he is not really satisfied yet and a fifth, *The Old Country*, which opens in the West End in September. "The telly plays are to do with behaviour whereas there are ideas in the stage plays. Whether or not they are any good I don't know; maybe I'm inflating them by saying this. I thought of trying to write a Northern play for the stage but it hasn't come to anything. I might still try and do that."

NOVEMBER 1961

The Good Companion

When the *Yorkshire Post* began its tradition of Literary Luncheons, the first guest at the Hotel Metropole in Leeds was JB Priestley.

"I like the North. Indeed, I could almost say I love the North. I speak the language. Indeed, it's the only language I speak properly. I think it's a fine language. We are able, in our Northern language, to keep our vowels open.

I love the country. I have been all over the world and still think the most beautiful, satisfying countryside is that of the Dales, beginning some 20 miles north of where we are now. I even like the towns – or I did before they began improving them. To me there was always a sombre dignity about those great black stone mills and warehouses and the way the lighted trams could be seen climbing the hills like little golden beetles – and the way the street lamps were like strange constellations against the sky. It had a certain beauty to me when I was young.

Market Street, Bradford, which I've been remembering because I'm beginning to write some reminiscences of my life there 50 years ago – Market Street, Bradford, which was rather wide and had these black buildings – the old George Hotel, now pulled down – was a fine street. But of course they've improved it, and the minute you bring in these white buildings, meant for the Mediterranean and southern California – buildings that look like sodden wedding cakes in the West Riding – then you ruin it.

A man rang me up from a Northern city to ask me a favour, and said, "You know, I must tell you quite frankly that I don't like your last book." And of course I could have said "Well, I haven't seen your face – but I probably wouldn't like that either." But I didn't because I under-stood him. He did exactly what I would do – and what I've often got into trouble for doing. He was being honest.

We have always had, in the North, a public image of ourselves as blunt, honest, independent men and women that you couldn't push around. I very much believe in this. That's the sort of man I am and I hope it's the sort of people you are. And I hope that when these young writers, who show a great deal of fine talent – these young writers you are producing now in the West Riding, display themselves as being blunt and honest and indignant, perhaps at times a little rude – a little awkward – you will remember that they are carrying this public image for you. You must welcome them. You must cherish them.

We live in a bad time and we are between two mill-stones – neither of them owned by God. We are between the new ant-hill civilisation of Communists in the East and, in the West, what I have called "ad-mass" – a way of life in which the masses have been manipulated for profit. I don't like either of them. I say "A plague on both your houses." Now we've arrived at such a situation that, if you criticise one, it is automatically supposed that you believe in the other. Both sides are so stupid now that they can't understand that you don't like either of them.

Let us take our own stand here. And writers will help us because litera-ture is the friend of man. In one part of the world a man is simply some-thing used by the state – one ant, one termite, among millions. On our side of the curtain, man is becoming a consumer – a customer – a unit of labour. Man, the individual, almost seems to disappear, except in litera-ture, which preserves the whole man. If you want to find the whole man he is there in books – that is why the writer is so important. And I do assure you – and this has got nothing to do with my feeling for my own profes-sion or my own situation – I do assure you with all the sincerity that I can command that never in Man's history was the writer so important as he is today.

It is one of the grimmer ironies of our times that, just when he is so important, the whole status of the writer is going down – particularly in this country. The British Establishment does not like the writer. But you in the North – if you are the people who deserve this public image – should be anti-Establishment. Whatever your politics may be, you should refuse to be one of the hypnotised sheep that are beginning to be accepted as British citizens. You should cherish your rebels, even if you don't agree with them.

You must! This is our hope of saving ourselves. And perhaps, by saving ourselves, helping to save the world.

There is an old story – and I don't tell it for its own sake – you probably all know it, that when gas-fires were very new a woman in Shipley bought one and the neighbours said, "'Ow are you getting on with t'gas fire, Mrs Sugden?" She said, "Ee! It's champion. We lit it a week last Tuesday and it's not gone out yet." Now, there's a spirit of individuality – there's a flame in the North – and we readers and writers should make sure it doesn't go out."

The Brontës, the Intelligencer and a fatal decision

The Brontë Parsonage Museum in Haworth and (below) Charlotte Brontë
Graham Lindley

One family who were particularly keen on the *Leeds Intelligencer* were the Brontës of Haworth. The Rev Patrick Brontë corresponded from the parsonage and also sent in verse. The youthful Charlotte wrote that the *Leeds Intelligencer* was "a most excellent Tory newspaper". She and the other Brontë children entertained themselves by creating a fictional world centred on an imaginary city called Verdopolis. The characters who live in Verdopolis read and discuss and reply to articles printed in the local papers, one of them the *Verdopolitan Intelligencer*. The real newspaper had clearly fed these young minds and inspired their writing. Later, Branwell followed his father's literary example by submitting his verse to the *Intelligencer* which obliged by publishing one of his poems about the Afghan War on 7th May 1842. It also printed a poem of Anne Brontë's in December 1848. There

was also a long and favourable review of Charlotte's novel *Villette* on 19th February 1853.

But the *Intelligencer* was to play a fateful and tragic role in the family's destiny. In 1824 Patrick Brontë spotted an advertisement in the newspaper for a charity school for clergymen's daughters run by William Carus Wilson at Cowan Bridge in Lancashire. In July that year he sent his daughters Maria and Elizabeth to the school. Charlotte and Emily joined them later. It was a disastrous decision. The school was in a damp area, sanitation was bad and there never seemed to be enough to eat. Maria was bullied by one of the teachers and then typhus broke out. Maria and Elizabeth fell sick and died from

consumption in 1825. Years later Charlotte told her biographer Elizabeth Gaskell that Lowood School in *Jane Eyre* was based on Cowan Bridge and that the minatory character Miss Scatcherd was based on the teacher who had made Maria's life a misery. When Mrs Gaskell's *The Life of Charlotte Brontë* came out in 1857 the *Leeds Intelligencer* joined in with newspaper condemnation of Patrick Brontë for his failings as a parent.

Maybe the school, which relocated in 1833 and is still going as Casterton School, was unfairly treated by Charlotte. One thing seems certain: it was no great shakes at talent-spotting. A report opposite Charlotte's name in a register of the time states that she read "tolerably".

And how did she write?

Humour in the Yorkshire Post

This page: Nicky Taylor's illustration for the
cover for the Yorkshire Show supplement, 2002

Opposite (clockwise from top left):
Eric Cantona by Graeme Bandeira
Cartoon by Morris from 1975
Jo Brand by Nicky Taylor
Clive James by Nicky Taylor
Bill Tidy's cartoon strip from 1989
Anne Robinson by Graeme Bandeira

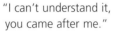
"I can't understand it,
you came after me."

GOD'S OWN COUNTY by Bill Tidy

EXCUSE ME, SIR. THIS SURVEY WILL ONLY TAKE A FEW MOMENTS.

DO YOU THINK THE POPULAR IMAGE...

..OF THE YORKSHIREMAN IS
A) LIKEABLE BUT BLUNT
B) DISLIKEABLE BUT HONEST OR
C) DON'T KNOW?

DON'T KNOW!

NO YORKSHIREMAN 'DOESN'T KNOW!'

The making of a picture

This photograph, which takes perhaps three seconds to look at, was three months in the making between the RAF and the *Yorkshire Post*.

Bruce Rollinson preparing for his flight and (above left) the Red Arrows pictured from the ground with Bruce Rollinson's Hawk aircraft shown detatched

The project started when Flight Lieutenant Matt Clark, a pilot and the press officer for RAF Linton-on-Ouse just north of York, spent a day at the *Yorkshire Post* offices in February 2004.

The RAF, like all the armed forces, acknowledge that public relations plays a big part in what they do and the Flight Lieutenant needed some first-hand knowledge of what a newspaper needs and how it works.

Over afternoon coffee with our picture editor, Ian Day, he asked what the RAF could do that would make a front page picture for the paper.

"Fly with the Red Arrows."

"Maybe to take you down the Yorkshire coastline?"

"No, over York Minster."

The wheels were duly set in motion. Eventually a date was fixed: 28th May 2004 at the start of the Red Arrows' 40th anniversary season. They were to begin it at Linton when 15 new pilots from 207 Squadron graduated. The director of flying training Air Commodore Glen Edge would present the pilots with their wings and then the Red Arrows would do their stuff. It was arranged for our photographer, Bruce Rollinson, to fly in one of 100 Squadron's Hawk T trainers based at RAF Leeming and to pick up the Red Arrows at Linton. Once the plans were finalised, all they could do was pray for decent weather.

This sort of flying is exacting on the body. Bruce Rollinson had to pass a medical with his own doctor, followed by another at RAF Leeming where he also had to undergo G-force training. It was potentially his most queasy assignment, so naturally in the squadron mess immediately before the flight they fed him fish and chips and mushy peas.

Special camera lenses had been hired that would give sharp images despite the aircraft vibration. This of course leaves out the human element. No sooner did Rollinson's Hawk meet up with the Red Arrows, than they were approaching York. At these speeds, there were to be no second chances. Once over the Minster he had just enough time for two shots, no more. After three months of groundwork, everyone was sky-high when the results appeared on our front page on 29th May.

● *A Nikon D1X was used for the picture, with 24-120 f4 VR Nikkor lens, 1/640th sec @f8. Rated at 400 asa.*

7 The competition for readers

Griffith Wright senior died in the autumn of 1818, the world he departed almost unrecognisable from the one he had known when he started in journalism. That December his grandson sold the business and retired to enjoy himself. A copy of the newspaper then cost seven pence, the highest it reached, and the new owners changed the title to *Leeds Intelligencer and Yorkshire General Advertiser*.

The stability of the dynastic Wrights gave way to an ownership of shifting business partnerships which seemed to dissolve every couple of years. Eight people, including a woman, Mary Robinson, were involved at various times. Hiring an editor as the job is understood now put Alaric Watts in the saddle in 1822, just as the *Intelligencer,* under new ownership again, moved to the handsome Georgian premises of the Leeds Library in Commercial Street. He was paid £300 a year, "more than had ever been paid to the editor of a provincial journal," his bosses assured the readers.

Watts was stung by an attack from Edward Baines, took him to court and won. It was only a technical victory. Baines's stock as an opinion former and political fixer continued to soar. Watts was a poet who wore his heart on his sleeve. After a visit to the Infirmary to see some of the casualties of the Industrial Revolution, factory-hands whose health had been wrecked by machines, he thundered out against the inhumanity of the mill owners.

A pile of letters promptly arrived from readers cancelling their subscriptions. Working men preferred the *Leeds Mercury*'s radicalism and clubbed together to buy a copy. For the badly off, seven pence for the *Intelligencer* was out of the question. Alaric Watts had misjudged his market and did not stay long.

He was successful however in bringing a literary flavour to the pages of the *Intelligencer* which was one of its attractions to the youthful residents at Haworth parsonage. The Rev Patrick Brontë gave the lead to his literary children when the newspaper used a satirical poem he had written on the Irish nationalist Daniel O'Connell. Charlotte, aged 13, confided in her diary, grandly titled *History of the Year 1829,* "Papa and Branwell are gone for the newspaper, the *Leeds Intelligencer*...We take two and see three newspapers a week. We take the *Leeds Intelligencer*, Tory, and the *Leeds Mercury*, Whig, edited by Mr Baines, and his brother, son-in-law, and his two sons..."

The *Intelligencer* would not have appreciated sharing her affections with Mr Baines. It targeted him with violent abuse, sneering that he was, *"still the same poverty-stricken adventurer that he was 30 years ago, when he wandered into Leeds, his whole fortune centred in a composing stick and his head as empty of learning as his back was bare of clothes..."*

Prosperity slightly eased the difficulties. The *Intelligencer*'s sales started to pick up. In the five years up to 1838, circulation

YORK MINSTER FIRE 1829

THE LEEDS MERCURY

YORK MINSTER BURNT.

THE ENGRAVING.

This Engraving gives a spirited and very correct delineation of the appearance of the Minster when the flames were at their height. The spectator is supposed to be standing near the south-west angle of the Cathedral, and the tower in which the fire originated is that from the top of which the flames are seen issuing. The portion of the roof of the nave betwixt the two western towers is that which was set on fire by the falling of the weather-boards. The ravages of the fire extended as far as the great lantern tower which rises over the centre of the Minster, at the intersection of the transepts with the nave and choir. The south-side aisle is shown by the lower tier of windows, in which is the rich stained glass; and betwixt the lower and the upper windows, though not distinctly seen in the Engraving, is the narrow roof of that aisle, which was set on fire about ten o'clock, but where the fire was extinguished.

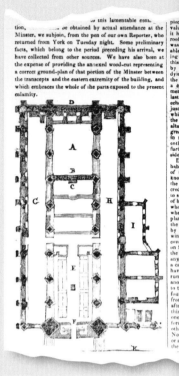

The *Leeds Mercury's* illustration of the burning Minster (left) and (above) a duller effort that appeared in the *Leeds Intelligencer*

Perhaps because there was a whole Baines brood to contribute bright editorial ideas and think of newsy angles, the *Leeds Mercury* seemed better equipped to raise its game when the big story broke – such as York Minster catching fire in 1829. This was how the *Intelligencer* covered it.

"Fire at York Minster.
It is our distressing duty to state that, on Monday morning, at an early hour, the choir of this splendid cathedral pile, was discovered to be on fire, and that the flames were not subdued till the whole of that part of the Minster, hitherto used for divine service, had been destroyed, and the roof, from the tower to the great East Window, had fallen in, burying under its remains, every monument of art and piety which crowded the space below.

The profound and melancholy impression, which such a catastrophe so sudden, unforeseen, and lamentable has made where ever it is known in this county, language cannot convey.

York Minster has been the just pride and the boast of people in Yorkshire – the architectural glory of the North of England – and as a gothic structure, equal if not superior in magnificence and preservation, to any in Europe."

For illustration, the *Intelligencer* carried a not very informative ground floor plan of part of the Minster.

The competition had a much better idea than this. Under the headline York Minster Burnt, the *Mercury* had found the time to commission an engraving (or at least had the wit to look out a stock engraving of the Minster

and add some flames to it). Their story boasted:

"This engraving gives a spirited and very correct delineation of the appearance of the Minster when the flames were at their height. The spectator is supposed to be standing near the south-west angle of the cathedral and the tower in which the fire originated is that from the top of which the flames are seen issuing..."

The fire-raiser turned out to be an extreme Methodist, Jonathan Martin. The last Minster watchman had been dismissed some time before the incident.

Closing the door after the horse had bolted, the following month the Minster's Dean and Chapter announced it had taken on "a watchman/ constable...to keep watch every night in and about the Cathedral".

climbed by 75 percent. It had acquired its first steam press, turning out about 800 copies an hour and now had a staff of 38. There was no let-up in the circulation war with the *Mercury* and on the 9th June 1838 the *Intelligencer* was clearly rattled by jibes from its rival that it had massaged its sales by inflating figures for blank paper purchases. It hotly denied fiddling its sales: *"We observe that one of our contemporaries insinuate that we sacrifice money by purchasing stamps which we do not use. The insinuation is false. Except to meet the probable inclemency of the weather at the beginning of winter, we give no extra orders and we have never more than a barely working stock in hand. All that we have received we have both printed and **sold**. We neither sell old papers by the ton to cheesemongers, nor at half price after the day of publication, nor do we cut them up as wrappers for new ones."* This final sentence unwittingly betrayed a too-explicit understanding of the art of puffing circulation. It was omitted when the newspaper ran the piece again the following week – and once more at the end of the month with the added complaint:

"The above statement was published four weeks ago, but the Mercury took no notice of it. At length, annoyed by its repetition, the Editor of that paper asserted, last Saturday, it was an exceedingly delusive and fraudulent article. The Intelligencer asks in wonderment, 'How can it be either delusive or fraudulent...seeing that the figures...were extracted from the Parliamentary return?'"

The editor had to concede that sales-wise, the *Mercury* was now the best in the country outside London, topping the Provincial News Press category. The *Intelligencer* however *"maintains its position at the head of the Conservative Press of Great Britain."*

There was more to this spat. The rivals were about to go to press with the story of decade – the June 1838 coronation of Queen

READ ALL ABOUT IT

"He do the police in different voices."

In Charles Dickens's *Our Mutual Friend* – first serialised in 1864 – the character Betty Higden marvels at the genius of her young servant, Sloppy. "A beautiful reader of a newspaper," she says. "He do the police in different voices." Sloppy's extemporised dramatisation of newspaper reports was a skill greatly prized among the many who could not read adequately for themselves.

In 1840, 30 percent of men and half the women in the country could not sign their names on marriage registers. Dickens's episode shows how in the 1860s enjoying a newspaper was still not a private habit although the demand for them was insatiable. Records based on the Parliamentary returns for the numbers of stamped sheets bought by newspaper publishers show an increase from 16,085,000 in 1801 to 54,769,000 in 1831. In reality, many more newspapers circulated than official figures indicate because some titles went out illegally on unstamped paper. Better schooling would eventually improve literacy but the rural and largely non-reading culture of old England was necessarily coming to an end as urbanisation spread. Even far out in the sticks, village life was being subtly changed by the arrival of printed matter, whether posters, pamphlets or leaflets. People who had been able to get by without understanding the printed word acknowledged they would be left behind.

Illiteracy was already dropping sharply before the first Education Act of 1870 introduced elementary schooling.

As to the impact the newspaper culture had on society, the *Mercury's* Edward Baines had evangelised about the benefits it was conferring. "Whoever looks at the influence of the newspapers...at this day...cannot but perceive that the press is now endowed with a power such as never existed before in any country...it is the most noble instrument for meliorating the condition and raising the dignity of mankind." Baines also struck a contemporary note for modern newspapermen, warning about government spin doctors, which he referred to darkly as "the rumour manufactory in Downing Street (that) was kept at work night and day."

Victoria – and the *Intelligencer* feared coming off second best. They had already got wind that the *Mercury* was planning something special for their coverage – an engraving of the big event – and knew that they could not match it.

In the issue carrying its coronation report, the *Intelligencer* ridiculed the idea that a newspaper should even think of using an illustration. *"In the Mercury of Saturday we find an announcement which has since been repeated in widely circulated placards that on this day, Mr Baines intends to give 'a well-executed engraving of the interior of Westminster Abbey representing the coronation of Her Majesty Victoria I'...we did not expect to see the dignified Mr Baines descend to picture days for the purpose of attracting the million and checking a falling circulation. Such, however, has always been our contemporary's course: adopting that tomorrow which he condemns today."*

The coronation had taken place the previous Thursday. The *Intelligencer* gave their story four columns on an inside page (without engraving) and it begins brightly enough. *"From an early hour in the morning of Thursday last, the 28th instant, all was bustle and animation in London and Westminster more especially at the West End of town."*

This was as much of a re-write of the officialese as the editor could manage. The rest of the *Intelligencer's* report reads with all the verve of a grocery list.

Leaving aside the master-stroke of the illustration, the *Mercury* won hands-down with some poised colour reporting which caught a real sense of national celebration. Note the clever insertion of the Yorkshire weather reference that gives it local resonance.
"The day on which the youthful Victoria was solemnly crowned...was as brilliant as the most loyal heart could have wished: and on that day millions of attached subjects testified their joy at the public recognition of her title to the sovereignty, by all the modes of rejoicing and festivity common in England. In the capital, the coronation itself attracted immense crowds, not only from the city and neighbourhood, but from all parts of the kingdom, to witness one of the most splendid and interesting ceremonials which the world can furnish...The morning of Thursday opened on the metropolis soberly and was by no means so cloudless as in Yorkshire. A few showers of rain fell early but before the procession began to form, the sun burst through in splendour and rarely has he looked on a gayer scene or one of more animation and delight..."

There was also a piece headlined, *"The Abbey (from our own correspondent, Westminster Abbey, 4 o'clock pm)"* which concluded with a final triumphant side-swipe at the attitude taken by the Leeds Tories, (meaning the *Intelligencer*) towards the day's momentous events.
"In Leeds a few – a very few – of the Tories had the good sense to join publicly in the celebration; but the great body of the party stayed as much aloof as if they were in alliance with the "Northern Democrats" and wished to bring the monarchy into popular disrepute! Other towns will scarcely credit the littleness and paltriness of the Leeds Tories..."

The *Intelligencer* continued to rumble on about its circulation figures until the end of the year, finally boasting in bold type in the first Saturday in December 1838 that its average weekly circulation had gone up to 3,461. But however much they huffed and puffed, the *Mercury's* was three times that.

The *Mercury's* superior coverage of the coronation, with the engraving depicting Victoria on the throne

FIRST FASHION PAGES, 1840

In April and May 1840, out of the blue, the *Intelligencer* seemed to wake up to the fact that it had female readers. It ran separate pieces on the latest Paris fashions with an illustration at the top of the page. After these two articles appeared, interest in fashion seems to have disappeared as abruptly as it arrived.

"The grand advent of the Spring fashions having passed, we are enabled to present our fair readers with what we fear they have long been waiting for: namely patterns of promenade wear. We cannot say of all the costumes we have inspected (and we have seen a great number) there is much to arrest the attention as new or striking. From a mass of plates we have selected those which are evidently the greatest favourites among tasteful wearers."

The article picks out for special note, *"the gradual introduction of Indian forms and colours into various portions of costume...Fashion having exhausted the resources of Europe, finding no shadow of taste in America, and turning away with a blush from African modes, has at length commenced her researches and exercised her powers of imitation upon Asia..."*

Yorkshire's Victorian style guide

1. **Paris public promenade dress.** Azure blue pou de soie pelisse, the body fits closely to the shape, is quite high at the back, moderately open at the bosom, and has the front embroidered down each side in a scroll pattern, with lavender bloom silk cord and buttons to match...

2. **Public promenade dress.** Pea green pou de soie dress, figured in detached flower in emerald green...

3. The dress is composed of gros de Naples, a drab-coloured ground, striped with brown, a deep tuck surmounts the hem, and each is headed by a rich silk cord...

4. **Evening dresses.** White tulle robe, and tunic over white pou de soie.

5. **Grand costume.** White satin dress, the body cut very low and pointed at the waist.

6. Presents a back view of the head-dress of Number 5.

7. **Evening dresses.** Robe of grey Gros de Tours, a low corsage, quite square at the top, and very deeply pointed at the bottom.

8. **Evening dresses.** Blue gros d'ete robe, a tight corsage, cut very low and trimmed round the top with three folds of white satin...

The full description of the first dress runs to over 250 words. Towards the end of the list the writer is allowed less than a tenth of that.

Perhaps one senses the impatient hand of an editor cutting the copy to make room for what really mattered to him – the story about the average price of wheat which follows.

A colourful chapter closed when Edward Baines died in 1848. He had been excoriated, often with good reason, by the *Intelligencer* as an adventurer and a plagiarist and William Cobbett had called him the Great Liar of the North. But 30,000 turned out on the funeral route and it was acknowledged – even by the *Intelligencer* – that a great man had passed.

Perhaps they felt magnanimous towards the reviled old enemy because they were doing well. The *Intelligencer* was sharing in the national feel-good factor which followed from Queen Victoria's opening of the Great Exhibition in Hyde Park on 1st May 1851. When the Great Exhibition finished, Joseph Paxton's building was moved to Sydenham and in June 1854 Queen Victoria was on hand again to open what was in effect the world's first theme park.

This was the point where the *Intelligencer* was able to announce some innovations of its own, explaining to readers: *"The Intelligencer is now issued with a half sheet supplement of 24 columns...Apart from the embarrassment to ourselves of having weekly an excess of matter beyond the limits of our space, and the mortification of being compelled to withhold matters prepared for publication, our readers had the additional inconvenience of finding the news generally, and especially the latest intelligence...printed so closely in small type as to be irksome to read..."*

Their supplement was not quite like those that drop onto doormats at weekends today. There were still no illustrations and despite their professed concern for readers' eyesight, the type was as cramped as ever.

The re-opening of the Crystal Palace however presented an opportunity for some magazine-style writing with a bit of flair. The *Intelligencer* sent along *Our Own Correspondent* to the 1854 event with the licence to insert his own personality into the scene. Anticipating crowded roads, he takes the river steamer from the West End to London Bridge where fellow passengers were *"chiefly clerks getting a cheap ventilation before losing themselves to the labyrinth of double-entry in the City"*. Instead of being excited, he complained they were *"grandly taciturn, or canvassing the past or speculating on the future news from the Baltic...*

Accustomed as we are at Leeds to be

Supplement to The Leeds Intelligencer.

No. 5228.   SATURDAY, MAY 27. 1854.   No. 5228.

SEBASTOPOL.   CONSTANTINOPLE.

Engravings of the Crimea, 1854

sensible of a stir and bustle, and a contagious excitement and curiosity spreading among all classes when any ceremonial of local importance is about to take place...it is difficult to realise the supineness prevailing amongst the Londoners concerning the inaugural ceremony of throwing open the Crystal Palace on Saturday last."

He notes *"the tall figure of the mayor of Leeds (John Wilson esquire) [who] merely decorated with the official chain was very conspicuous among their worships, and our excellent neighbour, the mayor of Bradford (Samuel Smith Esq) in his scarlet robe, made an impressive figure on the occasion...and we hope to see our towns and trade take its proper position in this vast emporium of the beautiful and useful.*

We regret to find that coffee is only supplied at sixpence a cup and indeed that, except an out of the way beer engine in an area remote from the main building, placarded second class refreshment room, there is no obvious provision for the people. A visit to the palace must occupy the greater part of a day and a crowning act of generosity on the part of the directors would be the making of absolute provision for letting a family group get a good supply of wholesome food and beverage at the lowest possible rate to yield a reasonable profit to the purveyor."

The *Intelligencer's* expansion into a supplement came with a cost – a cover price of fivepence from fourpence ha-penny.

Five months later, it had something more impressive than a day out at a theme park and complaints about the catering to justify its price increase. The editor had not sent a correspondent to the Crimea to write a colour piece about the Battle of Balaklava. But he had something even better for his readers.

The charge of the Light Brigade: The 13th Light Dragoons attacking the Russian batteries at Balaklava

An anonymous officer who had been in the charge of the Light Brigade on 25th October sat down and penned this first-person account at his camp near Balaklava. The paper ran it on 18th November.

"You will be glad to hear I am alive after our tremendous affair on the 25th. We were ordered to charge some Russian batteries and cavalry, and the light brigade went down – the 17th and the 13th leading the line; and the 11th were ordered to hang a little in the rear in support and the 4th and the 5th followed in a sort of third line.

We all knew the thing was desperate before we started, and it was even worse than we thought. In our front, about a mile and half off, were several lines of Russian cavalry and nine guns – to get at which we had to pass along a wide valley with the ground a little falling, and in itself favourable enough for a charge of cavalry; but sloping hills on each side gave the enemy an opportunity (which they used) of placing guns on both our flanks as we advanced; and not only guns but infantry with Minie rifles.

However there was no hesitation, down our fellows went at the gallop and through a fire in front and on both flanks which emptied our saddles and knocked over our horses by scores. I do not think one man flinched in the whole brigade – although everyone allows that so hot a fire was hardly ever seen. We went right on, cut down the gunners at their guns (the Russians worked the guns until we were within ten yards of them) – went on still, broke a line of cavalry in the rear of the guns...

But there our bolt was shot: the Russians formed four deep and our thin and broken ranks, and blown horses could not attack to break through them...We broke back through them however, and then had to run the gauntlet through the cross-fire of the artillery and the Minie rifles back to our own lines, with their cavalry on our flanks...

There is no concealing the thing – the light brigade was greatly damaged, and for nothing; for though we killed the gunners and the horses of nine 12-rounders, we could not bring them away. Nolan, (who brought the order) is dead. The first shell that burst hit him in the chest. He gave a loud cry, his horse turned, trotted back (with him still in the saddle) between the first and second squadrons of the 13th and carried him so for some way, when he fell dead. He was hit in the heart.

In the two leading regiments, including Lord Cardigan (who led in person) and his staff we had 19 officers. Only three came out of the action untouched both man and horse...

It was a bitter moment after we broke through the line of cavalry in the rear of their guns when I looked round and there was no support...You never saw men behave so well as our men did...All our dead and wounded were left behind, and so know not who are dead or who are prisoners. All this makes me miserable, even to write; but it is the naked truth...

I hear from a man who dined with Lord Raglan today, that they do us justice at head-quarters, and say that our attack was an unheard-of feat of arms."

8 A new daily is born

The buoyant *Leeds Mercury*, standard bearer for the Whigs and Liberals, became a daily newspaper in October 1861. The weekly *Intelligencer* seemed left behind in another age. Newspaper readers were demanding immediacy, Griffith Wright's world where London was four days away by stagecoach had been shrunk by the railways. It contracted further in 1846 with the start of electric news. The service offered by the English Electric Telegraph Company's link from London to Leeds may not seem remotely speedy to us. It took half a day for the *Intelligencer* to receive its first significant story by telegraph, the Queen's Speech on 23rd November 1847. The first of the 730 words arrived at lunchtime at five past one, and the last at five past six that evening. By the standards of the time this was lightning-fast. Within three years, most of Europe was wired up through an undersea cable. By 1866 we could pick up stories from the furthest-flung corners of the Empire via a trans-Atlantic cable. A second information revolution was underway.

The *Mercury*'s ambition was encouraged by a much kinder climate for newspapers as a whole. The tax on newspaper advertisements was lifted in 1853; stamp duty followed two years later and in 1861 the newsprint tax was removed. The ending of the much-resented "taxes on knowledge", together with a surge in advertising revenue brought about lower cover prices.

It offered a new opportunity to appeal to a wider readership and this was seized by a clutch of daily newspapers which now burst onto the scene in the English regions. The dailies

The first
Yorkshire Post,
2nd July 1866

Below left:
William Beckett
Denison MP,
first chairman
of the Yorkshire
Conservative
Newspaper
Company and
their 1865 share
prospectus

printed in Fleet Street and sent out by train could not provide an equivalent news service tailored for local needs. The pride and identity of England's major cities grew as newspapers like the *Birmingham Post* flexed their editorial muscles. The regions relished their new status as the significance of London diminished.

In Leeds, the Conservatives were by now acutely aware that their paper, the weekly *Intelligencer*, was being politically out-muscled. They were rattled further when they heard that the Liberals were to target the city for the 1865 General Election. To stiffen resolve with what was described as "the moral weight of the press", a move was made by a businessman, GA Boyce. He wrote from Liverpool to a WM Nelson about "a project I have in hand for establishing a thorough Conservative daily paper in Leeds to counteract the influence of the *Mercury*." He planned to buy the copyright of the *Leeds Intelligencer* if the owner, Christopher Kemplay, "will take any reasonable sum". Boyce invited Nelson to take shares and introduce the project to

59

"Beckett Denison and JL Fox Esquires, or any other suitable gentlemen." The banking dynasty of William Beckett Denison's family went back to John Beckett in 1770 and they were staunchly Tory. William Beckett Denison became the first chairman of the new Yorkshire Conservative Newspaper Company and the family was to play a key role in the fortunes of the business for the next 96 years.

The first edition of the new paper had four pages of seven columns. The first story, on page two, is Commercial News. Shock, horror has to wait until column five with a local double murder and suicide.

SUICIDE AND TWO MURDERS AT HALIFAX.

A shocking case of triple murder occurred at Halifax on Saturday. Ephraim Smith, carpet weaver, Old Lee Bank, returned home, having been to the Fair, and, finding the door of his father's house fast, raised the latch by putting his hand through a hole in one of the panes, and entered. He struck a match to obtain a light previously to retiring for the night; but as soon as he had done so he was horrified at the sight of his father sitting in a seat connected with the window, his head leaning upon the table, and his throat cut. The young man rushed out of the cottage and alarmed the neighbours. Two of them went into the house, and soon discovered that two of Smith's children, both girls, had also been killed, the one by having her throat cut and the other by being suffocated. The one who had been suffocated was named Emma, five years of age, and was found on a bed near the window upon her right side with only her chemise on. She was laid with her face downward, her nose flattened as if she had been struggling, and her right arm was marked as if from blows. The other daughter was named Elizabeth, about ten years of age, and was laid behind the house door with her throat cut from the windpipe to the back of the neck. At the feet of the father was a razor with which the murderous deeds had evidently been committed. Mr Hodgson Wright was sent for, and stated that the father had cut his own throat. Smith had for a considerable time been employed by Messrs Crossley, as a weaver. He has for some time been noticed to be depressed in spirits, but pursued his employment as if in good health. His wife has been in Wakefield Lunatic Asylum about two years. We need hardly state that the affair has caused very much excitement in the town. It is understood that an inquest will be held to-day (Monday).

A heat-wave the previous week, 85F degrees in the shade, had broken at the weekend (nothing new there then). Stories of severe storms which followed are carried from Selby, Barnsley and Filey where the only damage was to the flagstaff at the coastguard station.

Like Griffith Wright in 1754, the paper set out its stall in a preface. *"That opinion exists in this country at the present day subversive of that political and social system which distinguishes England from all other nations in the world, no candid observer can deny.*

That defects still exist in our institutions which may be amended with benefit to the public, is a truth equally indisputable.

By these two guiding facts, the political conduct of the Yorkshire Post will be regulated. It will be at once Conservative and progressive – a foe to democracy and revolution, but the firm friend of all constitutional reform.

The great social questions which in the present age divide, almost equally with politics, the attention of the thinking man, the relations between capital and labour, the sanitary improvement of our large towns, the punishment of crime, the reformation of vice, the diffusion of knowledge, and the relief of poverty, will receive...constant and serious consideration...

Every kind of national sport will be reported by the Yorkshire Post by writers of ability and experience. Racing, field sports, coursing, cricket, rowing and athletic amusements in general will be described in detail and illustrated by original comment. Sports more peculiarly interesting to Yorkshiremen will be made subject of especial care...

...a change has been effected in the conditions of the English press...which corresponds...with a change that has been taking place in English society. The old line of demarcation between town and country has been broken through. Railways and the electric telegraph have established a frequency of locomotion and a constant circulation of ideas which rob country society of all that inertia and incuriousness which were once its peculiar characteristics; and the highest questions of politics and literature are discussed with as much knowledge and vivacity in the country town or secluded manor house as in the smoking room of a London club...

London papers have grown less exclusively metropolitan. Country papers have grown less exclusively provincial...

The daily newspapers which are now published in the half dozen chief towns of Great Britain are, both in the influence they exert and the high character which they sustain, something totally distinct from the country newspsapers which amused the leisure of our grandfathers...

We enter upon our new duties at a moment when the political arrangements of Europe, which have existed substantially unchanged since the Treaty of Utrecht, are threatened with destruction..."

The newspaper's pride in being "a foe to democracy" rings oddly today. They interpreted it as mob rule. The "especial care" promised for sport was not in place for day one. Among local cricket matches briefly mentioned was one on Woodhouse Moor where Victoria were playing Leeds Morning Star. There was no report or scorecard, only the bare outline: the Morning Star 34; the Victoria 73 – of which Chester contributed 14. WG Grace does get better coverage.

As time went on, the *Yorkshire Post* was as good as its word in tackling defects in social arrangements and its sustained assault on public squalor amid private wealth in Leeds makes powerful reading.

It also believed that the provision of general education was *"the foundation of the way of living for the bulk of the community enriching the lives of the people and providing the best antidote for 'vice, misery and poverty'."* High-mindedness was touched with self-interest. A more literate population meant more newspaper readers, although whether the *Yorkshire Post* would be the one to win them was uncertain. The competition was severe. The leaders of the pack were the *Leeds Daily News* and the *Leeds Express* which easily out-sold the *YP* and the *Leeds Mercury*. Two other also-rans were the *Leeds Times* (a twopenny weekly) and the *Yorkshire Weekly Post*.

By 1870 the *Yorkshire Post* had a 20-strong editorial and commercial staff, out of 90 all told. But for someone who was part of that team, it all seemed a bit ramshackle. In 1870, a lad called J Neville was recruited for a job in the advertising department and rose to chief cashier. Years later, discussing those earlier days, he remembered the *YP* as, "a bit of a weakling...For some years after I joined, the paper had a struggle to keep alive. The

buildings were dilapidated and rat-infested. The work in the advertising office was certainly very dull – chiefly because so little business came in." With colleagues, he would rig up a pen round the desks where rats were let loose and dogs put in. He recalled, "Never was the fun interrupted by a customer turning up."

Rat-infested or not, the paper was quick on its feet when it had a big running story to report. After war broke out between Prussia and France on 15th July 1870, demand for hot news in Leeds was met by printing the telegrams of the latest battles on galley slips. These were taken onto the streets and sold with a copy of the paper for a penny.

Mr Neville reckoned the real turn for the better occurred with the arrival of a "live wire"at the helm in October 1882. This was the new editor, Charles Pebody, who promised to turn the *Yorkshire Post* into *The Times* of the North of England – "to reflect the genius of the people among whom it circulated, and to represent and identify itself with what was distinctive in the Yorkshire character." Three years on, in September 1885, its sales were up to 46,637 a day.

On 1st Sept 1890 the *Yorkshire Post's* sister paper, the *Yorkshire Evening Post* was launched with four pages and two reporters. A Mr Denham who joined the staff on that day recalled, "There was not much fuss about this new publication. I marvel at the modesty of that occasion."

It quickly became one of the most successful newspapers in the country. In Leeds, as in Manchester, the profitablity of the evening title was the bedrock on which the sister morning paper was able to build its influence and reputation.

The slickness of the production departments was tested in the early years of the new century by stop watch at the start of the flat racing season. This was on the day of the Lincolnshire Handicap at Doncaster. The name of the winner was called out in the case room and was printed in the small space for late news known as the Stop Press. The editor waited outside carrying the watch. The time that elapsed between the race winner being shouted, and the first copy of the edition carrying the result being sold in Basinghall Street outside the office, was 45 seconds.

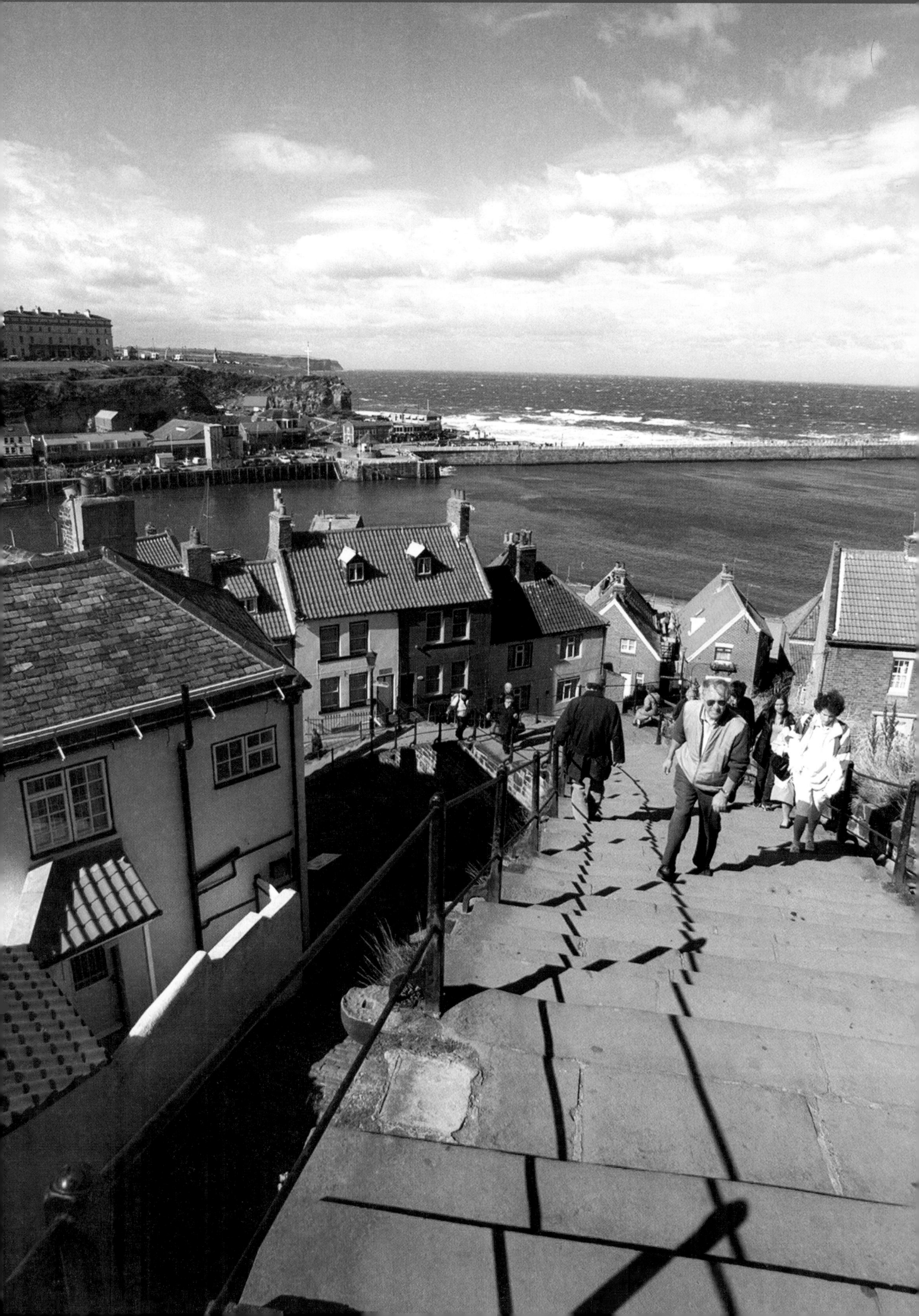

Coastal views

MARCH 1978

A *perfect boyhood*

Malcolm Barker recalled growing up in Thirties and Forties Whitby.

Each generation has its own Whitby to cherish; the Whitby as it existed over a limited period while that generation was brought up and shaped and moulded as it absorbed the myriad influences of the old town.

I left Whitby in 1949, but I have been lucky. Throughout the years I have been able to go back.

My parents provided the refuge, first at a four-square house of good red Grosmont bricks which my grandfather had built at Stakesby; then at a house at Sleights with a long narrow flower-filled garden stretching down to a lilac tree and, beyond, an unmade road, busy Littlebeck, and a cricket field where fine trees field deep at the beck-end.

Oh, those happy returns! First by steam train rumbling through the valleys from Pickering across a score of echoing bridges, then in clattering diesels and, latterly, by car across the moorland road.

Whitby always calls and is often answered. The old town may keep its head down beneath the cliffs, but it carries its badges high. There is the old Abbey, blunt and forthright, and – equally prominent – the Metropole Hotel, with four towers set above its curious roofline. Glimpses of them show miles from the town; the sight of them lifts the spirits.

In my younger days, Whitby was a great place for walking. Everybody walked everywhere. For example, we were High Church-folk in my family – grandfather named his house after a priest – and we walked to church three times every Sunday. We would set off from Stakesby down an old flagged monks' causeway leading through meadows and a succession of kissing gates, across Harrowing's Drive, over the bridge across the railway line leading to West-Cliff station, and down a long flight of worn stone steps to the road and the top of Chubb Hill.

We would hurry along St Hilda's Terrace and then turn down another long flight of stone steps running alongside Pannett Park to reach Baxtergate and our destination, St Ninian's. Harry Frank would urge us over the last lap of our journey by ringing the three bells, one of which was cracked – ding, dong, thump, ding, dong, thump.

St Ninian's was built by a group of Whitby folk, many of them ship-owners. At that time, years ago, ships were owned in 64th parts. The church-builders applied that idea to St Ninian's. In the 1940s our Sunday visits to St Ninian's for eight o'clock Holy Communion, for Sung Eucharist, and for Evensong, were like a family reunion. My grandfather was there. He was the Crucifier and for more than 50 years he sang in the choir. My father was there, singing bass, my mother contralto, my Uncle Bill tenor and my Aunt Edith soprano.

Whitby inevitably is bound up with the sea. At wartime evensong, lit only by candles because of the black-out, we sang *For Those in Peril* and mourned brave Whitby men lost on Atlantic convoys or perilous journeys to Russia. Some, like Arthur Spark were St Ninian's men. I don't think I properly appreciated it at the time but I was extremely fortunate in my father. He had succeeded his father as editor of the *Whitby Gazette* soon after the war, and in his quiet way he communicated his own love of the town and district to his children.

He seemed to know everybody. It sometimes took us nearly an hour to get through Baxtergate. We would walk down the Pier – my grandfather regarded a "Pier-ender" as a cure for all ills, whether of the mind or of the body – and best of all perhaps we would walk in the country.

There was a pleasant inevitability about Saturdays. We would meet father at the office, go to Wilcocks for the groceries, to Johnsons for the meat pies and to the Co-op for Grandad Fisher's tobacco, and then catch the Castle Park bus home. After listening to the lunch-time cricket scoreboard we would walk along Switchbacks, then a narrow-country lane enchanted by skylarks, to Four Lane Ends. Here we would catch a bus either up the Guisborough road to Egton, or perhaps up the moor road to Saltersgate or Goathland.

These were not aimless wanderings. We walked with a purpose. In high

Whitby today: the famous 199 steps leading to the abbey

Mel Hulme

A replica of the *Endeavour* sails into Whitby in September 1997, marking the 200th anniversary of Cook's expedition   Mark Bickerdyke

summer we filled baskets with bilber-ries, gathering them by the pound on the brow of the hill near Saltersgate. As the days shaded towards autumn, we would pick blackberries. I some-times thought father knew every bilberry patch and blackberry bush in Whitby district, but we never did find the fabled Blueberry Gill where the fruit was supposed to hang like cher-ries from bushes as tall as a man.

We did find mushrooms though – lots of them in a field at West Barnby. We would get apples, too, buying at farms or from the quaint old apple woman at Newholm. There were other fruits of these walks. We came to know every lane and track. We can still find most of them, although some have disappeared and many are over-grown. We usually just happened to find ourselves at a village cricket match when they were serving teas (Glaisdale teas were best) or at a tea-garden or, in season, a country show (Fryup, long gone, was our favourite).

I can never contemplate a perfect

summer day without remembering – smelling even – the scent of the allysum that grew in between the paving stones on the way towards Love Lane, Upgang and the beach.

I can never read a poem without remembering the strange, fey evening when I sat on the West Cliff and contemplated the old Parish Church, which seemed to be floating above the town like a blessing, and for the first time in my life I tried to put words together to express deep thoughts, half recognised among the confusion of facts gathered by schoolboys.

Whitby has changed, of course. I liked it as it was, all rigg and furr and with an old 1914-18 German field gun marking the spot where a shell had fallen during the 1914 bombard-ment. We were West Cliff folk, quite different from East Cliff folk – certainly not better, but different. The East Cliff folk and those who live on the Crag, where the narrow alleys always seemed to smell of Sunday

dinners, were in the main fishermen.

We were friends with them. They would, for example, fill my father's office with live crabs as gifts, and this often startled visitors. But we were not part of their community, nor the inheritors of their great traditions. Theirs was the glory of the lifeboat service, and theirs the eternal myster-ies of the sea with its successive seasons: crabbing, long-lining, salmon fishing and herrings.

Ah! The herrings! In the years after the war the Scottish fishermen came down for them and the harbour was packed from pier to pier with their varnished keel boats. They caught thousands of crans of herring in their ring-nets. They sometimes caught so many herrings that they couldn't sell them, and had to dump them back in the sea. They were marvellously care-less with their herrings. An agile boy down the pier before breakfast could collect a delicious fry by simply follow-ing one of the laden lorries from the quay. The fish fell to the road and we scrambled for them.

I think it right to say we West Cliff folk were proud of the fishermen and perhaps a bit envious. We used to make visiting friends climb the 199 steps, pointing out the street lamp with a different coloured light that was a guide to incoming vessels. We would talk of "our" town and "our" harbour although we knew deep down that they really belonged to the fisherfolk, the Storrs, the Leadleys and the Harlands.

Whitby was not planned as a beauty spot nor a holiday resort. It was developed first by the monks who came to the windshorn headland and raised their Abbey to the glory of God and in defiance of the elements. Then it was the turn of fishermen, who plastered their tiny cottages to the cliff-sides as cunningly as gulls crevice their nests.

The gloriously prosperous years came in the 18th and 19th centuries when they built ships and took them to the Arctic for whales or to distant Southern seas in search of unknown continents.

Whitby had a spring like the one which flushed Scarborough to success as a holiday resort, but it did not

Whitby harbour in the 1930s

"Monks came to the windshorn headland and raised their Abbey to the glory of God and in defiance of the elements"

pause to think about holidaymakers until George Hudson needed to create traffic for his newly acquired Pickering to Whitby railway line and built the grid-iron of terraces on the West Cliff.

All these elements of Whitby's history were borne on us in our childhood and we absorbed them unconsciously. They remain today,

sometimes fragmented but occasionally drawn together in a pang of pure nostalgia.

Even after nearly 30 years, neither my wife nor my son and daughter, nor my friends, have any doubt as to my meaning when I say I am going home. They do know where I am going. It is to Whitby.

Whitby Abbey

Mel Hulme

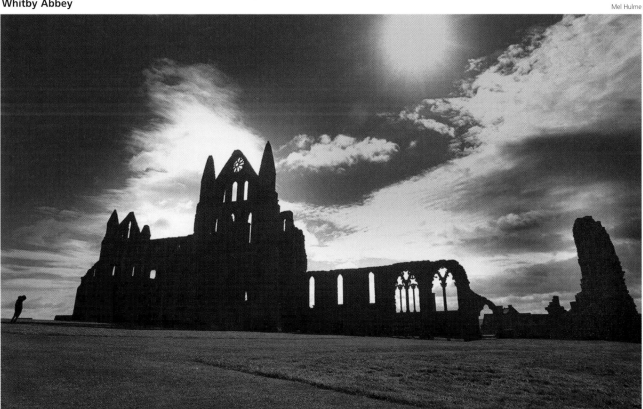

"What's up wi' yer? Are you all dead in here?"

Here's to you, Mrs Robinson. Geoffrey Winter looked at seaside landladies and recalled a memorable Bridlington boarding house of his youth.

In the summer of 1938, three impecunious youths, myself included, arrived in Bridlington for a week's holiday. We had booked into a boarding house called Kenwyn, 18 Marshall Avenue. Incredibly, even in those days, the terms for full board were 35s a week – five bob a day.

We walked with our bags from the station, and asked a policeman the way to Marshall Avenue. "You'll be wanting Kenwyn," he said, and we wondered how he knew.

The reason became apparent when we joined a queue stretching down the avenue from the gate of Kenwyn. Because of its rock bottom terms, that boarding house was Brid's most powerful magnet. Its nearest rivals went no lower than two guineas, and a saving of seven shillings was considerable then.

The landlady, Mrs Robinson, did not allow newcomers into the house until each weekend's departing guests had left the premises, hence the queue. Ruth Robinson provided comfortable beds and adequate plain food, but she was strict. If you were a few minutes late for breakfast you missed it.

Some of her guests slept in an annexe – a house up the road called Braganza – and late risers there would throw clothes on over their pyjamas, race down the street and arrive breathless at Kenwyn's breakfast tables, only to find that they hadn't quite made it.

Mrs Robinson's stock reply to all complaints was: "Well, what do you expect for 35s a week?" There was no answer to that. While you did not exactly rough it at Mrs Robinson's, the creature comforts were rationed and it was not advisable to buck the system.

Every Friday teatime, Mrs R would move round the tables, pouching the money from her guests in a black Gladstone bag. At these times her smile was at its brightest.

Even in those far-off days, Mrs Robinson and her sister, little Olga, who used to have to stand on a box to light the rings on the gas stove, sought the sun on the French Riviera when the rigours of each holiday season ended. Forgetting their months of drudgery and dragooning, we envied them.

Today, Ruth and Olga are long gone, but Kenwyn remains – upgraded to the "Kenwyn Private Hotel – and fully licensed." And it has doubled in size by the fusion of 18 Marshall Avenue with 20.

When Mrs Robinson left for that great guest house in the sky some ten years ago, a Mrs Violet Lunn bought Kenwyn and since her retirement her son, George, has run it. When I called, the season had

BRIDLINGTON
Bigger, better and bouncier than ever!
BRIDLINGTON
WE'VE SPENT OVER £20 MILLION TO MAKE BRIDLINGTON THE COAST WITH THE MOST

Bridlington harbour and fish market

Terry Carrott

just ended, the last guest had gone
and only a notice in the window
looked to the future: "Booking now
for Christmas."

George Lunn had left the previous
Saturday for a no-doubt much-needed
six weeks in Benidorm.

Many of the present members of
the Bridlington Hotels and Boarding
Houses Association remember Mrs
Robinson, the good businesswoman
with affection and respect. "She
favoured young people," they say.
The reason is clear to me. We were
light-hearted and easy going and
took all those stairs in our stride.
Mrs Robinson, bless her, provided
holidays we could afford and the
rules that made the low price possible
amused rather than irked us.

This summer minimum weekly rates
for bed and breakfast and an evening
meal have been £23 to £25.
Last summer the minimum was £19,
and the landladies themselves thought
the increase a bit steep. Business
suffered a little. Though inflation

Bempton Cliffs, north of Bridlington

Terry Carrott

is running at 15 per cent, Bridlington's
landladies have decided to try to keep
next season's increase down to
12 per cent (about £3) and bear
the brunt of the rest from their profits

in the belief that next summer the
cost of Continental holidays will
be prohibitive.

Dolly Mortimer, from Pudsey, has
been a landlady for the past 14 of her

67

59 years. This year her terms were £25 a week for bed, breakfast and dinner (at five o'clock). Dolly is good-natured, laughs a lot and likes to see people enjoying themselves. "Good food, a clean house and comfortable beds – that's all they really want. When I first came, nobody wanted a bath...well, nobody asked for one. People want a lot of baths these days. They're better educated nowadays, aren't they? They can have one or two baths free, but I charge 10p for extra ones. They can have them whenever they want, except when we're washing up. Then we need all the hot water.

"We have a regular weekly dinner menu – Mondays chicken portions, Tuesdays lamb chops, Wednesdays home-made chicken and ham pies, and so on, but we try to vary it for the second week of the fortnighters. To fill the plates up a bit, we serve Yorkshire puddings every day.

"The favourite sweet is a fresh cream eclair, ice cream, red melba sauce and a wafer biscuit. They think it's marvellous. It's nowt really, but it looks a right lot on your plate."

The Saturday change-over tends to be a little sticky. The new guests are shy of one another, and a hush falls over the sitting room when they assemble. Dolly carries in a tray of tea and biscuits and breaks the ice with: "What's up wi' yer? Are you all dead in here?"

Dolly's place was fully booked from the start of last summer. But, she says, she and her husband, Bert, couldn't manage through the winter without his wages as a fitter.

DECEMBER 2001

Seeing the Point

Frederic Manby offered a beginners' guide to the desolate beauty of Spurn Point.

Okay, this isn't an easy one. First you'll have to get there, and once there you'll not be able to spend much money.

Ah, that's got your interest. Spurn Point is the hook of land which curls over the end of the Humber estuary. We love it.

This is a fragile nose of an East Yorkshire coastline which is crumbling into the North Sea. It is a children's free-roaming paradise in a life menacingly occupied by VDU screens and other entertainment electronics. Get out a map, find Hull, then look right and down a bit, following the A1033 through Keyingham, Winestead and Patrington, into a landscape which will open eyes of all ages.

At Patrington, the A1033 veers north to Withernsea, and you follow the smaller B1445 to Easington. Spurn Point, or Spurn Head as the mappers call it, lies ahead.

So, why should you drag the family across many miles of Yorkshire or Lincolnshire to reach a fragile piece of land? Because of what you'll find when you get there. This is seaside with a difference. On the left, you

The former lighthouse and sea defences at Spurn Point

Terry Carrott

have the steely blue North Sea, on the right there are the calmer waters of the estuary, dotted with tankers and trading ships waiting to enter the docks at Hull or Immingham.
The pilot boat sets out from Spurn's pier. On this sheltered side you'll see the lifeboat station and their houses huddled low to the ground to avoid the worst winter gales. It is one of the county's remotest communities.

Unless you are there on a summery day when crab sandwiches are on sale, your only outlay will be a small admission charge to drive your car onto the land, which is owned by the Yorkshire Wildlife Trust. At the last measurement it was 320 hectares (790 acres) of which 194 hectares are covered at high water. Dogs are prohibited.

At the entrance there is a small shop and museum of interesting relics, and a list of recent bird sightings. Barry Spencer, the warden for nearly 40 years, runs the site. At this time of year he can promise lots of wading birds. You can park and walk, or drive to the far end and then walk.

Birds are what the place is all about,

but don't panic. You'll not be embarrassed by ranks of birders and twitchers. They never seem all that obvious, as discreet as one of the migratory creatures which flutter happily down after their ocean flight.

"Ahead is the lighthouse – an almost antique childhood memory which should be trapped in every young mind"

We've never been big birdwatchers. Nice to have them around, but ask me to tell a curlew from a whimbrel at 100 paces and I'm all sixes and sevens. For us, Spurn Point is the walk, and the bracing sea air, and this is why it is so good for children who spend more and more time locked into computers.

You may walk up the meandering spinal road, which changes from time to time as the sea cuts into the sandy

soil. This year, 2001, part of the old road was eroded but the new road was already in place and waiting to take over.

On this landlocked walk you'll see little but grassy dunes to your left. On the right are mud flats and then sand, and ahead is the lighthouse – an almost antique childhood memory which should be trapped in every young mind. The best walks are along the sands and the seaside of the peninsular, passing the weathered wooden groynes which run down the beach to control sand movement.

There are shells and rocks and tumbling concrete pillboxes from the Second World War: perhaps an opportunity to discuss the past and the future with your children? As you keep walking towards the physical point of Spurn Head the sea view changes because the shoreline is curving.

This explains why, almost suddenly, you are walking down the other side of the land mass, and you never noticed the tip, because, in a way, there is one and there isn't one. We like that bit.

69

Netting a loss

In Scarborough, Malcolm Barker talked to gloomy skippers in the herring fleet.

With 30 crans of herrings in his hold and the torn remnants of two nets on his deck, skipper Donald Patience brought his fishing boat, *Incentive*, into Scarborough Harbour yesterday.

Skipper Patience, a softly spoken man from Fraserburgh, Scotland, was not displeased with his catch. But he was indignant about his nets ruined by a foreign trawler operating within the 12 mile limit.

The incident happened as the herring fleets, British and foreign, jockeyed for position on a crowded sea not much more than ten miles from Scarborough Harbour bar.

It is out there that the 1968 Yorkshire herring fishing season is in the balance. So far it has been better than some dared to hope and not as bad as some feared. With the season moving into its peak weeks, landings at Scarborough and Whitby now total 4,103 crans for the year, all but 207 of them landed at Scarborough.

Last season, when the worst fears were realised, the total landing at Yorkshire ports was 7,735 crans.

These catches in retrospect seem pitifully small. It was a century ago last month that 135 railway trucks from Scarborough and 77 from Whitby rumbled through Malton Station laden with herrings on a single day. The fish traffic left the track so greasy that the first train out of Whitby the following morning lost 45 minutes slithering on the incline between Grosmont and Goathland.

There is no need to go back a century to point to the decline of the fishery. In 1947 nearly 30,000 crans – a cran, equals 28 stones – were landed at Whitby alone. Whitby's catch last week was two crans, not much more than an appetiser for the town's seagulls.

Although the fall in catches has reduced the size of the fleets, the Scotsmen have stayed loyal to Scarborough. Fifteen of them were alongside yesterday, as many as on any single day last year.

But the crucial importance of 1968 in deciding the future of the Yorkshire herring fishery lies on the fact that the Scottish skippers can hardly afford to

spend their late summers in Scarborough just because they like the town.

"If it is a flop this year...well," said Mr James Reid, of the *Watchful*, out of Gardenstown, Aberdeenshire. And he gave an expressive shrug.

The fish are out there, even though far fewer in numbers than in the golden years of the Silver Darlings. But so too are the foreigners, Dutchmen who enjoy a traditional right to fish within the 12-mile limit. From the Longstone, off Northumberland, to Flamborough Head they are permitted to fish to within six miles of the shore.

Last week, when they got among the shoals the Scotsmen played a canny game in an attempt to secure an advantage over their competitors. The chit chat on their radios died away to an occasional word.

But the Dutchmen were not slow to find the herring. "They know the grounds better than we do," conceded skipper Reid.

The Scotsmen lack none of the expertise of their rivals. Skilled fishermen, bred from generations of skilled fishermen, they rank with the finest herring catchers in the world.

Their complaint is that in the hunt for the herrings during the soft darkness of the North Sea summer nights they are not competing on equal terms. They use drift nets. The Dutchmen drag small mesh trawl nets along the bottom trapping the fish on their spawning grounds.

"The herrings are so thick on the bottom that a cod could not live among them," said skipper Patience. "The bottom trawling breaks up the trawling grounds. It is happening here."

The Scotsmen also complained that the Dutchmen are unscrupulous – latter Van Tromps who sweep all before them. Skipper Patience recalled the incident which cost him two nets and their contents.

Incentive had shot 75 of her 90 nets when the Dutchmen came up. He was showing no lights to indicate that he was trawling, said skipper Patience. He just went through *Incentive's* nets twice on a zig-zag course and

destroyed two of them.

Skipper Patience, who carries a camera in the hope of photographing such incidents noted the Dutch vessel's number. But he said he had little hope of compensation.

The Scottish skippers feel that if the Dutch continue exercising traditional rights it should be by traditional means, drift netting not trawling.

The future of the fishery is inevitably bound up with the behaviour of the fish themselves. Those that spawn off Yorkshire and on the Dogger Bank are from the Central North Sea stock. Scientists agree that the success or failure of the Yorkshire coast fishery has come to depend almost entirely on the number of three-year-old fish spawning for the first time.

Over the past four years fish in this category have represented on average threequarters of the catch. That meant, said Dr HA Cole, director of Fishery Research at the Fisheries Laboratory, Lowestoft, that there were scant reserves of older herring. The fishermen were virtually dependent

Rough sea at Scarborough in the Thirties

on the young first-year spawners.

It is also significant that the percentage total mortality of herrings has jumped from 37 per cent in 1948-53 to 75 per cent in 1962-66. There are far fewer fish and a bigger proportion of them are being killed.

A local attempt to have a close season for herring imposed within the 12 mile limit off the Yorkshire coast failed this year after representations to the Ministry of Agriculture, Fisheries and Food.

The North East Atlantic Fisheries Commission rejected a recommendation that herring fishing should be suspended for at least six and preferably nine years in the southern North Sea and English Channel. The Commission called for further scientific investigations and at the request of the British delegation it was agreed to extend research to the state of stocks in the central and northern North Sea. The scientific investigation continues.

As the fleet sailed from Scarborough on the tide last night it was an occasion to recall some words of Skipper Reid's: " I read somewhere that the time would come when herring would be as much a rarity as trout," he said. "That could well happen."

Scarborough's fishing fleet in its heyday

71

9 Snapshots of Yorkshire's war 1914-1918

In the early months of the war, armies clashing in Belgium and France converted into dramatic copy. On the home front, not much was happening and newspaper censorship operated in a faintly unreal way. One night, TH Hatfield, a senior sub-editor in the *Yorkshire Post's* London office in Fleet Street, was busy at 2am when the Leeds office got in touch. They had heard troops of cavalry were patrolling the cliffs in Scarborough. Hatfield recalled, "I was asked to submit this intimation to the Censor for confirmation or otherwise. I at once hurried to Whitehall to see Mr FE Smith (the late Lord Birkenhead) trying to imagine what the people in Burniston, Scalby, Ravenscar, Robin Hood's Bay and even Whitby were doing under the implied stress. It was a weary walk and on the way I did not see a soul until I came level with an armed sentry at Somerset House. The Censor was very courteous. He informed me there were no cavalry patrols on the Scarborough cliffs and that the inhabitants of the Queen of Watering places were, as far as he knew, sleeping peacefully."

Their peaceful lives really were interrupted a month or so later on 16th December with a savagery which FE Smith could not so casually dismiss. Out of the blue, German warships attacked the Yorkshire coast and the *Yorkshire Post* had an eye-witness, the world-renowned photographer of Whitby, Frank Meadow Sutcliffe, who lived at Sleights. In his extraordinary report, Sutcliffe recalled that shortly before the incident he had had a prophetic dream. It was about two German warships steaming into Whitby harbour and shelling the town. He wrote:

"So vivid was the dream that as soon as I arrived at Whitby next morning I went across the harbour to the East pier, that I might find out whether it were possible to get inside this stone structure and make holes in it from which torpedoes might be discharged at any possible enemy ships.

As it happened, some masons were at work inside the pier that morning and I went down too. Then I made straight for the coastguard station and asked the man on duty whether some plan of firing torpedoes from the East pier could not be devised, seeing that as far as the public knew the town was not protected by so much as a single gun.

The coastguard smiled, and then replied with the question, 'What about our Navy, Sir?' and after a pause added, 'No, Sir. I don't think we need worry about torpedoes,' and wound up by saying, 'Any German warship which found herself in British waters would be blown into the air before she knew where she was.'

With this comforting assurance I felt that the uneasiness which had prompted Sir Hugh Bell, the Lord Lieutenant of this district, to tell us where to make for in case of invasion, was not shared by this gallant sailor.

It was, I believe, to Stape, a hamlet on the moors between Goathland and Pickering, that the people about here were told to make for if the Germans landed. But how ten or twelve thousand folks were to be fed and housed on the top of a bleak moor we were not told, though we were forbidden to use the high roads and to keep to by-paths.

So I forgot all about my dream till a few mornings later when on December the 16th, about nine o'clock, there was an ear-splitting noise which we first thought came from an engagement between British and German ships. It was not till shells began to scream over the garden and drop into the fields and river below that we realised the engagement was one-sided.

As the train I went to Whitby by would be due in a few minutes, and as I had an appointment to photograph a child at 9.30, I made my way to the station [at Sleights]. At the bottom of the lane I found my youngest daughter, a VAD (Voluntary Aid Detachment) from the hospital on the other side of the river, standing on a gate watching the shells as they came and dropped into the fields round about.

BRIDLINGTON.

The Corporation of Bridlington desire to assure intending Visitors to Bridlington

That the alarmist rumours as to the state of things in Bridlington are absolutely without foundation.

That Visitors need have no fear about coming to Bridlington, as it is perfectly safe.

THAT THERE IS NO SHORTAGE OF FOOD.

The prices of Groceries and Provisions are about normal, and the charges in Restaurants and Cafes have not been increased.

All Entertainments, including Boating and Fishing, are in full swing.

No Visitors are being ordered to return home. No houses on the front have to be vacated for Territorials, nor have any lights to be extinguished.

All N.E.R. ordinary services, including tourist and week-end tickets, are as usual.

YOU CAN WITH SAFETY AND PEACE OF MIND SPEND YOUR HOLIDAYS AT BRIDLINGTON.

JOHN T. HILL, Mayor.
A. E. MATTHEWMAN, Town Clerk.

SCARBOROUGH AND THE EUROPEAN WAR.

OFFICIAL DENIAL OF MISCHIEVOUS RUMOURS.

The public are informed that there is no foundation for the many foolish rumours at present afloat with respect to Scarborough.

The Spa, Floral Hall, Theatres, and all other Amusements are in Full Swing, and there are no Increased Prices at Hotels or Boarding and Lodging Houses.

THE ALARMING RUMOURS ARE AS FOOLISH AS THEY ARE GROUNDLESS.

G. C. GRAHAM, Mayor.
SYDNEY JONES, Town Clerk.

Frank Meadow Sutcliffe

Left: 'Mischievous rumours' denied by Scarborough and Bridlington Councils

Below left: Shell damage in Scarborough

With her was one of the wounded soldiers, who said it was he who had insisted on my daughter leaving her post as the place was getting too warm, and the shells were too close for his liking. He added that in a barrage the elevation of the guns was gradually increased, the shells' bursts creeping further and further away from the gun.

Then the din stopped as suddenly as it had started, but there was no sign of any train at the station, and the signalman at the cabin said he had just heard that Whitby Abbey had been blown to pieces and that the west side of the town was in flames.

Then we had to wait till an engine had gone up the line to where our train was held up at Grosmont to see if any part of the line or any of the railway bridges had been hit.

When I got to my "Smithy", half an hour late, I found the girls sweeping up the broken glass which had fallen from the skylight, and in the yard I picked up a bit of shell, still warm.

In the waiting room was my small sitter and her mother, who had fortunately not been hit by any falling tiles or splinters on their way. After I had made the portrait I slung my camera on my back and went out to see what damage had been done. I saw where the coastguard had been killed, and saw, too, with great relief that the report about the Abbey having been blown to pieces was slightly exaggerated.

I saw also the bedroom window beside which a nephew of mine was shaving when the bombardment began. At a house close to, a friend of ours lay dying. Part of a shell had hit her.

I saw also the milk-girl who had pluckily stuck to her milk cart all through the affair, calmly stroking the terrified horse in the shafts. I saw, too, the school which had suffered so badly, but where fortunately not a single scholar was hurt, neither was the school gardener, though every bit of glass in his frames and greenhouses was smashed to smithereens.

Then came the reports of how Hartlepool and Scarborough had suffered far more grievously, both in loss of life and property than old Whitby, followed by one that the Germans were coming back in the afternoon to 'finish off' Whitby.

After lunch I filled my dark slides again

73

and went on to the cliff tops to get a photograph of the ships as they came back; though I waited till it was too dark for photography, they never came, thank goodness.

The hospital at Sleights had been filled to overflowing with women and children who had walked from Whitby. In the late afternoon they were persuaded to go home.

There were lean times in old Whitby after that, and to make things worse we had to pay 'Bombardment Insurance' at a high rate. Landlords said that if the Allies won the War the Germans would pay it all back with interest."

The full story of the bombardment had to wait another 20 years until it appeared in our pages as described by a special correspondent. "December 16, 1914, was a dull grey morning with a belt of mist off the Durham and Yorkshire Coast, and it was out of this bank of mist that five German cruisers under Admiral Hipper emerged to bombard the Hartlepools, Whitby and Scarborough. Twenty years have passed since the waking inhabitants of Hartlepool and West Hartlepool were startled by the sound of gunfire close at hand, but the memory will always remain with those who experienced the 42 minutes during which shells rained on the towns.

The casualty list comprised 112 civilians, nine soldiers and six naval men killed, while 400 persons were injured.

The bombardment of the Hartlepools was carried out by three ships, the *Seydlitz*, *Moltke* and *Blucher*, the other two – the *Derflinger* and *Von der Tann* – turning south to bombard Whitby and Scarborough. The two

Yorkshire coast resorts were, of course, undefended, but Hartlepool possessed two batteries, the Heugh and Lighthouse batteries, while at the South Gare Breakwater (Tees) there were two 4.7 guns within range of which the German ships never came.

Colonel L Robson, CMG, DSO, DL who as fire commander at Hartlepool, and is now 80 years of age, told me the other day the story of the unequal duel between the batteries and the German ships with their infinitely superior and more numerous armament.

"We received a warning the night before," said Lieut-Col Robson, "that a German squadron was in the North Sea, and ordering us to keep a sharp look-out. Tynemouth and Hull got the same warning, and similar ones were issued nearly every week. This particular warning impressed me, however, as being stronger than those usually received, and I took extra care to see that the look-out was well kept. About 7.55am the petty officer in charge of the port signalling station reported by telephone that three ships were approaching at speed.

"I could not see them myself from the battery because of the Heugh Lighthouse (it obstructed the view and masked the guns) and I asked if they were enemy ships. 'I think they are our own ships; they are flying the White Ensign and have answered our signals,' came the reply. Firing then became audible, for the German ships, as they proved to be, were engaging the five destroyers which left Hartlepool each morning at 5am for scouting purposes.

"We could not do anything but wait," said the Colonel, "and when the leading ship came into view she proved to be the *Seydlitz*, followed by the *Moltke* and the *Blucher*. The *Seydlitz* hit the battery with her first shot, killing Private Thomas Jones, of the 18th Battalion, Durham Light Infantry (Pals), who was the first soldier killed on British soil by enemy action in the Great War. A second shell killed three other men.

"From the Heugh Battery we engaged the *Seydlitz* and the Lighthouse Battery engaged the *Blucher*.

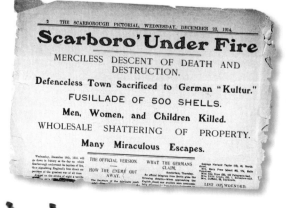

2   THE SCARBOROUGH PICTORIAL, WEDNESDAY, DECEMBER 23, 1914.

Scarboro' Under Fire

MERCILESS DESCENT OF DEATH AND DESTRUCTION.

Defenceless Town Sacrificed to German "Kultur."

FUSILLADE OF 500 SHELLS.

Men, Women, and Children Killed.

WHOLESALE SHATTERING OF PROPERTY.

Many Miraculous Escapes.

The Scarborough Pictorial Bombardment Number, 23rd December 1914
Left: A German shell blows a hole through Scarborough lighthouse

The latter was hit forward between her two 5-inch guns, which were put out of action and all her deck ammunition destroyed. The *Moltke* then came into view and the three ships engaged the Heugh Battery for about 15 minutes. The *Seydlitz* and *Moltke* then moved slowly north, firing on Hartlepool and West Hartlepool, leaving the *Blucher* to engage the batteries.

"It was extremely low tide and the *Blucher's* shells continually burst on the rocks. These shells were filled with black powder and created a smoke screen which hampered us. We kept firing from the Heugh Battery at the *Blucher* until she moved out to sea followed by the *Seydlitz* and *Moltke*."

The armament of the Hartlepool batteries consisted of three 6-inch guns, while the German cruisers used about 70 guns of varying calibres from 11.2, 8-inch and 5.9 down to small guns. In all they fired about 1,200 rounds against 123 fired by the shore batteries. The men engaged in this unequal duel were Territorials, the batteries being manned by the Durham Royal Artillery (Coast Defence) with a few reserve regulars, but the whole of the officers were Territorials.

The opinion was formed at the time that the German cruisers had mercantile captains on board who were familiar with the port. Colonel Robson, in conversation with the chief mate of a German ship a few months ago, asked if this was true, and was told there were German trawler skippers on board who had been into the Tyne, the Tees and Hull and were familiar with the Durham and Yorkshire coast.

While the batteries were gallantly replying to the fire of the *Blucher*, the *Seydlitz* and *Moltke* were dealing death and destruction upon the towns. Many children had started for school, most families were at breakfast, and although many persons were killed in their homes the greater majority of the injuries were received by people in the streets. There were innumerable instances of courage and disregard for personal danger. A typical one was that of a school teacher who, when a shell caused a gasometer to explode, was urged to turn back. "The children will be there waiting for me," was her reply, and to the school she went.

Admirable work was done by the VADs, most of whom had no experience at that time of cases of serious wounds. Rumours that a landing had been effected caused thousands of people to set out over the country with their most valuable possessions. Word, however, was despatched by the Mayor that the bombardment was over and there was a general return to their homes.

Mr Winston Churchill, then First Lord of the Admiralty, described how word of the bombardment reached him. "I jumped out of the bath with exclamations," he has written. "Sympathy for Hartlepool was mingled with what Mr George Wyndham once called 'the anodyne of contemplated retaliation'." Unfortunately, poor visibility prevented the retaliation.

Only two DSOs were awarded during the war for service in England, and both were earned at Hartlepool. Colonel Robson received the first for his services during the bombardment, and the second was awarded two years later to Lieut IV Pyott, the airman who destroyed the Zeppelin L34, which raided the port in November 1916."

Shell damage to Spring Mill, the Royal Hotel and the Grand Restaurant

YORKSHIRE'S PALS

FORWARD!

Forward to Victory
ENLIST NOW

For Yorkshire, the slaughter of World World I was felt nowhere more keenly than in the communities which provided the Pals Battalions. Earl Kitchener, who had been appointed Secretary for War at the outbreak of hostilities, had the idea of creating units which drew their entire strength from one particular town or city and in fighting terms, the idea of sending men off to war alongside their friends and workmates seemed to make sense. In West Yorkshire the recruiters urged Bradford men "to serve, shoulder to shoulder, with friends and colleagues in civil life".

Bradford eventually sent two Pals Battalions to war, the 16th and 18th (Service) Battalions of The Prince of Wales Own West Yorkshire Regiment. Kitchener's folly was in not forseeing how devastated an area would be if their fighting menfolk suffered mass casualties.

It was worse than anyone could have imagined. On the Somme, several Pals Battalions were virtually wiped out. Their deaths plunged entire communities into mourning. Local newspapers for many years carried lists of In Memoriam notices every 1st July on the anniversary of the 1916 Somme offensive.

The response to Kitchener's poster appeal "Your Country Needs You" was wholehearted throughout Yorkshire. Malcolm Barker reports on the Pals' finest hour.

In Barnsley, the recruiting office ran out of official forms, and those clamouring to join were told to be patient as "signing on was temporarily postponed until the arrival of another batch of papers".

Eventually, two battalions of Barnsley Pals, the 13th and 14th (Service) Battalions of the York and Lancaster Regiments were formed. They marched off to war under the leadership of local men. Lt Col Joseph Hewitt, a solicitor in the town and an ex-Territorial, was the driving force behind the recruiting campaign, and headed the 13th Battalion. He was replaced in November 1915, and survived the war to be awarded a knighthood and, later a baronetcy. The first commanding officer of the 14th Battalion was a Barnsley alderman, Lt Col William Emsley Raley.

His youngest son, Walter Hugh Raley, was killed in May, 1915, shot down by a sniper while serving with the Territorials. A month later his eldest son, Capt Harry Raley, was killed. Hardly surprisingly, Col Raley's health broke under the burden of grief and he returned to Barnsley.

By early 1916 the various Pals battalions were in France. Field Marshal Sir Douglas Haig, who had taken over as British Commander in Chief from Sir John French in December 1915, had 38 divisions at his disposal. The assembly of such a force was a remarkable achievement. When Britain went to war in 1914, it had only been able to deploy six divisions in the field, an army no bigger than that of Serbia.

More men were needed and as the Pals marched off to Flanders, the government abandoned the voluntary recruitment and with the Military Service Act of January, 1916, introduced conscription.

THE YORKSHIRE POST. WEDNESDAY, AUGUST 5, 1914.

ENGLAND DECLARES WAR AGAINST GERMANY.

BRITISH ULTIMATUM REJECTED.

ARMY AND NAVY MOBILISED.

TERRITORIALS EMBODIED.

BRITISH RAILWAYS UNDER STATE CONTROL.

Left: The *Yorkshire Post* report of the beginning of the Great War

Below: Leeds pals at Costerdale

"One man described a loud wailing 'as if huge wet fingers were being drawn across an enormous glass pane, rising and falling, interminable and unbearable. It came from a sunken road where hundreds of wounded were shouting, moaning and singing in delirium'"

YORKSHIRE'S PALS

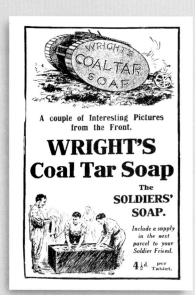

Capitalising on the war effort (above) and (below) the art of persuasion

Below right: Old Pal Arthur Dalby revisiting the hall in Leeds where he signed up in 1914

In terms of volunteers, the Pals were the last of many.

Haig's plan for 1916 was a Big Push. His main attack, on a 14-mile front between Maricourt and Serre, was entrusted to Sir Henry Rawlinson's Fourth Army. The plan was to destroy the German wire and front line defences with an artillery barrage of unprecedented ferocity, and then send the infantry across no man's land to break into open country beyond the trenches and end the Western Front stalemate.

The failure of this plan cost the Pals' communities a generation. Many of the Yorkshire Pals were serving with 31st Division which formed part of Lt Gen Sir Aylmer Hunter-Weston's VIII Corps. There were men from Hull, Leeds, Sheffield, Bradford, Barnsley, Accrington and Durham.

Their role was to take Serre and open the way for the seizure of Bapaume. Their battle orders set them up nicely as targets: "When advancing to the attack, cheering and doubling should not be allowed. The former advertises the fact that troops are attacking and the latter is too great an effort to men carrying heavy weights."

On part of the front, first advance was made by The 15th West Yorkshire, the Leeds Pals. As soon as the Leeds men went over the parapet, German machine-gunners opened fire. All the officers went almost immediately. Eleven were killed and 11 wounded. A few of the men advanced a hundred yards beyond the British wire, but were then either killed or wounded.

Undeterred by the slaughter, the Bradford Pals pushed forward in

support. One of them wrote later that he suddenly realised he was entirely alone, the rest of the company having melted away.

On another section of the 31st Division front the attack was led by the 12th Sheffield City Battalion, the York and Lancaster Regiment, a Pals unit known to some as the "Coffee and Bun Boys". They too were shot to pieces but some seem to have reached their objective, for months later, when Serre eventually fell, the graves of some York and Lancasters were found among the brick dust and shell holes – all that remained of the village. That night, with no man's land in front of Serre littered with the dead and the dying, Haig took up his pen and wrote in his daily diary: "I am inclined to believe that few of the 8th Corps left their trenches."

He soon learned otherwise. The Leeds Pals, in addition to 24 officers, lost 504 men. Only 47 of the Battalion answered roll call. The 16th Bradford Pals lost 22 officers killed, missing and wounded. Total casualties added up to 67 per cent. Its sister battalion, the 18th, lost 70 per cent.

In a brief part of a sunlit summer morning, the 31st Division lost 3,600 men, of whom only eight were prisoners. Its survivors, many of them wounded, sheltered in shell holes and the relentless German machine-guns continued sweeping to and fro.

One man described a loud wailing "as if huge wet fingers

were being drawn across an enormous glass pane, rising and falling, interminable and unbearable. It came from a sunken road where hundreds of wounded were shouting, moaning and singing in delirium."

Along the whole front, more than 57,000 British soldiers lay dead and dying on the uplands of Picardy. The sum of the anguish represented by the casualty figures is horrifying to contemplate. July 1 was not just pointless carnage. It was an epic of heroism that proved the moral quality of the Pals.

Attracting recruits in Leeds

10 Abdication and appeasement

"But for the Yorkshire Post we would have got away with it."

Arthur Mann came north from the editorship of the *London Evening Standard* in 1919. Taking the editor's chair at the *Yorkshire Post* was a step up. He was chosen by the soon-to-be chairman Rupert Beckett and his elder brother and fellow director Sir Gervase Beckett who was also tracking another recruit on his radar. This was an aristocratic Tory with a First from Oxford, a war hero with a Military Cross, called Anthony Eden.

The careers of the newspaper editor and the man who was to be Prime Minister were intertwined for the next 20 years. Arthur Mann set in motion the events leading up to the abdication of King Edward VIII and with Eden opposed his own party by calling on the nation to wake up to the true menace of Hitler.

In Arthur Mann's first ten years the paper's staff more than doubled to 1,269. He also assumed overall charge of the *Leeds Mercury*, acquired in 1923 but run as an independent title. Parts of the business still echoed the days of Griffith Wright and his carters trundling their newspaper bundles into the heart of bucolic Yorkshire. One of the paper's drivers, H Rogerson, described his day in 1929:

"On the 4am run to Pateley Bridge. There's a policeman waiting at Moortown...and with one flung to him and a bundle flung over the newsagent's gate I open out the open Talbot – a freezy, breezy experience these cold mornings – for Harewood. There's often a cheap dinner going on this road. A plump hare got caught in the headlines the other morning and later I ran him down...

I changed him later in the morning with a farmer for a chicken. I was once making a speedy run on this stretch when I just avoided something which turned out to be a horse sleeping stretched at full length across the road.

"At Harrogate there is always a good bit of business to do – catching trains, or delivering parcels to the villages if you miss them. The mail van is caught at Hampsthwaite and it is always a race with him. I have got the papers which he must collect from the newsagents to deliver.

"Some country hills we slide down and others especially on a frosty morning, we must be pushed up. At Dacre the mill hands often help to push the car up and in turn we then push up the mail van and a rival newspaper van and we are off again.

"At Pateley Bridge we are invariably asked for the "winners" and are given the day's "winners" in return – both lots being wrong. And then there is a little time to bargain for some eggs because country eggs are good and cheaper and finally before returning home there is that last copy of the *Yorkshire Post* to collect from a newsagent to be given to a farmer in person if we meet him on the homeward run and if we do not see him, well flying it goes over the hedge into his field."

By 1936, the relationship between Edward VIII and Mrs Wallis Warfield Simpson, the divorcee from Baltimore, was known to the British papers. Her name even appeared in the Court Circular, but since her husband's name was also included the facade of decorum was maintained.

The Newspaper Proprietors Association (NPA) and the Newspaper Society had come to a "gentlemen's agreement" about keeping up royal appearances and Howell Arthur Gwynne editor of the *Morning Post*, wrote to Prime Minister Stanley Baldwin, "The newspapers of the whole world are busily engaged in recording every incident of the King's friendship for Mrs Simpson. Some have urged me as editor of a newspaper which is the staunchest supporter of the monarchical institutions to break what they term

ANTHONY EDEN AND THE YORKSHIRE POST

In 1920 Anthony Eden was engaged by Sir Gervase (Ger) Beckett to write an occasional article "to bring freshness to the paper" for a fee of between five and ten guineas. An engagement of another sort followed not long after.

Sir Gervase, who like his father had become MP for Leeds, was a widower. He lived at Nawton in Kirkdale in North Yorkshire with four children from his first marriage and one of them, 18 year old Beatrice, struck up a relationship with her father's newspaper protégé. Anthony Eden proposed to Beatrice in July 1923 and a delighted Ger gave them 2,000 shares in the family business, Beckett's Bank, as an engagement present. The couple were married by the Archbishop of York and looked for somewhere to live in Haworth.

On 3rd March 1924, at Ger's suggestion, Eden wrote a political article for the YP. Arthur Mann wrote to him enthusiastically, "I believe a great many people will pay particular attention to what you say in relation to domestic problems." Eden confided to his diary, "This fills me with hope that I shall get the job of writing for them every week. It will be a considerable financial help."

The following year, the Empire Press Conference was being held in Australia and New Zealand in August and the YP invited Eden to cover it, paying £500 in expenses in return for articles about his travels. At the time his parliamentary salary was £400. On his return, Eden also got a book out of the trip titled Places in the Sun.

There was more good news to report in his diary on 9th February 1927. "Ger tells me that Mann is very pleased with my writing and says he must 'raise me to a higher scale of payment.' Splendid!"

The fee for his political notes went up from £3 to £4; the following year he was writing arts pieces and the year after that leaders. The relationship had a use beyond money for

Anthony Eden with his first wife Beatrice and their son Nicholas

Eden. He learned from Arthur Mann and other YP journalists about the interplay between the press and politicians.

When he resigned as Foreign Secretary in 1938, Eden sought out the Becketts in the Yorkshire Dales. When a letter of consolation from Lord Halifax arrived he confessed, "The moors in this glorious week do not exactly encourage me to contemplate a return to political life, ever." His marriage to Beatrice was not happy either (the couple were eventually divorced in 1950).

Eden did return to the political life with a vengeance. Churchill, made Prime Minister in May 1940, chose Eden as Secretary of State for War

where as a member of the Defence Committee, he shouldered the daily burden with Churchill.

The Conservatives lost the 1945 General Election and to make up for the loss of a Cabinet minister's salary, he accepted a directorship with Westminster Bank which had absorbed Beckett's Bank.

In April 1955 Eden stepped back into power when he became the first Foreign Secretary to succeed as Prime Minister in the 20th century. In less than two years his political career was over following ill health and the dispiriting outcome of the Suez crisis when his personal antipathy to Egypt's Colonel Nasser affected his judgement.

'the Great Silence'. In each case I have strongly urged on my friends the need for continued restraint and silence." He believed "that in such a delicate matter as this, the press should follow the government and not dictate to it."

One of the key players was Esmond Harmsworth, chairman of the NPA, a personal friend of the King and the most public supporter of his right to marry Mrs Simpson. Harmsworth was the heir of Lord Rothermere the owner of the *Daily Mail,* a paper sympathetic to fascism. A couple of years earlier, on 8th July 1934, the Mail had run a front page headline *"Hurrah for the Blackshirts"*, praising Oswald Mosley. Lord Rothermere had several meetings with Hitler and addressed him as "My Dear Führer" in correspondence.

The news about the couple finally broke across the British press on 2nd December 1936 when the *Yorkshire Post* picked up on a speech by Dr Alfred Blunt, the Bishop of Bradford. Arthur Mann was in the *YP's* London office. He was discussing what the next day's main leader article should be with his chief leader writer, Charles Tower, when the Leeds office alerted him to the contents of the Bishop's presidential address to the Bradford Diocesan Conference. The bishop had actually written it some months earlier – before he had ever heard Mrs Simpson's name. In private notes, Dr Blunt later confided that in November he had heard all about Mrs Simpson and the King through gossip at the autumn session of the Church Assembly. Should he change the completed speech to accommodate that?

The Duke of Windsor and Mrs Simpson meet Hitler. King Edward VIII had abdicated on 10th December 1936. (Below) the opening paragraph of Dr Blunt's private notes on the controversy over his speech

reference. So I delivered the words as originally written.....I had no idea that so much dry heather was lying about, waiting to be kindled; nor did I know that for some time the newspapers had been straining at the neck for the moment to break the news..."

Ironically, to avoid misunderstanding, Dr Blunt had a long-standing arrangement for the *Yorkshire Post* to receive these speeches in advance. He noted, "It ensures some adequate proportioning in the report of them. I did in this case what I usually do. They had the address at 3pm. I had it back at 5pm. Whether the Bradford office of the paper sent word to its Leeds office of what I was going to say, and so they were prepared with comment on it, I have no means of knowing and have never asked."

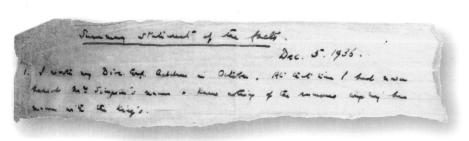

"For a moment I wondered whether I ought to alter the words I had written. I decided not to for the simple reason that as the words had no reference to the King's love affair, they could not be twisted to contain such a

These are the words that changed the destiny of the King and perhaps the nation. "The benefit of the King's Coronation depends, upon God, upon two elements: Firstly on the faith, prayer and self-dedication of the King himself; and on that it would be improper for me to say anything except to commend him and ask you to commend him to God's grace, which he will so abundantly need, as we all need it – for the King is a man like ourselves – if he is to do his duty faithfully. We hope that he is aware of his need. Some of us wish that he gave more positive signs of such awareness..."

This is how Arthur Mann and his leader writer Charles Tower interpreted that last phrase in Dr Blunt's address. The article they wrote sent ripples around the world.

"THE KING AND HIS PEOPLE
The Bishop of Bradford said yesterday that the benefit to be derived by the people from the King's Coronation would depend in the first instance on "the faith, prayer, and self-dedication of the King himself." Referring to the moral and spiritual life of that self-dedication, the Bishop said the King would abundantly need Divine Grace if he were to do his duty faithfully, and he added: "We hope that

he is aware of his need. Some of us wish that he gave more positive signs of such awareness."

Dr Blunt must have had good reason for so pointed a remark. Most people, by this time, are aware that a great deal of rumour regarding the King has been published of late in the more sensational American newspapers. It is proper to treat with contempt mere gossip such as is frequently associated with the names of European royal persons. The Bishop of Bradford would certainly not have condescended to recognise it. But certain statements which have appeared in reputable

United States journals, and even, we believe, in some Dominion newspapers, cannot be treated with quite so much indifference. They are too circumstantial and have plainly a foundation in fact. For this reason, an increasing number of responsible people is led to fear lest the King may not yet have perceived how complete in our day must be that self-dedication of which Dr Blunt spoke if the Coronation is to bring a blessing to all the peoples of the Empire and is not, on the contrary, to prove a stumbling block."

Arthur Mann explained the circumstances behind his leader article in a letter 22 years later.

"A few days before the Bishop spoke, Geoffrey Dawson (editor of *The Times*) invited me to call upon him at The Times offices. A talk between us on matters of common interest was not unusual, sometimes at Leeds where Dawson often called at the *Yorkshire Post* offices to pass the hour he had to wait for his train connection to his Yorkshire home, Langcliffe Hall, and at other times in London.

"At this meeting he told me of the impasse that had arisen between the Prime Minister and the King. There was as I knew already, a plot afoot sponsored by at least three chief proprietors of popular newspapers and more than one prominent politician to form a party known as "King's Men" designed to bring pressures to bear upon the Government and Parliament in favour of the introduction of a Bill to permit the King to contract a morganatic marriage with Mrs Simpson. It was one of the leading backers of the King's Party who was later heard to remark, "But for the *Yorkshire Post* we would have got away with it.""

In a further letter Arthur Mann said, "The *Yorkshire Post* did act alone in preparing a leading article early in the evening of December 1, 1936, the day the Bishop spoke and sending it to the Press Association for general circulation...As the historian of *The Times* newspaper points out, Mr Geoffrey Dawson, then its Editor, found a copy of the *Yorkshire Post* leader on his desk when he returned to his office from dinner that evening. After consultation with other London Editors, he decided not to comment upon the Bishop's address but simply to publish the address as a news item."

**Dr Alfred Blunt,
Bishop of Bradford**

As war loomed, the principal opposers of appeasement found their positions increasingly untenable. On 20th February 1938 Eden resigned as Foreign Secretary and just over a week later Arthur Mann wrote to him:

"I shall continue to think you were right until we have proof to the contrary. The Chamberlain line of approach to the dictators seems to me highly dangerous and unless it succeeds, its effect on this country will be damnable."

In April that year Eden wrote to Rupert Beckett, chairman of the *Yorkshire Post*:

"The sum of my criticism of Chamberlain's foreign policy is that his too patent eagerness to come to terms with the dictators encourges their aggressive tendencies...When we come to home affairs the position is no less anxious. Our rearmament programme is clearly inadequate to the dangers that confront us. If we are to live, other than on sufferance, in the next few years a united national effort is called for...For this a national leader is called for. Neville Chamberlain has none of the necessary attributes. He is essentially a party man... and lacks the imagination and personality for wider appeal.

For these reasons I believe it would be wrong to lend active support to the Government in its present form...they are unequal to the situation, perhaps the gravest we have known for centuries...

It may be true that the *Yorkshire Post* has sniped at the Government. I am sure that it is no less true that by their frank exposure of the plans of the dictators and the risks that accrue in consequence to the British Empire, they have done an immense service...the London press has been more sycophantic, but I am sure that the *Yorkshire Post* more truly represents national uneasiness...

The greatest risk of the moment is complacency. The British people are only too ready to believe that the international situation is easier, when it is not.

If I seemed to you reluctant, as indeed I am, to consider rejoining the present Government it is because I felt when I was in it increasingly out of tune with the blind optimism of the majority of my colleagues. It would be impossible for me to return to play the part of the ostrich, or to cheer on a party warfare which I regard as stupid,

if not criminal, at this time.

Hence I must wait; but while I wait I must speak out. For unless some of us, to whom the nation will at least lend passing attention, are prepared to do so, we can neither pave the way to that national unity that must come, nor do our duty by our countrymen."

Eden was alarmed to hear that an offer for the *Yorkshire Post* had been made by a big newspaper group that leaned towards appeasement and that a deal had tentatively been agreed. Eden saw Rupert Beckett to impress upon him that this would be unpatriotic. It would encourage Hitler. The *YP's* voice must continue to be heard.

But Arthur Mann's insistence that country must come before party met a hardening resistance from a significant section of his readership. Some members of the board became rattled. Linton Andrews, editor of the *YP's* sister paper the *Leeds Mercury*, was privately approached and told some directors wanted him to take over and bring in a more "reasonable" policy on appeasement.

On the last weekend of November 1938, the York Conservative Association met and voted to rebuke the paper in a letter. This was published, with a magnificent defence from Arthur Mann, on 26th November under the headline, *"Foreign policy and public opinion."* *"Freedom of speech means freedom, if need be, to express views unpalatable to those in authority...The existence throughout this country of anxiety concerning the foreign policy which the Government has pursued is too evident to ignore, and too widespread to be regarded as a mere manifestation of party politics...Since it is idle to deny the existence of this anxiety, a question that arises is whether, in the interests of the nation, newspapers should either obscure it or or express no knowledge of it, or whether the safety of the realm is not better served by candour. The claims of party loyalty are interpreted too narrowly if they demand the sacrifice of democratic principles.*

A resolution based on a number of misunderstandings of the attitude of this newspaper was passed this week by the executive committee of the York Conservative Association, in the following terms: "That this Executive Committee of the York Conservative Association resents and deplores the anti-Government attitude adopted by the Yorkshire Post ever since the resignation of Mr Eden from his post as secretary for Foreign Affairs, culminating in its recent attacks upon the Prime Minister for his efforts to bring appeasement to Europe, and is of the opinion that the present policy of the Yorkshire Post is doing a signal disservice to the country in general and to the Conservative Party in particular."

We have already denied that Mr Eden has any influence, direct or indirect, upon the policy of the Yorkshire Post beyond that possessed by any public man expressing views which we uphold...Since 1936 we have criticised certain aspects of Government policy with regard to Abyssinia, Italy, Spain and Germany. It appeared to us that the resignation of Mr Eden was followed by a relaxation of the attempt to establish orderly international relations and marked the institution of a new policy of capitulation to aggression which had its culmination at Munich. Having scrapped first collective security, and then the balance of power, we have sacrificed both our principles and our safety. There remains, as our only guide and hope, a policy of appeasement which means trust in the good will of those who even now are lashing us with contempt and hatred and whose triumph is the measure of our departure from those concepts of foreign policy in the past which the Conservative party has done so much to shape and inspire.

Believing that these issues concern the safety of the realm and must therefore take precedence over the claims of party loyalty, there has been no course left to us but to criticise the policy into which the Conservatuve party, has, in our opinion, been mistakenly led...

"Deep as is our regret to find ourselves out of sympathy with some members of the party whose welfare it is our sincere desire to serve and foster, we own, and can own, no other allegiance than that to our public and to the truth as we see it."

The disaffected Tories would have

none of it. The following month, 17th December 1938, the paper ran a report of a speech by Osbert Peake, Conservative MP for North Leeds, to his contituents:

"...as a Conservative who for years past has looked for guidance on great affairs to that great northern newspaper the Yorkshire Post, I have been a little surprised and pained by its attitude...I was very much pained by an article...containing a long and sustained attack on the Prime Minister..."

In the New Year, Sir Eugene Ramsden, Conservative MP for North Bradford, returned to the attack when the *Yorkshire Post* reported his election speech as chairman of the Yorkshire Provincial Area of the National Union of Conservative and Unionist Associations on 30th January 1939.

"I am very sorry about the attitude taken by the Yorkshire Post since the crisis. I do deplore the attitude they have adopted.

Winson Churchill with Anthony Eden in August 1939 and (below left) Arthur Mann

85

(Hear, hear)...We do expect from a newspaper of the type of the Yorkshire Post, if not active support, fair play, and quite frankly, I do not think we have received it...it would appear to me that their criticisms, instead of doing good, have only had the effect of making the task of the Prime Minister even more difficult...

I do not think there is any doubt the great mass of the people in this country are loyally supporting Mr Chamberlain and the policy for which he stands (hear, hear)..."

A couple of years later Sir Eugene survived being shot up by the Luftwaffe while he was sitting on a train at York station.

On Monday, 27th November 1939 the *Yorkshire Post* absorbed the *Leeds Mercury* and the cover price was halved to a penny. It explained to readers: *"We have decided to unite their forces and to present in the*

combined paper the best features of each. War conditions (especially the shortage of paper and petrol) compel us to reorganise on a thorough basis our methods of production and distribution."

In its leader column the same day it remarked: *"In recent years the paper has been unremitting in efforts to reveal the Hitler danger. It has been one of the most quoted papers in the world as a moulding force in British politics."* That it had been so was down to Arthur Mann.

In smaller type at the bottom of the page was this: *"The directors of this paper announce with regret that Mr AH Mann has notified his desire to relinquish his duties after 20 years of arduous work as the Editor of the Yorkshire Post."*

Taking over was Linton Andrews, editor of the *Leeds Mercury*.

German troops being greeted by locals in the Sudetenland on 1st October 1938

A REPORTER'S LIFE ON THE YORKSHIRE POST

John Halton recalled working for Arthur Mann in the Thirties.

"In those years the *YP's* Editor-in-Chief (note the "in-Chief") was Arthur Mann, a stern, tall character.

He had a gloomy, cigar-smelling room at the back of the old *YP* offices in Albion Street, Leeds, and to get to the Board Room (where files of old newspapers were kept for reference) you had to walk through Arthur Mann's sanctum and excuse yourself for the interruption, but he never seemed to notice. His desk was always strewn with proofs of tomorrow's newspaper and those not only littered the large old fashioned desk but festooned down to the carpet.

Mann was not a public figure. He spent a lot of his time in London, it is believed hob-nobbing with people like Stanley Baldwin. His home was 200 miles away in Sevenoaks, Kent, and in Leeds he lodged for years at the Mount Hotel, Mount Preston. His retreat from the YP office was the Leeds Club in Albion Place. He would be at the *YP* office during the afternoon and early evening for the daily editorial conference, retire to the club for dinner and bridge and return to the *YP* office and his proof-cascading table, in mid-evening where he would remain until perhaps midnight.

During those inter-war years, the *YP* was proud of its coverage of the North of England. The slogan "Twixt Trent and Tweed" was freely used. It had a great chain of local correspondents stretching from South Lincolnshire to Newcastle and specialised in "county" news. It was very interested in news of the many hunts (foxhounds and others) and was not afraid to display a contents bill containing the words "Grouse shooting prospects" outside a newsagents' shop in scruffy Burley Road, Leeds, which cannot have made many sales for the paper in those parts.

Some of its leaders were written nightly in Leeds at head office – others came over the wire from the

The sign outside the *Yorkshire Post's* premises on Albion Street

HL Mann

"The Yorkshire Post was proud of its coverage of the North of England. The slogan "Twixt Trent and Tweed" was freely used"

busy London office in Fleet Street. Great attention was paid to politics. Whenever a Prime Minister or Foreign Minister or leader of the Opposition came to Yorkshire, there would be a verbatim report. Those were the days before handouts of speeches and the news editor (William Finerty) would get together those reporters known to have reliable shorthand, form a "ring" and send them to Leeds Town Hall, Doncaster, Bradford or wherever the political VIP was speaking. Five reporters would write shorthand in turns (the ring) of three minutes each, write up between "takes" and hand the handwritten copy to a messenger who would whip it back to the office.

When one returned to the office, the speech was already set up in type – a terrifying sight for young reporters who were not first class Pitman writers and who wondered

what political crisis might ensue if they happened to mis-report. Usually there was a first-class shorthand writer who would take a check-note and be available for filling in gaps or correcting others' mistakes. The *YP* was strong on sport over a wide area, and, perhaps reflecting Arthur Mann's personal outside interest, gave great attention to horse-racing.

During the inter-war years, Leeds had several newspapers – the *YP*, *Yorkshire Evening Post*, *Yorkshire Weekly Post*, *Leeds Mercury*, *Yorkshire Evening News* and (for a time) the *Daily Chronicle*. Their editorial staffs frequented pubs like Powolny's Bar, the King Charles, the Ostlers' Arms in Trinity Street and especially Whitelocks Bar, an Edwardian establishment which attracted also a theatrical and musical clientele, the licensee then being Lupton Whitelock who played the flute in the Hallé Orchestra."

11 Snapshots of Yorkshire's war 1939-1945

First casualty: the Heinkel 111 shot down near Whitby in 1940 by Peter Townsend

Yorkshire was where the home front opened. The first enemy plane of World War II to be brought down was a Heinkel 111 bomber on 3rd February 1940 near Whitby. The RAF fighter pilot doing the shooting was Peter Townsend – the man destined to be the post-war love of Princess Margaret's life. He was a Flight Commander based at Acklington in Northumberland when they were scrambled one Saturday morning. This is how he told it.

"On the morning of the 3rd of February, in a cutting wind, the other pilots in my flight and I, went for our Hurricanes dispersed on the far side of the airfield. Far away at Danby Beacon Radar Station, the duty operator picked up the phone, it was 09.03 – the operator had seen a blip, then another – unidentified aircraft, some 60 miles out to sea, were approaching at 1,000 ft. Moments later, blue section of 43 Squadron were scrambled and on their way from Acklington airfield to intercept. Myself with Folkes and Sgt Hallowes in my wake – "Vector 190, bandit attacking ship

off Whitby – 'Buster' – with throttles wide open, racing south at wave-top height and spreading into search formation, Hallowes on my left and Folkes on my right.

Suddenly there it was, a Heinkel just below cloud, 'Tally-Ho two-o-clock', banking right in a climbing turn, it came into my sights – I pressed the button – I was firing at Missy, Wilms, Leuschake and Meyer (the names of the Heinkel's crew) who at Schleswig only a few hours earlier had been shovelling snow and enjoying coffee and sandwiches. It never occurred to me that I was killing men. I only saw a Heinkel with big black crosses on it, but in that Heinkel, Uffz Rudolph Leuschake was already dead, Uffz Johann Meyer, his stomach punctured by bullets was mortally wounded – closing in fast, I passed it as it entered cloud – seconds later Folkes, the Heinkel and I tumbled out of the cloud almost on top of one another, then the German turned shorewards with a trail of smoke behind him and force-landed."

The Heinkel came down at Bannial Flat

Farm, Whitby, at 09.40. Special Constable
Arthur Barratt dashed up to the Heinkel
and saw Fw Wilms, the pilot, burning the
aircraft's papers – it took five fire extinguish-
ers and a shovel full of snow to put the fire
out. Uffz Meyer was screaming in pain, Uffz
Leuschake had died instantly, shot through
the head, Uffz Missy, the upper gunner had
been grievously wounded, with one leg
broken and the other terribly mutilated,
cried out in agony as he was pulled clear.
Peter Townsend visited him in hospital. Later
the Squadron buried Rudolph Leuschake and
Johann Meyer at Catterick with a wreath:
"From 43 Squadron, with sympathy".

GROUP CAPTAIN PETER TOWNSEND

The photograph below
is about as close as
Peter Townsend (in
the cap) and Princess
Margaret (emerging
from the vehicle) could
be pictured together.
He was a married man,
twice her age, with two
children when he first caught her eye. She
had nothing to do with a break-up of his
marriage but the conventions of the State
and the Church of England still stood in the
way. If she wanted Peter Townsend she
would have had to give up everything else.
In 1955 Princess Margaret issued a statement saying that "mindful of the Church's
teaching" she would not marry the group
captain. Five years later she married
Anthony Armstrong-Jones.

THE YORKSHIRE POST AT WAR

The first winter of the war brought the bitterest
weather for years. Most Yorkshire rivers froze
and the ice was thick enough for people to
walk across the Ouse at York and the Wharfe at Otley.
When the fire brigade attended a fire in Leeds the
water froze.

All this was a state secret. Newspapers could not report
the effects of the severe conditions since that might be
giving useful information to the enemy. In January 1940 it
was not just Yorkshire's weather which was a talking-point:
in many other parts of the globe the weather was also
doing unexpected things and these events the newspapers
could discuss freely. Since a direct statement about the
domestic situation was not allowed, the *Yorkshire Post* tried
the oblique approach with this tongue-in-cheek leader
referring to the stories it had been carrying of a spate
of weather-related accidents.

*"Buses and cars were colliding in dozens for no apparent
reason. Men were falling down in the streets and breaking
their legs – just as though they had never learned to walk.
And – most uncanny of all – quite a number of people
walked across ponds and then suddenly sank. It shows what
remarkable things may pass almost unnoticed if you fail to
keep your eyes open at your own doors and pay too much
heed to the extravagant goings on in Moscow, Budapest,
Athens, Kenya and Buenos Aires."*

Instructions to editors defining news that was forbidden
were seemingly endless, although the censorship was voluntary. If there were doubts about interpretation, copy was
submitted to the Censorship Division in London. But getting
the copy passed could be irritatingly slow and deadlines
were often missed. The *Yorkshire Post* resisted official
suggestions that it print misleading news to confuse
the enemy.

On Tuesday 15th October 1940 a 500 pound bomb
smashed into the *Yorkshire Post's* London office in Fleet
Street and penetrated as far as a cellar where three staff
were sleeping and eight sub-editors and telegraphists were
working. It did not explode and everyone went on working
until told to evacuate the building three hours later.

When Hitler was finally defeated the *Yorkshire Post*
was found to be on a secret list in his headquarters.
Some assumed that Hitler had intended to destroy the
paper that had warned Britain against him during his rise
to power. Possibly he just planned to take it over. When the
European war came to an end on 9th May 1945, the centre
of Leeds on VE Day was a bit of a let down. It rained and
there was not much by way of celebration for the
newspaper to report.

YORKSHIRE CITIES BLITZED

On Friday, 24th and Saturday, 25th May 1940 Middlesbrough became the first industrial town to be attacked by the Luftwaffe with Dorman and Long's steel plant the first of their industrial targets. Within weeks Yorkshire's towns and cities were under attack from the air.

York

The Baedeker raid on York on the night of 28/29th April 1942, brought the horror of the blitz to the old city. John Scott talked to a family 50 years on about how they survived it.

As the bomb fell on No 19 Nunthorpe Grove, Mrs Edna Blakeborough had a cup of tea in her hand and her three-year-old daughter, Ann, sitting on her lap. "The next thing I heard was a voice saying, 'don't move or you'll fall down to the bottom of the crater'." The air raid warden had seen a hand sticking out of the rubble in the side of a huge pit – all that was left of No 19 and its adjoining 'semi-detached'.

Five years later Mrs Blakeborough and her husband Frank moved back into their rebuilt home and they have lived there ever since.

There had been six people huddled together when the bomb fell. Mrs Blakeborough, her daughter and the ATS (Auxiliary Territorial Service) girl billeted with them had been invited next door as the bombing started. Mrs Blakeborough's husband was on night duty and the army major billeted in the adjoining semi urged them to go next door for company. Also there were Mrs Webb, the owner of the next door house, and ATS girl, Dorothy Thompson.

The 500lb bomb sliced sideways through the house and buried itself in the front garden before exploding. The major found himself lying

Destruction in Coney Street

Damage in the Leeds suburbs
and (below) evacuation orders

CITY OF LEEDS

EVACUATION

(1) SCHOOLCHILDREN may be registered to be sent out when evacuation of the district is considered necessary.

(2) EXPECTANT MOTHERS may register for evacuation. They will be evacuated when they are within one month of confinement.

(3) PRIVATE ARRANGEMENTS.

(a) *Unaccompanied children* whose parents can make arrangements for them to stay with a householder in a reception area can get a free travel voucher and a billeting allowance will be paid to the householder with whom the child stays. Billeting allowances will be continued if it is clear that the child cannot be maintained without hardship.

(b) *Mothers with children under 5* who can make similar arrangements in a reception area can get a free travel voucher and billeting allowances will be paid to the householder with whom she stays. She may take with her also any of her children who may be of school age.

Northern Ireland or Eire :—Mothers with children of school age or under may go to Northern Ireland, or, provided they satisfy certain conditions, to Eire. It is not necessary that they should be accompanied by a child under 5.

(4) HOMELESS PERSONS, MALE AND FEMALE, whether or not they are normally resident in an evacuable area, may go to any area except some towns on the East, South and South-East Coasts, or the Metropolitan Evacuation Area. If they are employed persons they will be expected to remain near their work and will not be assisted to move to a distance from it.

NOTE.—The Metropolitan Evacuation Area includes certain Thames-side and Medway towns. The Officer in Charge of the Rest Centre will tell you if the district to which you wish to go is within this area.

WHERE TO APPLY FOR INFORMATION.

(1) *Schoolchildren.* At a school or at the Education Offices, Calverley Street.

(2) *Expectant Mothers.* At the nearest ante-natal clinic.

(3) *Persons making private arrangements.* At the Housing Department, 107, Portland Crescent.

Billeting Allowances are payable to the householder with whom you are billeted. For unaccompanied children the rates vary from 8s. 6d. to 15s. a week according to age and provide for board and lodging. For adults the rate is 5s. a week and for children under 14 accompanied by adults 3s. a week providing for lodging only.

If you have not enough money to buy food and other necessities you may apply to the Office of the Assistance Board in the place where you are billeted. The billeting officer will tell you where this office is.

O. A. RADLEY, *Town Clerk.*
A.R.P. Controller.

---

relatively unhurt in the street. Four injured were dug out of the debris, but Dorothy Thompson was missing until her body was discovered weeks later down the crater.

Mr and Mrs Blakeborough had only the clothes they wore. And Mrs Blakeborough, although she did not realise it immediately, was seriously injured. She walked with her child to the top of the street, put her hand to her forehead and found a hole in her head. She needed brain surgery, and spent months in hospital.

Edna's husband Frank saw York station bombed and later borrowed a bicycle to reach home. A policeman stopped him at the entrance to Nunthorpe Grove. He looked down the hill and saw the lamp post outside his house had disappeared. He looked again and saw his home had gone.

He did not know that Edna and Ann had been rescued. ARP (Air-Raid Precautions) men had formed a human chain and pulled them out. After frantic inquiries Frank found that his wife and daughter were in hospital. "But I was hardly recognisable," said Mrs Blakeborough. "I was black with soot and soil, bruised all over and with my teeth broken."

Mrs Blakeborough, in hospital at York until August, was transferred to Sheffield for further checks. Friends took in Ann, and others helped with clothes. The family had lodgings before getting a council house and stocking it with second-hand furniture. The Red Cross supplied blankets and there were patch-work quilts sent as war relief from Canada. From the government Frank

---

"The air raid warden had seen a hand sticking out of the rubble in the side of a huge pit – all that was left of No 19 and its adjoining 'semi-detached'"

---

received £200; Edna £100 and Ann £25 – a total of £325 to rebuild their lives and their home.

Mrs Blakeborough felt the war robbed her of her youth. "I was turned 40 before my injuries settled down and I was out of pain. I still have a silver plate in my forehead. In hospital the nurse said to me: 'It is now up to you. Will you promise me to fight back?'"

Edna and her husband did just that. But returning to the house where it had all happened had not been easy. "I thought I would never go back and live there again. But after the war all the neighbours were having a street party and they invited us. The trees were out and the house had been rebuilt and we just suddenly decided. The only thing that hit me was that this was where Dorothy had been killed, but we settled back in here and have never regretted it."

Daughter Ann is married and lives in America and the Blakeboroughs have four grandchildren and two great grandchildren. Edna's happy memories of the war are of the camaraderie in distress and people's kindness. She has no bitterness. The German pilot who dropped the bomb was someone's son. "I have visited Germany and I have some wonderful German friends. I would not be a Christian if I was bitter about it."

YORKSHIRE CITIES BLITZED

Sheffield

Blitzed Sheffield

Thursday 12th December 1940:
Eileen Reed of Glapwell, Chesterfield, recalled the day.

"The warning sirens screamed out across the city at 7pm. They had sounded often with nothing happening and many shrugged their shoulders and carried on as normal. About five minutes after the sirens had sounded came the dull roar of enemy bombers, followed by the thud of heavy anti-aircraft guns. Incendiary bombs lit up parts of the town for the waves of planes that were to follow.

Our house was only ten minutes walk from the city centre and by now we were getting very worried about my father, who hadn't returned home from work. We still hadn't gone into our Anderson shelter when he came rushing in and without any hesitation bundled us straight into it.

I shall never forget the sight that met my eyes as I set off for work the next morning. The devastation was unbelievable."

Eileen Wadsworth was working as a nurse at Fir Vale hospital, Sheffield on the night of the attack.

"Somebody told us the city was on fire and I was standing on the bedroom window sill looking at the flames when a land mine dropped a street away from where we lived in Crookes.

I literally jumped downstairs, and got to the stair-head, as we could not make it to the shelter. We heard clearly the planes machine-gunning the outside toilets and all the windows and doors were blown out.

I felt something hot land in my lap and thought it was a piece of shrapnel, but I realised it was a black cat which had been blown in. I sat with it on my knee all night – I really did feel it was the end for me. When the all-clear went, a whole street had been wiped out and many of my friends had just disappeared for ever. Next day, it took me two to three hours to pick my way through Sheffield city centre and once I arrived at the hospital we stayed for three weeks without relief."

Sunday 15th December 1940:
Cyril Wilson of Kimberworth, Rotherham, recalled the air raid.

"Sirens sounded about 6.30pm and my mother, my grandfather and I locked the house door and went a hundred yards down the road to a reinforced cellar beneath a corner shop. I was ten years old. Mother had decided that we should go there after the Blitz the previous Thursday when we had spent nine hours on our cellar steps. She thought we should seek a safer place next time.

At seven o'clock the German bombers arrived and the Shirecliffe guns set up a noisy reception. The people in that public shelter chatted and sang at first until the shrieking and thumping of bombs quietened them as they realised that they were much nearer to us than they had been on the first raid.

About nine o'clock a huge explosion smashed in the door at the top of the shelter steps, to be followed by a blast that made folk gasp for air. Women screamed, the lights went out and then came on and I recall a mother throwing herself across her baby's portable Mickey Mouse gas shelter.

We went home in the afternoon and my pals were astonished to see me, for rumour had it that I had been killed, along with others, in the public shelter beneath Maybury's shop.

We were soon going round the district collecting shrapnel, incendiary bomb fins, parachute chords and shreds of the canopy from two of the 14 landmines that had been dropped on Sheffield. Barrage balloons, shot down by German planes, were sought after for their material, which women made into shopping bags and left-over linen, fastened over broken windows by council workmen, were put to many uses.

We visited the demolished stable where Ernest Sutcliffe, greengrocer, kept his horse; the animal had broken out during the raid and was found grazing in Firth Park. Mrs Pogson's fruit and vegetable shop was a pile of rubble, but the oven of her Yorkshire range stood among the ruins. When we opened its doors it was found to contain a blackened pie! For several days we were on edge, waiting for the third Blitz, but it never came."

Hull

The day after war broke out, at 3.20am on 4th September 1939, the air raid sirens sounded in Hull. That was a false alarm. Those that came after were not.

The first to cause casualties was on 25th August 1940 and they continued for almost five long years until the last attack on the night of 17/18th March 1945 when twelve people were killed in east Hull.

The climax came on the nights of 7th and 8th May 1941 when 400 people were killed. More than 300 bombs falling over a twelve-hour period, virtually destroyed King Edward Street and gutted Riverside Quay. The fires started in the centre of Hull were so intense, RAF pilots flying over Denmark reported being able to see them.

The dislocation to everyday life was severe. Reserve food stocks had to be rushed to Hull and mobile canteens were brought into use in the worst-hit areas. On 19th May 1942, one huge bomb killed 50 people in Scarborough Street, off Hessle Road.

The street which the Luftwaffe hit in every single raid throughout the war was James Reckitt Avenue, a long straight thoroughfare pointing towards the docks which their pilots probably picked up to guide them on their bombing run.

Altogether, nearly 1,200 were killed and over 85,000 buildings damaged or destroyed in 82 air raids on Hull. In the early days it was planned to evacuate 100,000 people to the East Riding and Lincolnshire. Only a third ever went and most of them soon returned.

Bomb damage in Hull and (below) the report in the *Yorkshire Post* from 5th June 1941; Left: gas masks for children

"Altogether, nearly 1,200 were killed and over 85,000 buildings damaged or destroyed in 82 air raids on Hull"

THE ALTERNATIVE WARTIME 'YORKSHIRE POST': THE KRIEGIE EDITION

This page and opposite: excerpts from the *Yorkshire Post* produced by prisoners of war in Stalag Luft VI

Above: R Booth, secretary of the camp's White Rose Club

Right: A portrait of camp leader James 'Dixie' Deans

Below: The edition's front cover

Opposite page, bottom right: *Kriegie* editor Richard Pape

A unique issue of the *Yorkshire Post*, dated May 1944, stands as a remarkable tribute to the men who produced it. The Kriegie Edition was written in Stalag Luft VI, a prisoner-of-war camp at Heydekrug, Lithuania on the bleak Baltic coast (Kriegie was adapted from Kriegesfangene – Prisoner-of-War). It was produced by Yorkshiremen in the camp – 254 in all – who had formed a White Rose Club in February 1944 and this was to be their house journal.

The editor, Richard Pape, wrote that adopting the *Yorkshire Post* title was by "general consent" although some of the more diplomatic members had approached him "fearing we may offer offence to other county newspapers by favouring the name of one journal only."

The camp leader, Sergeant Pilot James "Dixie" Deans, wrote in the foreword to the edition: *"Having lived in Yorkshire since early 1937, I have travelled about the county a great deal and learned to know intimately the Yorkshire dales and moors...I have been lucky enough to obtain a Yorkshire lass for my wife...and I have chosen Yorkshire as my home...I look forward to the time when we shall all be able to meet together as members of Stalag Luft White Rose Club...at home in Yorkshire."*

Dixie Deans of 77 Squadron had taken off from RAF Linton-on-Ouse on 10th September 1940 in a Whitley

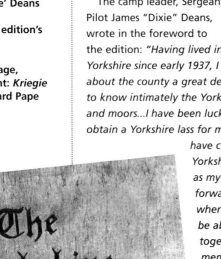

bomber P5042 to attack Bremen and was shot down in Holland. At Stalag Luft III – of Wooden Horse fame – he held weekly meetings with the Germans on behalf of the commissioned and other rank PoWs and had a system for passing back information to the UK to MI9, the intelligence branch responsible for escapes and evasion. The Kriegie edition was said to have played a part in that.

In March 1945, he took charge of 12,000 PoWs on a month-long march towards the approaching British armies in the North West. A section of Cornelius Ryan's 1966 book *The Last Battle* is devoted to Dixie's exploits.

In Stalag Luft VI, Dixie secured from the Germans, paper, Indian inks, brushes and water colours. Pen nibs, especially small mapping ones, were forbidden – the Germans being well aware what skilful RAF forgers could do with them. A former instrument maker made superb flexible nibs out of the steel tape that bound the Red Cross crates sent to the camp.

The *Kriegie Edition* contains 30,000 hand-drawn words with articles on subjects ranging from sport to cinema organs, motoring and mental hospitals. Water-colours of Yorkshire landmarks are mixed with cartoons about camp existence and caricatures. Once completed, it reached England in a little over five weeks, via Sweden by undisclosed means. After vetting by military authorities, it went to the *Yorkshire Post*, which printed souvenir copies for the next-of-kin of the fliers of the White Rose Club.

Both the Minister of War and the Minister of Information praised the Kriegie Edition. Winston Churchill wrote: "It is an interesting and moving record of the talent shown by these prisoners during the years of their captivity."

Dixie Deans became the first chairman of the RAF Ex-PoW Association and died aged 76 in 1989.

The Yorkshire Post

KRIEGIE EDITION

YORKSHIRE CRICKET by P.F. PACEY

Taking a glance at records and making a rough guess, one may say fairly safely, that cricket began in Yorkshire in the 18th century. The Yorkshire County Cricket Club was formed in 1863, and ten years later, when the County Championship competitions started on an organised basis, the 'White Rose' was among the entrants. On a point of interest Nottinghamshire were the first champions.

For many years Yorkshire was just another county, but in 1893, the eleventh year of Lord Hawke's captaincy, the championship was ours. Since then, out of the 63 competitions held, Yorkshire have held the title 21 times, followed at a respectable distance by Notts 12 times, and the 'Red Rose' club 11 times.

Lord Hawke by the way, captained the county for 28 years and did much to build up the prestige of Yorkshire Cricket. Whilst on the subject of captains, one of the most successful of all is Brian Sellars, our present leader. Major Sellars took over in 1932 when only 25 years of age. His appointment caused much consternation among the supporters and members, owing to his apparent lack of experience. However, he proved his worth by, in 1932, not losing a match. True in 1932 Yorks were defeated twice, but on both occasions Greenwood was captain in Sellars' absence. In the eight seasons prior to the war, that he was in command, Major Sellars steered the county six times to the top. Seasons 1934 and 1936 might also have been ours, had not Test matches sadly depleted the team.

Looking back on Cricket, Yorkshire has produced many names that will always remain fresh to followers, even though many of us are too young to have ever seen them play. Brown and Tunnicliffe, for instance, a really grand opening pair, which most of us have heard of yet few seen. Tunnicliffe of Pudsey, the town that also produced 'Erbert Sutcliffe and Len Hutton, and will, with luck, give us young Bill Sutcliffe soon. Young Bill, I think 16 years old now, is playing well

.....and Wisdens, who are rarely wrong, predict an even greater opening batsman than his famous father.

Percy Holmes Sutcliffe's county partner for many years, must not be forgotten. Holmes, had it not been for the maestro Hobbs, would undoubtedly have been Sutcliffe's test partner also. His share of the 555 runs against Essex in 1932, and the 11 more than '50 runs partnership with Sutcliffe prove him to be a player of no mean ability.

Another amazing fact about Yorkshire is the county's ability to produce left-hand spin bowlers. Peel, Rhodes and Verity, to name three, that are classed the finest of their particular period, and now Verity has gone another has to be found to keep up the peculiar record.

Verity took on when Rhodes left off and proved himself to be equally as great. Continued overleaf

---

Advertising Card in country shop:
"To Cyclists and Photographers Try our 1s.6d. luncheons A dark room is provided for developments"

'A Journalist,' said G.K.Chesterton, is a man who announces the death of Lord So-and-so to people who never knew he was alive........

Letter to Editor of Correspondence Column. "I am only 19 and I stayed out till two the other night. My mother objects. Did I do wrong?" Answer 'Try to remember.'

THE LAST FLIGHT OF AMY JOHNSON 5TH JANUARY 1941

"At Squires Gate aerodrome they tried to persuade Amy not to take off, pointing to the thickening clouds. But at 10.45am she said: "I am going over the top.""

Amy Johnson's Fatal Crash

'Plane Sinks in Thames Estuary

Miss Amy Johnson, the well-known Yorkshire airwoman, was killed when her 'plane came down off the Thames Estuary on Sunday, writes Drew Middleton, Associated Press war correspondent in London, in an eye-witness account.

"There was no possibility that Amy could have survived," he states. "I watched the machine glide gracefully down into the water, smash on a wave, and sink before help could reach her.

"A seaman from a balloon ship dived into the icy waters of the estuary. He is now lingering between life and death. He was half-dead from exposure when pulled aboard a lifeboat. No one could live for more than half-an-hour in that water.

Miss Amy Johnson

The incident occurred in mid-afternoon, when the ship in which I was a passenger was nearing the Thames Estuary.

"We sped through the shallow waters towards the wave-swept wreckage. As we neared it I thought I saw someone clinging to the fuselage, but the look-out said, 'No, it's just part of the machine'."

A Ferry Pilot

Miss Johnson was a ferry pilot for Air Transport Auxiliary, which is responsible for delivering aircraft from factories to RAF airfields. There are several women pilots with the organisation.

Mr J A Mollison, her former husband, was recently stated to be among men pilots with Air Transport Auxiliary.

Mr and Mrs J W Johnson, the airwoman's parents, live at Bridlington. She was their eldest daughter, born at Hull and educated at Sheffield University. Mrs Molly Jones, a sister, is the wife of Mr Trevor Jones, town clerk of Blackpool. Miss Johnson married Mr Mollison in 1932.

Remarkable Flights

By her remarkable flights to Australia, to America, to Japan and China and across Africa and the Equator to the Cape, she proved that women could achieve and maintain a high place in aviation.

Below is the *Yorkshire Post's* account of the death of Amy Johnson, and (left) as it originally appeared in the paper.

"Miss Amy Johnson, the well-known Yorkshire airwoman, was killed when her plane came down off the Thames Estuary on Sunday, writes Drew Middleton, Associated Press war correspondent in London, in an eye-witness account. "There was no possibility that Amy could have survived,"
he states. *"I watched the machine glide gracefully down into the water, smash on a wave, and sink before help could reach her.*
"A seaman from a balloon ship dived into the icy waters of the estuary. He is now lingering between life and death. He was half-dead from exposure when pulled aboard a lifeboat. No one could live for more than half-an-hour in that water. The incident occurred in mid-afternoon, when the ship in which I was a passenger was nearing the Thames Estuary. We sped through the shallow waters towards the wave-swept wreckage. As we neared it I thought I saw someone clinging to the fuselage, but the look-out said, 'No, it's just part of the machine'." After describing how lifeboats put out, Middleton says: "A ship went over the spot for nearly half-an-hour after the rescue attempt, but saw no sign of a body."
Miss Johnson was a ferry pilot for Air Transport Auxiliary, which is responsible for delivering aircraft from factories to RAF airfields. There are several women pilots with the organisation. Mr JA Mollison, her former husband, was recently stated to be among men pilots with Air Transport Auxiliary.
Mr and Mrs JW Johnson, the airwoman's parents, live at Bridlington. She was their eldest daughter, born at Hull and educated at Sheffield University. Mrs Molly Jones, a sister, is the wife of Mr Trevor Jones, town clerk of Blackpool. Miss Johnson married Mr Mollison in 1932. After their marriage was dissolved she re-took her maiden name.
By her remarkable flights to Australia, to America, to Japan and China and across Africa and the Equator to the Cape, she proved that women could achieve and maintain a high place in aviation. British aviation owes to her a great debt, for she took to the air at a time when foreign rivals were making great efforts for supremacy."

20th August 1957: Amy Johnson's husband James Mollison reflected on the mystery of that fatal flight.

The death of my first wife, the magnificent Amy Mollison, remains a mystery to this day. Although our marriage had been dissolved and she had reverted by deed poll to her name, Amy Johnson, she had my deep and sincere respect, not only for her immense courage but for her skill as a pilot.

When it was reported to me that she had run out of petrol at a point 100 miles off her course during a relatively short flight across England I could not credit the details.

At that time German fighter aircraft were making "sneak raids" on this country. I thought that one of them must have pounced on her defenceless aircraft and shot it down. Even now after reconsideration of all the available evidence, I feel that this possibility has not been eliminated. Poor Amy's aircraft was never recovered from where it fell into the Thames Estuary, and both she and the brave Naval officer who dived to her rescue lost their lives.

Amy Johnson, to use her maiden name which she made famous throughout the world, was born on July 1, 1903, daughter of a Hull businessman. She learned to fly while working as a secretary to the City and not long afterwards made an historic solo flight to Australia in a Moth light plane. I, of all people can testify to her skill at the controls and as navigator since she afterwards flew as co-pilot with me across the North Atlantic and later to India.

After the outbreak of war, Amy joined the Air Transport Auxiliary in the summer of 1940. She took the Royal Air Force Central Flying School course at Upavon, and "converted" to twin-engined machines, which she ferried until the end of the year, together with Spitfires and Hurricanes which were so vital to the successful outcome of the Battle of Britain.

The first days of 1941 were bitterly cold. Most of the country lay under snow. England was weary after months of the Blitz and lay under the threat of the German invasion. On January 4 Amy was sent to Prestwick to collect a twin-engined Airspeed Oxford, which she had to deliver at Kidlington, just north of the city of Oxford. She was forced down by bad weather at Blackpool, where she stayed the night with her sister and brother-in-law whom she told that there was something wrong with the compass – adding that she could, however, "smell her way anywhere in England."
This I fully believe.

Flying conditions had improved only slightly the following morning, Sunday, January 5. Visibility was about four miles, but the cloud was down to 2,000 feet. At Squires Gate aerodrome they tried to persuade Amy not to take off, pointing to the thickening clouds. But at 10.45am she said: "I am going over the top."

This was her last recorded statement. By 11 o'clock she had climbed out of sight into the clouds.

But from that moment the hours ticked away remorselessly with no news of her arrival. Darkness drew in early on that cold winter's afternoon. Meanwhile, poor brave Amy had met her mysterious destiny in the Thames Estuary, near the sandbanks of Herne Bay. At 3.30pm Lieutenant-Commander WE Fletcher, RN, was on patrol in the trawler *HMS Hazlemere* when he saw a parachutist drop from the cloud

wrack into the sea.

Almost immediately afterwards an aeroplane with dead engines spun down crashing into the icy waters nearby and breaking up. Fletcher altered course and put on full speed. There was a heavy swell and strong currents raced round the sandbanks. The trawler grounded. While the engine was put to slow astern, the port lifeboat was manned and lowered. As it went round the bows, the parachutist, believed to be a woman, was swept past, some 20 yards away.

The courageous Fletcher ran from the bridge and jumped over the side. From which moment reports from the tragic, twilight scene became confusing. One report was that a man as well as a woman had fallen from the plane and that Fletcher reached and supported one of them for a time. But the lifeboat well-nigh unmanageable in the heavy seas, did not reach Fletcher who was next seen swimming alone. Another boat picked him up but he died of exposure.

The country was swiftly flooded with rumours that Amy had carried a passenger in the aircraft. This was indignantly repudiated by the late Miss Pauline Gower, chief of the women pilots in the ATA, herself a most experienced pilot and a dear friend of Amy. Miss Gower declared categorically that there was no passenger taken on at Blackpool, nor had the aircraft landed at any other aerodrome.

Miss Gower added that it was impossible to land the Oxford and take off at any place other than an aerodrome. This I fully endorse. Her conclusion was that Amy had been looking vainly for a break in heavy cloud and that by bad luck she ran out of petrol over the sea.

Yet how can one credit that the experienced Amy could have wandered to this spot, a full 100 miles off course, in such a relatively short journey? In any case I agree with Miss Gower when she said that the falling door of the Oxford, which had to be jettisoned by a pilot before baling out may have given rise to the idea that there was a second occupant of the machine.

Village greens

Edward Hart reflected on the pleasure of pulling on a pair of white flannels again when village cricket resumed after the last war.

26th April 1791: "Leeds Cricket Club. The members of this club will hold their first meeting of the season."

Mike Cowling

Chapeltown Moor was originally where cricketers pitched their stumps. Here the first recorded cricket match in Yorkshire was played in August 1765 between Leeds and Sheffield.

On Tuesday, 26th April, 1791, the *Leeds Intelligencer* carried this notice (it looks as if the season started later and dinner was what we would now call lunch):

"Leeds Cricket Club. The members of this club will hold their first meeting, for the present year, on Thursday the fifth day of May next, at the Bowling Green house in Chapeltown. The wickets will be pitched at eleven o'clock. Dinner upon the table at three o'clock."

"**S**een and heard through the trees, the village cricket match is surely the loveliest scene in England and the most disarming sound". Sir James Barrie's views have been repeated by generations of players, and never more so than in the years following World War II. After years of being deprived of their favourite game, and the relaxation of petrol rationing, village cricket flourished. It was an ideal way of visiting. Friendships, old rivalries and plentiful teas returned under a summer sun.

I played for Spout House in Bilsdale, officially called the Sun Inn. Its walls are still covered with photographs of famous cricketers connected with the locality including, inevitably, WG Grace. At Archbishop Holgate's Grammar School in York, games master Max Ebbage and others drilled into us that, "the game's the thing, and if you lose, do so gracefully". At Spout House I soon learnt that it was better not to lose at all, especially if the opposition came from 'the low side'. This was a generic term for teams from the fertile plain beyond Helmsley, some of whose players had a slightly condescending attitude towards we dalesmen.

Harome was top of the league, and we played there immediately after the coronation celebrations for Queen Elizabeth II. We lost the toss and were surprisingly asked to bat first. Then came a tea of limitless proportions, comprising rounds of roast beef, apple and pork pies, sponge cakes oozing cream, trifles and other leftovers from the festivities. "Eat your

fill," smiled the mothers, sisters, wives and sweethearts who provided this magnificent repast, after which we staggered out, unable to bowl well or run in the field. Dark inferences were made – Glencoe in minor key – but what were two lost points set against that wonderful feast?

By contrast, the catering for the team at Knayton, near Thirsk, was presumably done by 'incomers'. I still recall the mixture of disbelief and distaste on my team mates' faces as they sampled the wafer-thin cucumber sandwiches and small puff pastries. To dalesmen reared on standing pork pies and thick beef sandwiches, this was no joke.

Normanby in Ryedale had a flat ground with a huge stone trough so far inside the square leg or extra cover boundary that it counted two, to the chagrin of mighty hitters smiting its unyielding exterior.

Pockley on the edge of the North York Moors was a late May fixture, often coinciding with Buchan's Cold Spell. The wind descended from the Arctic, and John Willie Noble from the warmth of his car said, "I'd give anything not to have to play tonight". He did play, of course, with the swing and swerve that could have brought him a Yorkshire place had his sponsor not died suddenly. John Willie delighted in the late cut and watching the ball curve to the boundary.

It was always sunny when we played at Helmsley, its castle brooding in the background. The pitch had been newly mown, and the scent of half-dried grass wafted into the

and whites

pavilion. Churchill said: "A smell is the best mnemonic", and new-mown hay anywhere takes me back to that well-tended Ryedale ground, white figures against green, and the drives through May blossom and bluebells for those early games. The first question was: "How are Yorkshire doing?" followed by, "How many did Hutton make?" The memories of my team mates amazed me. Ainslies, Nobles and Browns were long-established dales families who knew every strength and weakness of opponents for miles around, and warned me accordingly.

"Don't let the ball hit your pads no matter where you stand," they said on approaching Kirkbymoorside. "Their lame umpire raises his walking stick to give you out, which he does for every rap on the pads!"

We never passed the old pitch above Rievaulx without them recalling the wicket keeper there. He squatted right over the stumps and tickled a

bail off with his pads given half a chance. Another team from the low side brought their own umpire, who awarded six lbws against Spout House in a semi-final. A flush of resentment crossed my informant's face; only later did I realise it was 25 years ago.

Passions could run high. At one final, a snick into the keeper's gloves and given not out was heard right round the ground – and continued to be down the years. Some 'couldn't bide being beaten', and would be up to any dodge to get a wicket. As Emmott Robinson said: "We don't play this game for fun."

We couldn't bowl as fast as him but we admired the way Emmott had gone about things. In 1936 he bowled a corker to take the wicket of the Surrey captain, the Right Honourable Smythe-Foulkes, who said, "Well bowled, Robinson, a wonderful delivery." Emmott replied, "Aye', 'it were bloody wasted on thee.'

In our matches, umpires played their part. "He was more out t'first time!" one said raising his finger after reject-ing my appeal for the first ball of the match, when he was not fully focused. Yet the overriding memories are of fun and companionship in Yorkshire at its best. At Gillamoor, Kirkbymoorside, a vista of mile after purple mile of heather unfolds. The team wore green caps like the Australians, and here a retired farm worker told me of how they would walk twelve miles to a match, sleeping under a hedge as they returned.

A forestry worker playing for Lockton, Pickering, lived two miles up a rough track. The opposing bowler was the local postman. "Give me a long hop to leg, or I'll send myself a postcard every day for a fortnight!" sallied the batsman.

Summer evenings on village cricket grounds are near heaven for most of its players.

Headingley: Yorkshire's field of dreams

Jim Moran

Headingley became the main first class cricket venue on 27th May 1890 when Leeds played Scarborough in front of 5,000 people.
The first county cricket game, Yorkshire versus Derbyshire, was in June 1891 and that August was the first county championship fixture, Yorkshire versus Kent. In this arena some of the greatest cricket of all time has been played: Sir Donald Bradman scored triple Headingley centuries in 1930 and 1934. It was here on a chilly afternoon in 1981 that England's heroes – having been forced to follow-on – snatched victory from the jaws of defeat against Australia. Ian Botham scored 50 and 149 runs and took six wickets for 95, while Bob Willis took eight wickets for 43 to defeat the old enemy by 18 runs.

APRIL 1990

The heroes' hero

Sir Len Hutton, newly installed as Yorkshire's president, was asked by our cricket correspondent Robert Mills to cast his mind back and to look forwards.

One spring day at Headingley just before the start of the 1939 season, a Yorkshire committee man wandered up to coach George Hirst and suggested that the batsman practising in the nets looked good enough to have a trial with the second team.

Since that batsman was Len Hutton, who had made the small matter of 364 for England against the Australians at The Oval the previous summer, it can at least be said that the gentleman's judgment of a player was rather more reliable than his knowledge of the Yorkshire staff of the time.

It must also be comforting to the present occupants of office in the committee room that one of their pre-war predecessors was capable of such a monumental gaffe. No change there.

Hutton was then preparing for a campaign in which he scored a dozen of his 129 centuries, piled up 2,883 runs – just five short of his best season in 1937 – and averaged 62.67 with a top score of 280 not out against Hampshire.

By the end of that season he was probably at the zenith of his powers but little suspected that his prodigious run-making achievements for county and country were about to be cut short by a more lethal contest against Adolf Hitler.

The 1939 season marked the end of the first glorious phase of his monolithic career and he admits that cricket for him was never quite the same after that, in part because his team-mate and close friend Hedley Verity, who nursed Hutton through each interval during his record-break-

ing 364, did not come back.

We can only wonder what might have transpired had Hutton ever come face to face with Herr Hitler. In fact, he spent much of the war years face to face with nurses and surgeons in hospital in Wakefield and there were times during the global conflict when he feared that there would be no second phase.

PLAYER'S CIGARETTES

L. HUTTON

As Ronnie Burnet, who became Yorkshire captain in 1958, said, it is hard to imagine what he might have achieved, how many more centuries he would have scored, but for the enforced interruption. "You see, that 364 was the turning-point of his career." said Burnet. "Until then if he and Herbert Sutcliffe had put on 100

you could reckon that Herbert would get 60 and Len 40. After that he dominated and it could be 70-30 in his favour. Of the players I knew he was simply the best. There has been nothing to match him since."

Sir Leonard, now 73 and Yorkshire's president, explained the circumstances surrounding the war-time accident which left him with a left arm almost two inches shorter than the right. "After serving at Aldershot and Catterick, I was sent from Lincoln to do a commando course at York and on the last day some matting slipped from under my feet as I landed on it.

"The fall threw me off the mat on to the floor. I suffered a dislocation and a fracture, a bad one, and after a short time in a military hospital in York I was transferred to Pinderfields, where I spent the next two years.

"I had three operations, any number of plaster casts, and I gradually got to know from the nurses that things were not looking good for me.

"It left me with a 50 per cent disability in the arm, which is of course the more important one for a right-handed batsman. As time dragged on I started to think I would never be fit to play good class cricket again and I owe everything to a Leeds surgeon called Reg Broomhead, who became a dear friend."

Sir Leonard is growing old as he batted, with quiet determination and grace. Although some cricketing memories are fading, he has not forgotten the many friends made around the world. The impression is of a man who needed to be loved as well as admired and who perhaps took criticism a shade harder than he cares to admit.

"I would never tell anyone not to read newspapers but you have got to sort out what bits to take notice of. I was sometimes criticised for slow scoring and being too dour but I don't think it got to me. I knew that the bloke having a go one week might be praising me the next. You have to take the rough with the smooth. Often I didn't score quickly but that was because I learned my cricket on bad wickets. I had to build up my defence, it was a question of self-preservation."

His talent, already obvious when he opened for Pudsey St Lawrence at the age of 16, was nurtured by George Hirst, "a lovely man". He remembers the day Hirst told him he would be making his debut for Yorkshire Seconds and the feeling that he had let him down when he made nought against Cheshire at Halifax.

"Then we played Lancashire Seconds at Park Avenue – another nought. Cyril Washbrook made 200-odd for Lancashire that day and I thought 'what will George think of me now?' I had a nervous problem as a schoolboy and it took me a long time to develop the confidence an opener needs. I know when I first came into the first team I was frightened to death of running Herbert out. I was in awe of him.

"That's why I envied Don Bradman. He had no problems in that respect. Herbert was the best opener I played with, Walter Hammond the best England batsman and Don was just the best. Like Fred Astaire on his feet, amazing."

Hutton after the war became to England what Bradman was to Australia: when he was out cheaply the country seemed to shake with the shock of it. The consensus seems to be that whereas Hutton could at times break free to make any kind of bowling look inadequate, Bradman could actually destroy the contest between bat and ball.

"That double hundred and a century I got against Lindwall and

The Sir Len Hutton Gates, installed at Headingley in 2001

Miller were the best innings I played – much better than that 364. I don't like to talk about that too much, it makes me tired just thinking of it."

He is sad about the disappearance of the amateur captain and warns youngsters of today against the temptation of seeking the responsibility of leadership. "They should be wary. My advice is not to plan or scheme for it because they might not know what they are letting themselves in for. That sort of power never really appealed to me. It can be a burden and I don't have any regrets that I never had the Yorkshire captaincy."

That, perhaps, is Sir Leonard being diplomatic, for the appointment of Billy Sutcliffe for the 1956 season must have hurt and – troubled by lumbago – he retired before its start.

He is determined not to be an old-timer who moans about the modern game, much though it has changed. "Life has changed. I had already played for England when I got my first car, bought and paid for, in 1939, and money seemed to be conspicuous by its absence.

"But I would have loved to play one-day cricket. I think it would have given me the chance to play shots I never tried in my time. And the fielding nowadays is superb."

He lives in Kingston-on-Thames but still hankers after Yorkshire and admits that he sometimes wonders whether he did the right thing in dropping anchor in London.

"Nothing would give me greater pleasure than to see Yorkshire on top again – I know it would be good for England. And oh for another Verity and Bowes. That would be lovely."

NOVEMBER 1989

Fred: the fire within

"And as for Yorkshire County Cricket Club, I'll never have anything to do with them again as long as I live. Ever!" – so said Fred Trueman to Roger Cross.

It is a perfect, almost primeval rhythm, quite startlingly simple in execution, uncomplicated, timeless, and still explosively unnerving at the moment of delivery.

Fred Trueman, as he always did, starts running in slowly, the momentum building effortlessly until, those dark eyes locked on yours, he leans slightly forward and then rocks back before letting one go with violent intent.

"That...from Woolley? That... from Woolley? That...has helped ruin Yorkshire Cricket. And as for Yorkshire County Cricket Club, I'll never have anything to do with them again as long as I live. Ever!"

Yorkshire and England's greatest living fast bowler slumps back in his chair, pulls deeply on his giant briar pipe instead of rubbing the ball on his flannels, and thinks carefully about his next delivery.

Frederick Seward Trueman, South Yorkshire miner's son transformed over the years into legendary cricketing hero/villain (delete where applicable), will soon be 60, but some things never change. He may have retreated to a far pavilion in a secluded corner of the dales, yet the fierce fires of competitive fervour upon which his whole fast-bowling career was built, while dampened down much of the

time now, have not expired.

It has been said that FS Trueman, followed closely by Australia's D Lillee and M Marshall of the West Indies, had, quite simply, the most naturally fluent bowling action of all time. A run-in and delivery of almost poetic perfection, a thing of great beauty. He was also endowed with a fierce independence of spirit, a predeliction for calling a spade a spade, and a refusal to step back from controversy. Indeed, it might almost have seemed to many that he had a quite robust appetite for the ever-present side dishes of internecine warfare and bilious in-fighting which has made Yorkshire cricket the best and saddest music hall act around in post war years.

His on-field deeds will remain enshrined for all time, the first man to take 300 Test wickets, the winner of endless games for his county and his country. His extravagant personality, with the help of more apocryphal stories than Errol Flynn or even Ian Botham together had ever to contend with, has guaranteed a high profile public perception which is not always flattering.

The fall out with the Geoffrey Boycott faction (that aforementioned "person" from Woolley) finally ended with Trueman being voted off the Yorkshire Committee almost five years ago, although his sometime idiosyncratic commentaries as part of the Radio Three Test Match Special team have guaranteed a continuing, if ephemeral, role in the great game. His, usually angry, column in a Sunday tabloid has now helped fan the embers of controversy for more than 30 years.

But there has been a price to pay for being, as Harold Wilson once put it, the "greatest and most famous living Yorkshireman".

He lives in almost splendid isolation in a large and rambling and finely furnished one-storey house down an unmade track not far from Gargrave north of Skipton. The vista across a lovely garden and secret valley has replaced three ruptured cricket stumps as his very favourite view.

There is a Rolls in the garage and he made a comfortable living as a sought-after dinner speaker, a raconteur who can earn £1,000 a time for largely cricketing anecdotes which last for two and a half hours, he says, before he has to repeat himself. His legendarily patient wife Veronica takes care of all the administration involved in the business of his being Fred

Trueman, Yorkshireman Emeritus.

But the Boycott affair has left its scars, and although Trueman is patently content with his lot in the later years of his eventful life, there is still a sense of sadness. There is, not surprisingly, no indulging in self pity, but it must be a matter of some considerable inner pain to have abandoned Yorkshire CCC forever, the club that opened up a wonderful sporting and social life for him.

"When I broke the World Test Wicket-taking record in New Zealand I had telegrams from all over the globe, and every cricket club but one – Yorkshire. I am told I am the greatest fast bowler the county has ever produced, but when you go to their headquarters at Headingley there is hardly any sign that I ever existed as a player," he says, somewhat wistfully.

He goes to church most Sundays, obviously worships Veronica, his second wife of 19 years around whom there was so much media interest when their affair first became public knowledge, but they don't go very far beyond a close knit group of old and loyal friends in a social sense.

"I used to go in a local pub or two for a couple of pints last thing at night, but not any more. Your reputation seems to go before you and people won't really leave you in peace. If I saw Elizabeth Taylor in Skipton, I wouldn't dream of speaking to her, but folks seem to think you are public property, and that they can say the most outrageous things to you. And they have tended to get very personal since all the troubles at the club. I am happy to stay at home or go to a pal's house for dinner occasionally. We lead a very quiet and simple life."

They have five grown up children between them, and now there are grandchildren. The Trueman's home is hardly a shrine to his cricketing greatness, but there is a magnificent oil painting by John Blakey and a bronze bust which looks uncannily like the late Elvis Presley.

Despite a tendency to repeat himself on the radio Test commentaries, Fred Trueman is wonderful value in his own home. Quick witted and vastly entertaining about cricket and life and not least about one particular resident of Woolley.

"The Yorkshire members chose to vote me out of the club and replace me with someone with a deaf aid from Keighley. When I tell you that the majority of the so-called Reform Group have all apologised to me since for being hoodwinked by Boycott, then you can understand why I am not impressed.

Justin Lloyd

"As far as I am concerned Yorkshire cricket started going downhill from the day Boycott was made captain"

"As far as I am concerned Yorkshire cricket started going downhill from the day Boycott was made captain, and is still suffering, and will continue to do so. But we live in a democracy, even though some amazing strokes have been pulled behind the scenes, so the members must live with the consequences.

"It saddens me, of course. Of course it does, but I feel at peace with myself. You might find this hard to believe, but I don't even know where Yorkshire finished in the championship this summer."

He is endlessly creative and inventive in his assessment of Boycott, but as this is a family newspaper it must be left to the readers' imagination. Of one thing he is in no doubt, however, and the old fast bowler's hackles are positively rigid as he recalls the darkest hours of his stand against Boycott.

"I and my family were inundated with dirty, filthy hate mail. Drawings of men and women's anatomy, as they vilified me for daring to criticise the man from Woolley. Most of the post marks were from places like Rotherham, Barnsley and Wakefield. Veronica has told me since that she tore up the really offensive ones."

Whatever your opinion of Fred Trueman's views about Yorkshire Cricket, there is an aura of humbleness these days about him that, as far as all known records show, has never produced signs of breaking through the ozone layer about Woolley.

Digby, a big and engaging daft Old English Sheepdog, rescued from an animal shelter in Lancaster, sloppily licks the face that glowered at a thousand trembling batsmen.

"I am getting older, and sometimes I do feel tired, but it only seems like yesterday that I was playing in the street as a kid in Scotch Springs, a brick terrace in Stainton, near Maltby. I'd like to say that I would do it all again, and not change a thing, but some days I can't be absolutely sure about that."

Boycott: when the best was still to come

One Sunday morning Richard Dodd went to meet Geoff Boycott and found a singular and solitary man who told him, "What I want most is respect".

The Yorkshire and England opening batsman, still in his pyjamas, dressing gown and cricket socks for our Sunday morning appointment at his home, was not wearing his spectacles and I almost failed to recognise him.

Geoffrey Boycott shook hands delicately, and gave a friendly smile. His close-cropped hair made him look like a smaller version of the all-American college boy.

Cricket writers have described him variously as cold, calculating and a 'sphynx in glasses'. The truth is that he is probably more emotional than most and suffers more from nerves than the actor making his first stage appearance.

He said firmly: "Any batsman who says he does not suffer from nerves is either a liar or a fool. The difference is that top-class players can control it."

Boycott is the only famous resident of Fitzwilliam, a mining community about a mile and a half from Nostell Priory and, between cricket, he lives with his parents in a terraced house. It is a homely place with cricket souvenirs in a corner cupboard and cricket photographs hanging proudly on the walls in the front room.

Children in the community – it cannot be called a town or a village, says Boycott – will eagerly volunteer to lead you to the red front door of their hero's house in Milton Terrace.

"As a professional sportsman," said Boycott, "what I want most from people is respect for my ability, even if they don't like me, although I would love them to like me if they can.

"I think that to some extent I'm not easy to get to know, but what is also true is that not many people take the trouble to get to know me.

"I practise like mad whether I'm playing well or not. I don't drink or smoke and I still like to get plenty of sleep. When I first came into the game, certain people thought I was a nut and said it was a gimmick and wouldn't last.

> *"Any batsman who says he does not suffer from nerves is either a liar or a fool. The difference is that top-class players can control it"*

"When I was a second team player, senior officials looked down their noses at me and made rather offending comments because I was not like the others. I would be unnatural if I didn't want people to like me. I would become bitter and twisted. But I care far more about having the public respect me as a player and a person of integrity."

Boycott reached the top in cricket by hard work and his own initiative. He played for Barnsley when he was 15 and went to work in the town for the Ministry of Pensions and National Insurance after leaving Hemsworth Grammar School.

About four times a week he would practise in the nets. He was always first to arrive with the aim of having two knocks. "I played with Barnsley until 1961, and then went to play for Leeds. I was 21 and felt I was not getting an opportunity to play in the Yorkshire Second XI because I was not being seen. There were more prominent people around at Leeds.

"Within seven weeks of going to Leeds, I got my chance. In the first month I scored 12 runs (0, 4, 0, 8), but then began to play very well and finished the season by topping the second team averages.

"The first team were playing poorly at the beginning of the 1962 season and I was picked to play at Bradford against Pakistan. I had been averaging about 200 at this time but I got out for 4 and 4 and thought that was it.

"I played four more first team games that season but mainly it was 12th-man. I was very pleased to do it and for the opportunity of seeing first class cricket. I made the best of it by sitting, watching, listening and picking everyone's brains. I didn't waste my time."

Boycott gained a regular place in the county side in 1963, partly because of injuries to other players, and easily topped the averages with 1,446 runs. He was second in the national averages and was voted "Young Cricketer of the Year" by cricket correspondents. But he was still uncapped.

"It surprised me and I found it strange that this had happened," said Boycott. "The same had happened that season to John Hampshire, who scored nearly 1,000 runs and Tony Nicholson, who took 65 wickets.

"It was difficult to understand, but we knew we had to prove our ability to get our caps. A few good innings were not enough. But they did come, a month after the season ended. We were given them in mid-October and were told they had been back-dated to October 1."

Boycott's success had been rapid and within five weeks of the following season he had been picked to play for England in the first Test against

he will treasure for the rest of his days.

"There's no occasion like it in the world," he said. "It's a wonderful moment when you see all the colour and people rushing for their seats ...and all the noise. I love any kind of cricket but Test matches are the thing. The tension is tremendous.

"When you are opening and they have a new ball and it's bouncing all around, it's fabulous. I wouldn't swap it for anything. You are waiting for the first ball...just you and him.

"I often think that footballers ought to experience that kind of feeling and then there would be none of this swearing back at the referee. If they had to accept a decision like us and walk back in a proper manner, full of emotion and charged up, there wouldn't be a lot of this unruly behaviour which affects the crowd."

One particular innings by Boycott, witnessed by 25,000 spectators at Lord's and millions of TV viewers, will long be remembered. It was in the final of the Gillette Cup against Surrey when he scored an aggressive 146 during Yorkshire's win.

Wisden recorded: "After an indifferent season and without a first-class century, he cast aside his troubles and played forcing shots all round the wicket. He struck three sixes and 15 fours. He completely mastered Surrey's attack."

Boycott said of that innings: "People had begun to categorise me as a selfish individual, as a man who was definitely a defensive player. That innings, for the first time, showed the people the other side of my character.

"I know it was a very great moment. If I could play another half a dozen like that for my county or country I would die a very happy man."

In 1967, Boycott scored 246 runs in the first Test against India and was dropped for the second Test because of slow play. Amid the ensuing storm, Boycott, typically, refused to make any comment.

He had this to say to me: "It wouldn't do for me to discuss it too much except to say I was very, very disappointed. I felt at the time that everyone was saying too much about it and in all honesty I don't think that sort of publicity does any good for the game of cricket.

"The same applied to the d'Oliviera and Brian Close affairs. I decided it was best for cricket if I said nothing. I suffered it. I paid for it and I was still going to prove to them that I was the best."

Geoff Boycott at the re-opening of Headingley's West Stand in 2001   James Hardisty

Australia. He opened the innings, scored 48 and broke a finger when a ball from McKenzie hit him.

"I didn't have time to think about coming up quickly," he said. "In that first Test I didn't really know it was me. I didn't have time to think it was anything difficult and it seemed to be all action and go. There wasn't time to stop."

The long, lonely walk from the pavilion to the crease to open a Test match is an experience unequalled in any other sport, says Boycott, and one

There's no one to help you.

"What is different from other team games is that always in the back of your mind you know that if you fail it's a long walk back on your own.

"Footballers are different. They all walk off together. In fact, they run off. A cricketer has to hold his head up and walk that 150 yards like a man.

"The worst is Johannesburg. There are more than 80 steps from the pavilion to the field and then 90 yards to the crease. I've failed there twice and the walk back is agonising.

The century's greatest

Geoff Boycott's 100th hundred was in the fourth Test at Headingley, against Australia. Our cricket correspondent Terry Brindle watched a unique achievement.

History was a mass of dancing spectators, a roar which refused to subside until almost ten minutes had been wrenched out of the fourth Test, and a man in a paper cap, as Geoff Boycott came home to 22,000 hearts at Headingley last night.

The clock which has ticked regimentally through many of his finest hours showed 5.47 when Boycott leaned into a delivery from Chappell and the ball scurried away on its mission to the long-on boundary. Hundreds of youngsters and many of their fathers too, enveloped a hero they had waited all day to acclaim.

The first man to reach a century of centuries in a Test was swallowed from view, trying desperately to shake a hundred hands at once, trying equally desperately not to be hoisted onto a dozen pairs of shoulders. And when the more delirious of his admirers left, Boycott faced a swell of congratulation which echoed and re-echoed round the ground until it seemed it would never end.

Boycott, the man who had never lost his composure during the most exacting 320 minutes of his chequered cricket life, had somehow lost his cap, emerging beneath a white paper replica of the real thing until the young culprit raced up blushing, to hand him back his lions.

There may have been quicker centuries and more strictly-classical innings at a ground steeped in memo-

Main Stand (Football Stand End)

The four that made the century

Where Boycott scored his runs

ries of men like Bradman, Worrell and Hammond but not many. And there has never been a more emotional moment, a more complete demonstration of acceptance for a man who has smarted in his darker hours under a sense of rejection.

Few of us are fortunate enough to recognise the happiest moment of our lives in the instant that it occurs. Boycott will never have a moment's doubt. Slices of destiny are not cheaply won and Boycott's path to an historic

century and an unbeaten 110 at the close was never easy. His personal challenge was clear and so were his responsibilities to an England side which still walks in dread of batting failure...Boycott's responsibilities were sharpened by the failure of Brearley, who was caught behind off the third delivery of the day from Thomson...Batsmen played and missed, battling through the difficult hours when determination and character were tested as severely as ability...

There was a sense of history in the air and Boycott drove towards it while the spectators willed him on, laughed away their own nervousness and waited for the century which would release them from tension as surely as the batsman himself. In an hour after tea Boycott pieced together 15 runs and crept to 94.

Chappell replaced Walker...and Boycott took a single. Another single off Pascoe, four deliveries from Chappell and then that straight, strident boundary which released a sigh of relief and a tumult of acclamation. His century took 320 minutes, included 14 fours and was made off 232 deliveries: statistics have never meant more or mattered less.

He and Roope carried their partnership to an unbeaten 51 at the close...The applause re-doubled, Boycott's every appearance on the balcony brought a roar of welcome from thousands who had stayed behind to cheer. Had he been prepared to stay all night, they would still be there...

Yorkshire's top batsmen and their hundred hundreds

Two other Yorkshire greats also made 100 centuries. JM Kilburn writes of Sutcliffe and Hutton.

Character expressed through cricket was never better illustrated than in the batsmanship of Herbert Sutcliffe, the first Yorkshireman to achieve a century of first-class centuries.

Sutcliffe's batting reflected the man in philosophy, social and economic standing and personal appearance. It was calm, self-assured and immaculately groomed.

A Sutcliffe century was impressive because Sutcliffe at the crease was always impressive. He drew the eye, exuded presence, even in moments of immobility, when he leaned on his bat between overs. He stood with an air of prosperity; he moved with an air of purpose.

Sutcliffe batting was Sutcliffe consciously in business. He walked briskly to the wicket, brown faced, brown-armed and with black hair gleaming. He took guard and inspected the field-setting as though he were opening the morning's mail at an executive desk. "Now," he indicated to waiting bowlers and spectators, "what have we on hand today?"

That Sutcliffe should make 149 centuries in a career covering the 20 years between World Wars was not in the least surprising. Heavy and consistent run-getting was his business and success was in his nature and his means of accomplishment. He was not a cricketer to squander talent and opportunity.

He stepped confidently through every doorway opened to him. He made five centuries in his first season as a Yorkshire player. He announced himself at international level with a century partnership in his first Test. His first visit to Australia was a personal triumph, crowned by centuries in each innings of one Test and a day-long unbroken partnership with Hobbs.

His entrances were never allowed to wither into anti-climax. Herbert Sutcliffe the batsman and Herbert Sutcliffe the cricket personality were not threatened with obscurity at any time. He was a leading player on his stage until the day he left it.

By statistical measurement Sutcliffe's achievements are awe-inspiring, but full assessment of his talent and significance needs consideration of how and when his greatest innings were played. He was the rock against which seas of spin washed in vain at the Oval in 1926 and at Melbourne in 1929 when pitch conditions promulgated a batting impossibility.

He was scourge of the hapless in times of urgency, as at Scarborough when he advanced his personal score from 100 to 194 in 40 minutes against Essex or at Bradford when his hundredth 100 was made in 115 minutes because the state of the game against Gloucestershire called for hurry.

Sutcliffe the imperturbable, Sutcliffe the tireless defender was also the Sutcliffe who hit more sixes for Yorkshire than any of his contemporaries.

Fittingly, Sutcliffe sponsored by acclaim the second Yorkshire batsman to score 100 hundreds. In 1934 Sutcliffe publicly prophesied coming greatness for the 17-year-old Leonard Hutton.

Master and apprentice played together and made centuries in partnership before war brought one career to an unwanted end and threatened the other with premature extinction.

Hutton lost nothing by comparison with any batsman in technical accomplishment or the urge to succeed, but he missed a playing privilege that Sutcliffe enjoyed. It was the period of joyous assurance that marks mastery of the medium in coincidence with full physical vigour. In three home seasons and an Australian tour, Sutcliffe feasted himself on nearly 10,000 runs between 1931 and 1933. Hutton was allowed only time to taste.

In England in 1938 and 1939 and on tour in South Africa, he displayed all the glories of his

supreme ability. He had the freedom given by membership of strong teams and the scope to explore the whole range of enormous ability.

Briefly Hutton knew cricket as a golden game and spectators saw batting close to the classical ideals. How many runs Hutton would have scored and with what relish had there been cricket from 1940 to 1944 must remain for conjecture. From 1945 he was a prisoner of circumstances.

For county and country he was called to stern discipline. Yorkshire and England passed through a period of weakness and Hutton was compelled to put aside the lance and raise the shield. For season after season he represented virtually the whole authority in Yorkshire's batting and in Test matches his was the wicket most earnestly sought. Wherever he played he was under persistent bombardment. He, above all others, was the batsman expected not to fail.

He made the centuries expected of him in England and across the world. He provided the bulk of Yorkshire totals. Sometimes in a county match of no championship significance he could play to please himself and his batting trailed clouds of glory, with full measure of marvellous stroke-play generously given.

These were not the historic hundreds, but they were probably the happiest in the making. For the longer part of his career Hutton had to bat with awareness of the end-product.

His runs were needed.

He supplied them through the vast resources of technique and temperament. He made them beautifully as a model and mentor. He made them as much through an introspective mind as by the light of natural gift. He could rarely bat at ease and his triumph is that he did so much so magnificently under such challenge.

Sutcliffe strides out to bat at Scarborough in 1938

FEBRUARY 1999

Robert Mills discussed the past with Brian Close, Yorkshire's outstanding sportsman of his generation.

I f you submitted Brian Close's life story to the editor of *Boys' Own* he would probably think it too far-fetched to put into print and even if he deleted the expletives Michael Aspel would be able to fill two of his red books for *This Is Your Life*.

Here is a man who played professional football as an inside-forward for Leeds United (alongside the emerging John Charles), Arsenal and Bradford City until his career was cut short by injury; he captained Yorkshire and England at cricket (what England would do for his track record of six wins and one draw from seven Test matches in charge) and became one of the county's greatest all-rounders; he played golf to a two handicap right-handed and then switched to

Close encountered

left and played even better; he once beat the world billiards and snooker champions (Leslie Driffield and Joe Davis) at their own games in one afternoon and he played table-tennis, tennis and squash to a standard well beyond any normal human being.

Close, who in the coming week celebrates his 68th birthday, is no ordinary man.

Indeed, the word extraordinary

might have been invented to describe him and he still talks with passion and with phenomenal recall of the days which shaped his life and times.

It is tempting to try to think of the outstanding Yorkshire sportsman of the 20th century and I make no apology for saying that my vote would go to Brian Close.

He still has a handful of company clients as an insurance adviser but has

recently branched out into a new line, promoting a product designed to make car engines last longer to dealerships and fleets throughout the country. His two vices are smoking and gambling, which on the face of it do not make for the ideal insurance man. "I love horse racing. There is nothing like watching magnificent animals take those fences – it is the glorification of movement. I know one or two of the lads in the game and they give me the odd pointer." Judging by the outcome of many of his bets, he does not know quite the right ones.

The only job I reckon would be beyond him would be as a member of the diplomatic service, mainly because he is perhaps a better talker than a listener and certainly because his speech has often been too blunt for his own good.

Any regrets? "No, not really. I have always played sport for the honour of it. If I had been a bit more selfish I might have been better off financially but I would not have been a better person.

"I was never ever selfish. If I had been I reckon I would never have been out of the England side as long as I was on my feet."

Honour and high principle have been the themes running through Close's career, precepts instilled in him as he grew up at Aireborough Grammar School, on the border of Yeadon and Rawdon, from the age of 11.

"If you were at a grammar school and had some physical and athletic ability and a bit of intelligence you had the ingredients to be a leader and there aren't enough of them now, particularly on the cricket field.

"It is a great thrill to get to the end of a game you have won and know that you outwitted your opponents. There is nothing like it and when you win at an individual sport like golf it is not the same.

"Unfortunately, the media has invented this word "pressure" as an excuse for the failure of their favourite players. It's rubbish. The trouble is these days that the players are running sport. They want more money for more time off."

Close can still remember the one not out he scored on his debut for Rawdon juniors against Guiseley and then taking 5-19 in the next game at Horsforth. He hit the cricket scene like a meteor, did the double of 100

wickets and 1,000 runs in his first season for Yorkshire and earned an England call at the age of 18 years 149 days. He is still our youngest Test debutant.

By then he was also playing professional football at Elland Road but in November 1949 had his thigh smashed in a collision with Newcastle's Ted Robledo in a reserve game and did not play again for 18 months.

"It was the end for me when Major Buckley took over as manager and I signed for Arsenal. We got to a Combination Cup final but it clashed with the first day of a Yorkshire game at Lord's and they would not let me leave in time.

"I did the double with off-breaks in '52 but that November I did my knee playing for Bradford City and missed the next cricket season.

"A couple of years later when Yorkshire's game against the Aussies was rained off a few of us went to Ogden for a game of golf but we had a car smash and that was another two months out."

Sometimes cars and Closey have not been good mixers, mainly because he had a habit of trying to light up a cigarette while driving down country lanes.

Close was officially made county captain in 1963. He was asked to lead England in the last Test against the West Indies in 1966 and did an outstanding job, which continued the following summer.

"The selectors wanted me to take the side to the West Indies but the MCC overruled them, which could not happen now," he said.

"It happened because I had an altercation with a spectator at Edgbaston which was blown out of all proportion by a Sunday paper and then I was accused of time-wasting in the last hour of the same game, which was untrue.

"But for that I reckon I would have been captain for 10 years and England would not have lost a game.

"One of the best moves I made was to bring back Ray Illingworth to Test cricket. The other captains like Colin Cowdrey and MJK Smith did not know how good a player he was and he was badly used.

"In fact Raymond was a better bowler under me than he was under himself."

In 1968 he said 'no' to a move to Leicestershire even though they offered to double his wages. They subsequently signed Illingworth.

Close's Yorkshire career, which included three consecutive titles from 1966 but involved him in several visits to the committee chamber to confront Messrs Sellers and secretary John Nash, ended ostensibly because of his outspoken opposition to the Sunday League.

"I could put up with the Gillette Cup but the Sunday game I knew would ruin our cricket. I said then if we were going to play like clowns we might as well dress up like them and that has come to pass.

"Even so, I could see it was here to stay and I wanted to win cricket matches, so when we lost in the last over against Lancashire I was furious when I came off the field because we should have won.

"This bloke came up to me a minute or two later when I was still emotional and I told him that Lancashire had been rather fortunate, though I did not use those words.

"It turned out that he was the Lancashire president, he told Sellers what I had said and I was carpeted in the car park.

"I think they used that incident against me and even Lancashire were upset that they did.

"Some time later I was summoned into the offices, I thought to discuss the following season, and Sellers said: "Well, you've had a good innings" and my heart sank.

"I resigned at first but later changed my mind and made them sack me, but I have had a good innings.

"It's been fun."

Vaughan to lead

When Michael Vaughan was chosen to captain England in Test matches, Robert Mills profiled a man who brought to the job attributes not easily found among today's top sportsmen – such as a refreshing modesty and helpfulness.

JULY 2003

Michael Vaughan is the classic example of a cricketer who has had greatness thrust upon him.

This is not to say that he has not worked for it, and only the timing of his accession to England's Test captaincy will have been a surprise to him. But he has never openly or outwardly sought it, or shown any obsessional ambition to hold this coveted position. It has just sort of happened.

He should make a good captain, but no one knows. There is not as yet much evidence to go on. He has already had some success as England's one-day captain, but that is a very different matter.

Because of the dizzying amount of international cricket these days – a matter the authorities will have to address sooner or later or risk overkill – we are in this bizarre situation. Yorkshire's vice-captain, Matthew Wood, now has more experience of leadership than his own captain, Anthony McGrath, who has become an England footsoldier. Both have more experience than Vaughan, who has captained Yorkshire in one game,

against Cambridge University at Headingley some years ago.

By the time Vaughan gets to Leeds for the fourth Test match of this series against the South Africans he will thus have been England's captain more times than he has been Yorkshire's. In the (good) old days a player could generally only rise to this exalted role after a grounding in the county game. There are exceptions, notably Len Hutton, who was captain of his country but not of the county.

Vaughan is a sharp, intelligent cricketer who will sift through the advice and sort it out for himself. He knows, from the early stages of his batting career with Yorkshire, that you can have too much advice, which becomes confusing rather than helpful.

Vaughan is a good communicator, polite and helpful, and is very popular with the media. This may seem to be a peripheral matter for an England captain, but in fact it is vital these days. How you come across through the media to the general public is important in the modern sporting world.

Nasser Hussain never shied away

from comment, but latterly showed a tetchiness in the face of criticism, especially of his determination to hold on to the No 3 batting berth in the one-day side. He became the stern face of English cricket; Vaughan will lighten things up. He is serious about his cricket, that's obvious, but he enjoys every minute of it and wants everyone else to do the same.

How tough he can be, I do not know. He will need to be, and people who have played with him say that he is not short of a hard streak. But I doubt whether there will be any shouting and yelling or chest-prodding in the dressing-room. Of his Yorkshire predecessors, he is much more like the mild-mannered Norman Yardley than Brian Close, who had a bit of a temper if he thought a player was not pulling his weight.

We have to be careful about the "Yorkshire" connection. He is a Yorkshire player (on and off, anyway) but not a Yorkshireman. He was born in Manchester but learned his cricket in the Sheffield area, always supported to the hilt by his parents, Dee and Graham, who remain ardent Yorkshire supporters even though

there are bigger fish to fry these days.

It was mainly because of Vaughan that Yorkshire changed their policy to permit the club to sign players who, though not born in the county boundaries, had learned their cricket in the Broad Acres. Many of you may know my views on central contracts, which are that it has become a sledgehammer to crack a nut and has had a dire effect on the county game which is England's production line. But Vaughan is, to be fair and right about it, one of the shining successes of the system. He was plucked out of county cricket after a season in which he had often failed and tended to blame the conditions (notably at Headingley, where the pitches were bowler-friendly).

The management deserve credit for not going by statistics alone. They recognised class, they treated Vaughan well and handled him sensibly, batting him in the middle order at first, then at No 3 and now as an opener, which has always been his natural position.

He has an uncomplicated view of the game and has pared his batting down to the bare essentials. He was once a fairly dour and defensive player, which seems hardly believable when you see him now. He recognised that the better players, or at least the ones he thought were better than him, like Marcus Trescothick, were so because they were more aggressive. He taught himself to come out of his shell and hit the ball.

He learned much about his technique and his stance from Martyn Moxon, with whom he batted often, and took advice from Darren Lehmann about running more positively between the wickets. This, he reckons, has alone increased his scoring by about 10 runs a session.

In this respect, Michael Atherton (Michael seems a popular christian name for England captains) says that his cricket betrays his Lancashire roots more than his Yorkshire ones. I might take exception to that, but I know what he means.

Now a world-class performer specialising in big hundreds, Vaughan has come a long way since making 14 for Yorkshire's Academy in 1991, an innings which, though hardly eye-catching, persuaded coach Doug Padgett to get him into the Second X1. The rest is glorious history.

111

JULY 1989

The Special Representative

For 40 years the legendary JM 'Jim' Kilburn wrote lyrical essays about cricket for the _Yorkshire Post_. Soon after retiring a dark shadow fell across his magical life when he suddenly went blind. On his 80th birthday he talked to Roger Cross.

Even now, almost exactly 55 years on, and with the determined suspension of disbelief he has practised regularly during periods of introspection and reminiscence, Jim Kilburn has moments when the events of 1934 defy his comprehension. He was 25, had a degree in economics from Sheffield University following his time at Barnsley Boys' Grammar School, where he says he spent most of his days playing cricket, insisting that he was so deficient at the sciences the master simply ignored him, and had latterly worked as a teacher at a family-owned prep school in Harrogate where he saw not the slightest prospect of advancement.

Happily, through playing some cricket with the parents, several of whom were influential in the Bradford League, he was befriended by one Reginald Bailey, later to be Sir Reginald, a wool merchant and also the Vice-Consul in Bradford for Finland and Sweden.

During the winter of 1933/34, and armed with letters of introduction from his new friend, the tall and distinguished-looking Englishman travelled throughout Finland, which in those days was a little like going to the moon. So much so that, emboldened by hearing that speculative travel-style pieces he had penned for the _Barnsley Chronicle_ had been used, he fired some off to the _Yorkshire Post_ and was, again, delighted when four or five of them were published.

In the spring of 1934 the then editor of the _Yorkshire Post_, Arthur Mann, to whom he had written a letter of introduction with no great expectation, not only replied but invited him to call and see him.

"I was tentatively probing about opportunities in journalism, while not knowing the first thing about the required skills or any of the day-to-day problems. Arthur Mann was friendly enough but our conversation did not appear to be going anywhere until I happened to mention I was a bit of a cricketer. So, it seems, was he."

In those days there was no sports department as such, or cricket correspondent, but Mann staggered young Kilburn by casually suggesting he might go to Yorkshire's next match, which happened to be the Whitsuntide encounter against Lancashire at Sheffield. Details about style, length and content remained a mystery. "It was remarkable, really. We didn't even take the _Yorkshire Post_ at home so I simply had no idea of what was expected. Arthur Mann put me on three months' probation at £3 per week, although I didn't tell him I would have done it for nothing."

So he went to Bramall Lane and did the only thing he knew how, which in effect was to write an essay at the end of each day about events on the field. It went off by telegram (80 words per shilling) and appeared each morning under the legend "By A Special Representative." Arthur Mitchell made a century, Yorkshire won comfortably and Jim Kilburn wound up his report of the final day with the words "Duckworth miss-hit to mid-off and Turner doubtless said 'Thank you, George for a soft catch' and brought the proceedings to a close."

"I had absolutely no idea of whether I was getting it right or wrong and when the game was over I didn't know what to do. I didn't know the first thing about journalism. I hadn't been told to go on to Yorkshire's next game so I thought I had better return to Leeds and report to the news desk." Once there his burgeoning sang-froid received another rap on the pads.

"Unbeknown to me, my reports had been very well received by the readers and the red carpet was out. I was greeted like some sort of hero, albeit a bemused one. The newspaper had received telephone calls and letters asking about the 'Special Representative' and everyone seemed very excited". One of the letters was addressed to the "Cricket Correspondent" and contained an apology for not knowing his real name. It was postmarked Manchester and was from one Neville Cardus.

Even now, and despite his great successes over the subsequent years, it is difficult to imagine how Jim Kilburn must have felt on being told by the world's most famous and gifted writer on the beautiful game: "To my mind yours is the best cricket reporting today. Congratulations, and I hope we may meet." The rest, as they say, is history.

"The edict went forth from the editor that henceforth, I be attached to Yorkshire cricket. Although I was never told personally, apparently Arthur Mann also said that I was to be totally left alone and my copy not changed or cut." And so it was that that summer, as well as being left alone he had the visiting Australian tourists, the great Don Bradman and all, to report.

Jim Kilburn at Harrogate Cricket Club in 1989

Bruce Rollinson

He went to Lord's for the first time ("the royal palace of the kingdom of cricket"). His breakfast was disturbed the morning after the first day of the Headingley Test, for by now the *Yorkshire Post* was required reading at the Kilburn household.

"I settled down to, naturally, read my own stuff first but it was with rapidly increasing panic that I scoured the sports pages and couldn't find a line. I thought they had rumbled me at last, but then, almost by chance I noticed my piece on the main news page which was opposite the leader page in those days. It was the first time such a thing had happened, apparently, and they also gave me the 'By JM Kilburn' by-line for the first time."

As if all that was not enough, of course, it should also be remembered that Jim Kilburn's honeyed summer of '34 also coincided with one of Yorkshire cricket's truly great ages. The county won the Championship four times out of six and he daily wove his prose around the deeds of such god-like creatures as Sutcliffe, Leyland, Verity, Bowes, Mitchell, Barber and the rest. Soon was to

come Hutton, and later Close, Wardle, Trueman and company. A truly remarkable voyage for a cricketing idealist and stylist.

There were to be tours accompanying England to Australia after the Second World War, seemingly endless books, and a devoted readership. He wrote his prose with a fountain pen almost to the end of his *Yorkshire Post* career, his spare, upright and always immaculately attired frame almost symbolic of a vanishing age.

Jim Kilburn is still spare and upright and immaculate and most days strolls the short distance from his home in a quiet and leafy avenue to the nearby Harrogate cricket club ground. It was there 12 years ago, when he was asked to be the man of the match adjudicator in a Harrogate Festival game, that he faced a pervasive truth. He declined because he realised that his rapidly-blurring sight meant he was not sure which player was which. I went to see a specialist who said I shouldn't worry, that I wouldn't lose my sight. Six weeks later I was blind."

He made lasting and enduring friendships within cricket in particular, and to this day exchanges letters

every six weeks or so with Sir Don Bradman, who was also 80 earlier this year, and with whom he shares a love of classical music. He also regards him as simply the finest batsman who ever lived.

Mary, his dynamic and pragmatic wife goes with him most weekends to Harrogate cricket club to act as his eyes, talking him through each delivery.

"When I went blind she just got on with it and has made my life as comfortable and easy as possible, although I try and keep from under her feet. When I hear the ball hit the bat I love it when it is middled. I love to hear a good shot, or the stumps rattled. I am about as right as I can be in all the circumstances, but there are days when I have an ache in my heart, and look heavenwards and say 'Why me?'"

His legendary disdain for anything that didn't happen on the pitch may have irritated colleagues occasionally, but he blames it largely on his total lack of, "I think it's called a news sense," and a still firm conviction that sportsmen's private lives were nobody's business but their own.

12   A tyke takes charge

William Linton Andrews, the first Yorkshireman to edit the *Yorkshire Post*, had ink in his veins. He was still at school when he started making money from his pen, charging a fee to school fellows who did not have his facility with words, for writing their letters home to parents. He was at his public school on a scholarship but the family printing business in Hull was in such poor shape they could not even find the rail fare for him to come home in the holidays.

He was in his early teens when he left the classroom and started work as a junior on 7/6d a week on Hull's *Eastern Morning News,* having already taught himself shorthand. It was a news-beat where death and violence were a regular part of the daily round. A life-long teetotaller, whose lunchtime preference was for gingerbread and cocoa, Linton Andrews initially found the casual brutalities of daily life around Hull port hard to take. He learned and moved on.

He was a serious, even ponderous man – not the cavalier type. Yet his early career was marked by all sorts of scrapes. At 17 and by then working in Huddersfield, he picked up a story in a cafe over his gingerbread about a hunt up on the moors for the murderer of a gamekeeper. The weather was desperate but he set off to pursue the lead on foot and alone – without map or compass – across rainswept moorland between Marsden and Buckstones. After struggling through mud and flooded gullies he was surrounded by armed police trackers who suspected he might be the murderer of a second game-keeper whose body they had just discov-ered. Later, rushing to the scene of a rail crash, Linton Andrews went to the assistance of a passenger trapped under a wheel who died in his arms.

Recruited by the *Sheffield Telegraph*, he signed a contract agreeing, if he left, not to work for any other paper in a 20 mile radius of Sheffield Town Hall. When the paper tried to enforce the clause after he joined a Sheffield evening paper, he took them on with the help of the newly formed National Union of Journalists and won a celebrated court case.

Tired of journalistic drudgery and deter-mined to be a writer, he threw up his job and took the train to Paris intending to complete a novel. Finding he lacked the imaginative spark, he haunted Fleet Street where there was no luck either. At low moments and desolate at his inabilty to land any job, even as a library assistant, he would take himself down to the Thames Embankment.

The start of World War I found Linton Andrews back in journalism in Dundee and enjoying himself. He promptly gave it up to volunteer for the Black Watch and served almost all the war in the ranks on the Western Front. All his life he was diligent at getting newspaper copy out of almost every situation and this continued in the trenches. Pieces he wrote from the front line were used by the *Daily Mail*, who promised a job after the war.

When he arrived at the Mail in 1919 it was still under the minute-by-minute, line-by-line scrutiny of the man who had created a new sort of popular journalism, Alfred Harmsworth, Lord Northcliffe. Those who worked there inhabited a world not unlike *The Daily Beast* in Evelyn Waugh's *Scoop*, ruled by the alarming and capricious Lord Copper. Everyone had to call Northcliffe the Chief.

In 1921, the Chief visited the British Army on the Rhine and the paper announced they would be printing his articles about Germany. The first arrived late: Linton Andrews was the news executive under instructions to rush it through for the first edition. He gave it the once over and advised the night editor it should not be used. Nobody would believe it was written by a sane man. The article gave the impression of a hostile Germany full of pregnant women under orders to raise children for the next war. The thought of spiking the Chief's copy filled the Mail newsroom staff with dread. In the end, they followed Linton Andrews' advice. When Northcliffe returned to England his mental instability deepened. He died the following year.

In 1923, Linton Andrews then aged 37, a bright young spark on the nation's sparkiest newspaper, was approached by Arthur Mann, Editor-in-chief of the Yorkshire Conservative Newspaper Company. Mann wanted him as editor of the company's new acquisition, the *Leeds Mercury*. The *Mercury* was no longer the gloriously influential flagship of radical-

liberal opinion in West Yorkshire as it had been for so long under the Baines family when its soaraway sales had caused the *Leeds Intelligencer* such anguish. Its political clout had dwindled and it was now a small downmarket tabloid, although strong on local news and racing.

When war came, plans were secretly laid to merge the *Leeds Mercury* and the *Yorkshire Post*. Arthur Mann's long-standing opposition to appeasement had won many outside admirers but cost readers. He was to leave and Linton Andrews, who had broadly supported Mann's political line, would take the editor's chair. On the evening of Sunday 26th November 1939, the decision was announced, to the surprise of the staff. Even the *Mercury*'s chief sub-editor did not know until he turned up for work that the shift he was about to start would be his last. The victims of the merger got three to six month's pay in lieu of notice. Rupert Beckett contributed £5,000 out of his own pocket.

The war, as always, brought good business. There were days when the *Yorkshire Post* sold 120,000 copies. But six long and frustrating years of censorship and shortages wore everyone down.

Making a paper (clockwise from top): Setting the reporters copy in type; making up the pages; rolling off the press; checking the paper

When the war ended and the *Yorkshire Post* edition announcing it was put to bed, there were no handshakes in the newsroom. Not even a bottle of beer was opened to toast the victory. Linton Andrews suggested to Rupert Beckett he might take a month's holiday. The chairman demurred: he thought now was the time that newspaper editors needed to be especially on their toes to meet the peacetime challenge.

The place appeared exhausted when Derrick Boothroyd arrived as a new reporter. Boothroyd wrote later that the *Yorkshire Post* appeared to him like a gentlemen's club and the reporters room like a reading room in Pall Mall, occupied by venerable gentlemen with white hair. In this desultory workplace, no-one turned up before 10.15 in the morning and at 11am they all went out for coffee. To shake things up, the *Yorkshire Evening Post* brought in an editor from Fleet Street, Barry Horniblow, who applied London's

hire and fire culture to Leeds; 40 people lost their jobs. Linton Andrews warned the board that Horniblow was not fit to be an editor. It came to a head with the three principals in the drama in a room adjoining the board's deliberations. Horniblow emerged white-faced and stormed off. He was to leave immediately and Linton Andrews continued doing things his way. He became one of the first chairmen of the new Press Council and was

knighted just before the *Yorkshire Post's* 200th anniversary. Even when he retired, aged 75, the ink in the veins of this still influential Edwardian ran strongly and he continued to write signed articles as Editor Emeritus. He died in 1972, aged 86, a widower without children, and bequeathed a large part of his £100,000 estate to his secretary Edith Weir who had been with him since her teens.

117

THE POST-WAR FREEZE-UP AND A DEVASTATING FLOOD

Dry Ghyll near Tan Hill Inn in March 1947

1947   **As Britain emerged from the shadow of war, Yorkshire stoicism was tested again as the weather closed in.**

Yorkshire, like the rest of the country, was longing to get back to something like normality.

But we were desperately short of the necessaries of life. Goods that weren't rationed were often unobtainable. Pits were working flat out because coal provided 90 per cent of all fuel. Like everything else the mines had been run down during the war and couldn't cope with demand. With coal shortages, people switched on electric fires or lit the ovens in their kitchens, leaving the doors open to keep warm. As winter came on, fuel shortages started to bite and the last thing we needed was a spell of severe weather. What we got was one of the worst winters of modern times. The first blizzards hit in the last week of January. We entered a freezing dark tunnel and it was to be mid-March before we saw any light at the end of it.

1953   **Several days of bad weather came to a head on the night of 31st January when the east coast was devastated by the worst peacetime disaster to hit the UK.**

More than 300 people died when freak weather drove a wall of water – the waves were 18ft high off the Lincolnshire coast – down the North Sea. It was unstoppable and the sea defences were breached in 1,200 places. Some 30,000 people who were in harm's way had to be evacuated. In the grim days that followed, householders returning to the 24,000 homes that had been flattened or flooded tried to face up to the overwhelming task of making them habitable again and re-building their lives. In today's money, the total damage caused by the sea's violent incursion was estimated at over £5bn. The east coast has always been at risk. In 1953 the cause was a storm surge – the high winds pushing the sea towards the coast – coupled with low air pressure which raised the sea level. It was reckoned to be a "once-in-250 year event". Afterwards Anthony Eden's Conservative government started one of the largest programmes of building and strengthening of sea defences.

Today, on some parts of the east coast, the threat of flooding is being managed by letting the sea back in. The recreation of saltmarshes is claimed to be a more cost-effective and sustainable sea defence which also supports a rich variety of wildlife. Farmers who have to hand back their land to the sea don't always agree.

Reporting the east coast floods (far left) and the devastated sea front at Mablethorpe

LIFE AT THE YORKSHIRE POST: BARBARA TAYLOR BRADFORD

Barbara Taylor Bradford came to work in our old offices in Albion Street in Leeds when she was 15. At 18 she was Woman's Page editor of our sister paper the Yorkshire Evening Post. She is now one of the world's best-loved authors.

"I WAS born and brought up in Armley, Leeds. I loved reading as a child, and started writing stories when I was still quite small. My mother sent one of my stories, about a girl and a pony, to a children's magazine when I was ten years old. They printed it, and I was thrilled. A few years later, I decided that writing books was probably too speculative, and turned my ambition instead towards journalism, deciding that might eventually be the route to other kinds of writing. I learned shorthand and typing at school when I was older, and a friend with a friend at the *Yorkshire Evening Post* fixed me up with an interview for the typing pool.

When my parents found out they went berserk. They wanted me to go to Leeds University, not leave school at 15 to work as a typist. But I persuaded them, and agreed that if I didn't like it I would leave and go back to school then try for university. I started the job, and at first it was terrible, because I couldn't read my own shorthand back, and nor could anyone else. I wasted a lot of paper with my rubbings out, and had to take the wasted paper home secretly and burn it.

I did settle down after a while, and began to write up little stories I'd found on the quiet. I'd do sessions typing up stories phoned in by staff reporters, and would put the odd one of my own through under the name B Taylor. After a while the accounts department queried who this unknown freelance was, and the truth came out.

The editor, Barry Horniblow asked to see me, and seemed to find the whole thing quite intriguing. It took a while, but he gave me my chance, a while later, to work part-time in the features department as a writer, and after that I officially became a cub reporter. I was 16 and the other staff were extremely sweet to me, especially the lovely Keith Waterhouse.

I went on to write for the women's pages and became women's editor. While I was working on the *YEP* and learning my trade, the *Yorkshire Post* was seen as the posh paper, which everyone on the *YEP* was in awe of. It was the most important paper in Yorkshire, and was held in very high regard.

Years later, after I left for Fleet Street, moved to America and started writing novels, I 'stole' the *Yorkshire Post* and turned it into the newspaper that Emma Harte owns in *A Woman of Substance*. The location of her department store in Leeds is where Marshall and Snelgrove once stood. I'm sure people remember that store on Commercial Street, not far from the old *Yorkshire Post* and *Evening Post* office in the city centre.

I didn't have a great social life outside work. I did long hours, read a great deal and still lived at home in Armley with my parents. When I did meet up with friends, it was usually in one of the many coffee bars dotted around the city centre. Although I didn't have a huge social life, I was always well-dressed in clothes that a seamstress friend would copy from fashion magazines. At weekends I would often go to Ripon, where my mother was from.

I look back very fondly and cherish my years working in Leeds. They are the foundation of my successful career as a novelist. Although I inherited my drive and work ethic from my parents, Winston and Freda, it was in the newspaper office that I learned what makes a good story, how to shape it in the writing, about deadlines, and research. The training also gave me a great understanding of people.

When I visit Leeds now, the part of me that's very sentimental about the old days feels a little cheated by how much the city has changed. On the other hand, it's wonderful that it has had such a rebirth and is regarded as so stylish and exciting now. Whenever I am in Yorkshire I make a point of catching up with the local papers, and I still think the *Yorkshire Post* is the best newspaper in the north of England."

Barbara Taylor Bradford in Leeds in 1981

LIFE AT THE YORKSHIRE POST: SIR BERNARD INGHAM

Sir Bernard Ingham was Prime Minister Margaret Thatcher's chief press secretary from 1979 to 1990 and head of the Government Information Service. He started in newspapers in Yorkshire in 1948 straight from school at 16 and spent nine-and-a-half years on the Yorkshire Post.

"I was going to be a geography teacher. When I was in the lower sixth form, wrestling with calculus, I saw an advert for a junior reporter on the *Hebden Bridge Times*. I replied and got it. They paid thirty bob a week (£1.50). I haven't looked back since.

My parents were all in favour. There was no tradition in my family of going to university or training college. My father Garnet was a cotton weaver (and a town councillor) and they thought it was wonderful I wasn't going into the mill or a weaving shed.

It was an entirely different era. Newspapers were still pretty small because of newsprint restrictions. The paper was in an old 18th century baptist chapel. You walked through a graveyard to get into the building. They didn't spend too much money on it. There was a tide mark three feet up the wall from a flood we had.

There were only three of us. It meant I had the best training because I had the personal attention of the chief reporter. I went to night school for shorthand and typing and later for things like constitutional law.

It was a wonderful place to work because you had to do everything. Even designing the page and putting the slugs of type into the formes for printing. It was also a printing shop – they were only interested in making money out of printing – so if we didn't take care with the paper no-one would.

I really thought this was for me. I could have stayed on a weekly paper forever. You were thought pretty well of because of what you were doing for the community. There is not the same sense of community now – far more of the .people don't know each other. It was a serious paper, nothing frivolous, with a circulation of about 5,000. At the age of 20 I was effectively running it editorially.

I'd seen Tom Dickinson, the chief reporter in the *Yorkshire Post's* Halifax office, when we were covering the courts. He had apparently thought me a likely lad because in August 1952 he asked me to come and replace his son who had gone to edit *Sea Breezes*, a journal for master mariners. The pay was £7.50 a week. The *Yorkshire Post* office was on Horton Street. After the *Hebden Bridge Times* it was positively clean – lino, nice desks, decorated in the company's colours. Upstairs was a dancing school. I used to phone my copy over to head office in Leeds to the sounds of Victor Sylvester.

Between us we prided ourselves on covering the back page – our edition page – with stories that the local evening paper would follow. Tom Dickinson's first love was Halifax Town so I covered rugby league. Because I was probably the furthest west of the *Yorkshire Post's* district reporters I was sent to cover a lot of matches In Lancashire and Cumbria.

It was a very good news area. One weekend – in 1953 – we had an FA Cup tie against Cardiff City – which Halifax Town miraculously won – followed by hooliganism; a fire which wrecked the Palace Theatre; and really terrible weather with high winds. But we didn't get the kind of show we expected in the paper on Monday because the winds had help bring on the devastating east coast floods. Too much had happened in one weekend.

In the autumn of 1958 I started to be called over to do shifts at the *Yorkshire Post* in Leeds. They became more and more and it got rather wearing. I might not get the last bus back to Halifax. It wasn't fair to me or Tom Dickinson. I think I'd been in Halifax too long – seven years – and in August I went to Leeds permanently as a general reporter. By then I had a wife and child and we lived in a lovely flat provided by the *Yorkshire Post* in Shadwell in north Leeds.

The offices in Albion Street were a bit shabby. The reporters' room was

Mike Cowling

"I envied the debonair types in the office who appeared not to have a care in the world. Journalists were not self-confident then"

under a whitened glass roof, there was no ventilation and that year seemed an endless summer – it lasted from April to October.

People worked in reverential awe of Sir Linton Andrews. It was the later stages of his editorship. Reporters thought they worked for an institution headed by an institution. The editor was the captain of the bridge to be obeyed implicitly – although in my case he was quite benign.

He had his foibles. One day, I missed something about a cat stuck up a pole. The night editor came over and said in a reprimanding tone, "The editor likes cats." I giggled and with a colleague, made a face and said, "Oh, the editor like cats..." But it was what the editor said which mattered, whether sensible or not. You'd be told to do something "because the old man says so" – when he'd probably never heard of it. There was a lot of that.

You got damned silly instructions which didn't leave you a chance to make judgements on the ground. I was covering the Tailors and Garment Workers Union in Scarborough where someone announced they were wearing clothes worth £250 – a huge sum at the time. I didn't believe a word of it. The night news editor – who reflected the slavish approach in editorial – said they'd got this story through from elsewhere. It was on the tapes. I told him, "I don't care if it's in the Bible. This chap's a bloody show-off and I don't see why we should run around after him."

Linton Andrews was an indulgent editor in his last years. You couldn't argue the *Yorkshire Post* was the tightest-organised ship. I was on duty on a Sunday night once and they didn't have a feature page article for the next morning. They came over and said, "have you got a book we could possibly use?" and I was set to writing a review of something I'd read. Rising to the challenge of filling space.

It was a pretty proper newspaper to work for. There was too much deference around. But it did produce some good journalists and some good newspapers. And I mean *news* papers. I envied the debonair types in the office who appeared not to have a care in the world. Journalists were not self-confident then. That is not the case now when people have been liberated from the terror of losing their wage packet because they can always go and find something else.

After Linton Andrews, a new editor, Kenneth Young, brought more discipline to the production of the newspaper. He coarsened life, made it disturbing for people. In 1961 he made me industrial correspondent – a good job because the paper took the subject seriously. I had a very good year writing about regional development and economics and I also had a Monday column.

Kenneth Young was very good on literary matters but he was out of his depth producing a great newspaper. He'd got no idea how to manage people. One of our feature writers, Geoff Winter, refused to go shopping for his wife.

I was happy in my work but I couldn't ignore the atmosphere around me which was very unsatisfactory. I was the Deputy Father of the National Union of Journalists chapel and the general manager came down to the stone where I was working and asked me if I thought the NUJ would go on strike. Things came to a head over the sacking of two sub-editors. I said (to the chapel) going on strike wouldn't serve anyone's purposes.

In January 1962, I was offered a job in the *Guardian's* Leeds office and took it. Later I moved to their London office. It was a hell of a lot easier working in London. People fell over themselves to tell you things. In Yorkshire, it's much harder getting stuff out of people.

I'd no desire to leave the *Yorkshire Post*. I'd rather enjoyed myself. It's a regional voice that has to be reckoned with.

Anything worth its salt in Yorkshire must be its own man – awkward, challenging, difficult – even cantankerous."

Murder in mind

West Yorkshire has an unenviable reputation for breeding some of the country's most notorious killers. The Ripper began where the Black Panther left off, in 1975. Michael Sams followed within 20 years.

Peter Sutcliffe and 12 of those whose lives he took, as reported in the *Yorkshire Post* in 1981

Opposite page: Donald Neilson (left) and Michael Sams

Wilma McCann   Emily Jackson   Helen Rytka   Yvonne Pearson

Irene Richardson   Patricia Atkinson   Vera Millward   Josephine Whitaker

Jayne MacDonald   Jean Royle-Jordan   Barbara Leach   Jacqueline Hill

It was Britain's biggest ever manhunt. At last the Yorkshire Ripper was captured and on 22nd May 1981 he was jailed for a minimum of 30 years for the murder of 13 women and the attempted murder of seven others. Peter Sutcliffe's five-year reign of terror began in the summer of 1975 in Keighley and continued until November 1980. By then, fear gripped neighbourhoods across West Yorkshire.

Roger Cross, who led the reporting team which kept the *Yorkshire Post* ahead of the field, wrote: *"Two years before Sutcliffe had been arrested, a Yorkshire Post journalist was offered £10,000 to pass on the name and address to a national newspaper if he happened to get the information first.*

In the event, the Yorkshire Post did get the information several hours ahead of everyone else and spent many hours with Mrs Sutcliffe's parents before and after

Peter Sutcliffe made his first appearance in Dewsbury Magistrates' Court three days after his arrest. At one stage there were almost 100 reporters outside the house and offers of payments for Sonia Sutcliffe and/or her parents of several hundred thousand pounds were pushed through the letter box.

As the 17 weeks between Sutcliffe's arrest and his trial passed, the competition mounted with large sums of money exchang-

ing hands for the relatively few photographs of the mass murderer.

Once the Yorkshire Ripper had been identified, tabloid hysteria engulfed Bradford and Bingley where Peter Sutcliffe's relatives all lived. Chequebooks were produced and money handed out to almost anyone who seemed to have a link, however tenuous, with the killer. One tabloid had almost 20 journalists based in a hotel in Bradford with the instructions that money was no object."

A subsequent Press Council inquiry condemned newsmen who "ferociously and callously" harassed relatives of Sutcliffe and his victims, detailing alleged offers between £50,000 and £1m made to Mrs Sutcliffe for her story.

MAY 1981

The Ripper's day of reckoning

At the Old Bailey, Roger Cross captured the drama of the start of the Ripper trial.

Peter Sutcliffe being taken into Dewsbury Magistrates' Court, 5th January 1981

Peter Sutcliffe turned into the Yorkshire Ripper after hearing what he believed was the voice of God in Bingley Cemetery in the mid-1960s.

He was working there as a gravedigger when the voice, echoing and distant, seemed to come from the top of a stone cross.

The inscription on the gravestone, at the Catholic end of the cemetery, was in Polish, but Sutcliffe interpreted one word that sounded like "Jesus".

Sutcliffe, 34, claims that over the next 16 years he received hundreds of "messages", not all religious, including those that led him to kill 13 Northern women since 1975.

Sutcliffe's startling claims were revealed at the Old Bailey yesterday on the second day of the trial at which he has admitted killing the 13 women and attempting to murder seven others.

He has denied murdering his victims, but pleaded guilty to manslaughter on the grounds of diminished responsibility.

The six-man, six-women jury, who face the task of deciding whether Sutcliffe knew what he was doing at the time of the attacks, were offered an amazing insight into the mind of the Yorkshire Ripper.

That insight came first through the 17-hour statement he made to West Yorkshire Police after his arrest. It was a chilling, calmly-dictated account of five years of terror for the women of the North in which he described himself as "a beast".

And then, late in the day, they were handed the 35-page report on the Ripper by the Bradford consultant psychiatrist, Dr Hugo Milne.

Dr Milne had examined Sutcliffe at the request of the defence, explained Mr Harry Ognall, QC, for the Crown, but his report was being placed before the court early in the proceedings to provide the basis for debate about the Bradford lorry driver's mental state.

Dr Milne, who interviewed Sutcliffe 11 times between 14th January and 9th April this year and other psychiatrists from both sides who had seen him were agreed on their diagnosis.

Sutcliffe was suffering from paranoid schizophrenia. Dr Milne believed his schizophrenia pre-dated his first offence and had gradually developed to the extent where Sutcliffe was devoid of insight.

Dr Milne's report says: "He believes he has a mission to fulfil to kill prostitutes, and that it is at the direction of God with whom he is in constant communication." He believed the mental illness had substantially diminished Sutcliffe's responsibility for the attacks.

The Attorney General, Sir Michael Havers, who is leading the case for the prosecution, said the Crown had analysed the dates of Sutcliffe's interviews with Dr Milne.

He believed the jury might find it of interest to note that it was not until 5th March – two months after his arrest and the seventh interview with Dr Milne – that Sutcliffe spoke of his "mission" to kill prostitutes.

"The grave incident, the beginning of it all, not a word about that to Dr Milne until 12th March, the eighth interview," said Sir Michael.

"If it was a compelling reason for this man's murderous attacks of five years that he was acting under the

The Yorkshire Ripper's trail of horror, 1975-1981

1975: **July 5th.** Anna Rogulsky attacked in Keighley.

1975: **August 15th.** Olive Smelt attacked in Halifax.

1975: **October 30th.** Wilma McCann killed in Leeds.

1975: **November 23rd.** Joan Harrison found dead in Preston.

1976: **January 20th.** Emily Jackson killed in Leeds.

1976: **May 9th.** Marcella Claxton attacked in Leeds.

1977: **February 6th.** Irene Richardson found dead in Leeds. Tyre track found at scene of murder

1977: **April 23rd.** Patricia Atkinson killed in Bradford (the only victim killed indoors)

1977: **June 26th.** The first murder of a non prostitute when Jayne McDonald is killed in Leeds. George Oldfield, Assistant Chief Constable (Crime) of West Yorkshire police, is put in charge of the Ripper investigation.

1977: **July 10th.** Maureen Long attacked in Bradford.

1977: **October 1st.** Jean Jordan killed in Manchester. Killer leaves a £5 note on her body.

1977: **November 2nd.** Peter Sutcliffe interviewed by police for the first time – one of the 5,493 interviewed by police who they think could have received the £5 note as part of their wages.

1977: **November 8th.** Sutcliffe interviewed again about the £5 note.

1977: **December 14th.** Marilyn Moore attacked in Leeds.

1978: **January 21st.** Yvonne Pearson killed in Bradford.

1978: **January 31st.** Helen Rytka killed in Huddersfield. The only victim with whom Sutcliffe had sexual intercourse.

1978: **March 8th.** First Ripper letter sent to Assistant Chief Constable George Oldfield.

1978: **June 18th.** Second Ripper letter sent to *Daily Mirror* in Manchester and George Oldfield.

1978: **March 26th.** Yvonne Pearson's body discovered in Bradford.

1978: **May 16th.** Vera Millward killed in Manchester.

1978: **August 13th.** Sutcliffe interviewed by police for third time over his car being spotted in the red light districts of Leeds and Bradford.

1978: **November 23rd.** Police examine tyres of Sutcliffe's car to see if they match the tracks found at scene of Irene Richardson murder. Sutcliffe had replaced the tyres.

1979: **March 8th.** Police receive third Ripper letter.

1979: **April 4th.** Josephine Whitaker killed in Halifax.

1979: **April 16th.** Police go public about receiving Ripper letters and link them with the murderer.

1979: **June 18th.** Police receive Ripper tape.

1979: **June 26th.** Police play Ripper tape to Press for the first time. Publicity campaign begins.

1979: **July 29th.** Sutcliffe interviewed by police for the fifth time.

1979: **September 2nd.** Barbara Leach killed in Bradford

1979: **October 23rd.** Police interview Sutcliffe about his car being seen again in red light districts.

1980: **January.** George Oldfield taken off the case.

1980: **January 13th.** Sutcliffe again interviewed by police about £5 note.

1980: **January 30th.** Sutcliffe questioned about earlier statements.

1980: **February 2nd.** Sutcliffe questioned again about £5 note.

1980: **August 18th.** Marguerite Walls killed in Leeds.

1980: **September 24th.** Upadhya Bandara attacked in Leeds.

1980: **November 5th.** Teresa Sykes attacked in Huddersfield.

1980: **November 17th.** Jacqueline Hill found dead in Leeds.

1980: **November 28th.** Trevor Birdsall, a friend of Peter Sutcliffe, sends anonymous letter to police at Leeds Incident Room naming Sutcliffe as the Ripper. Birdsall interviewed by police in Bradford next day. His claim that Sutcliffe is the Ripper is set aside.

1981: **January 2nd.** Sutcliffe arrested in Sheffield and appears in Dewsbury magistrates court on 5th January.

1981: **May 22nd.** Sutcliffe sentenced at the Old Bailey to life imprisonment, with a recommendation by the judge that he serve at least 30 years.

The police photofit of the Ripper

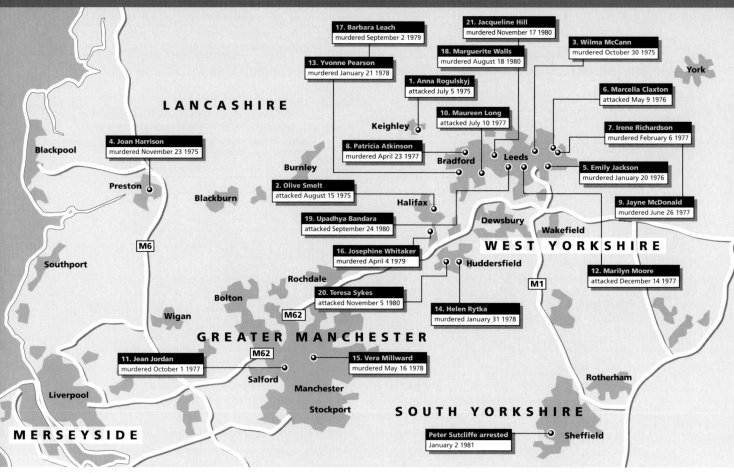

17. Barbara Leach
murdered September 2 1979

13. Yvonne Pearson
murdered January 21 1978

21. Jacqueline Hill
murdered November 17 1980

18. Marguerite Walls
murdered August 18 1980

3. Wilma McCann
murdered October 30 1975

1. Anna Rogulskyj
attacked July 5 1975

10. Maureen Long
attacked July 10 1977

6. Marcella Claxton
attacked May 9 1976

8. Patricia Atkinson
murdered April 23 1977

7. Irene Richardson
murdered February 6 1977

4. Joan Harrison
murdered November 23 1975

5. Emily Jackson
murdered January 20 1976

2. Olive Smelt
attacked August 15 1975

9. Jayne McDonald
murdered June 26 1977

19. Upadhya Bandara
attacked September 24 1980

16. Josephine Whitaker
murdered April 4 1979

12. Marilyn Moore
attacked December 14 1977

20. Teresa Sykes
attacked November 5 1980

14. Helen Rytka
murdered January 31 1978

11. Jean Jordan
murdered October 1 1977

15. Vera Millward
murdered May 16 1978

Peter Sutcliffe arrested
January 2 1981

LANCASHIRE • Blackpool • Preston • Blackburn • Burnley • Keighley • Bradford • Leeds • York • Halifax • Dewsbury • Wakefield • Huddersfield • WEST YORKSHIRE • Rochdale • Bolton • Wigan • GREATER MANCHESTER • Salford • Manchester • Stockport • SOUTH YORKSHIRE • Sheffield • Rotherham • Liverpool • MERSEYSIDE • Southport • M6 • M62 • M1

The Ripper's trail across the North of England, and (below) the appeal for information from the police

will and control of God, which started with a vision and which then became a mission, ask yourselves this – why did it take him so long to tell the doctors?"

Dr Milne also interviewed Sutcliffe's 31-year-old wife, Sonia. She had suffered from schizophrenia in the past. In 1972 she had had to give up her teacher training course in London because of the schizophrenic illness.

She had spent 22 days in a Bradford psychiatric hospital and, says Dr Milne's report, had suffered delusions and been excitable and disturbed for some time. She recovered and eventually was able to return to work.

Dr Milne's report says he found her temperamental and difficult when he had interviewed her earlier this year.

"She admitted that she teased and provoked her husband who said himself that the marriage had its ups and downs. He told me that she was over-excited, highly strung, unstable and obsessed by cleanliness.

If he wanted to read a newspaper she would shout at him, swipe him and, as a result, he would hold

her but never hit her."

Sutcliffe told Dr Milne that Sonia made him embarrassed in case the neighbours heard her shouting at him; would not allow him into the house with his shoes on; spent hours cleaning specks from the carpet and pulled

the TV plug out when he was waiting for his tea.

Dr Milne said the couple had "an intense relationship – on the one hand loving, but at the other extreme becoming very angry." Sutcliffe had said their sexual relations were "very satisfactory."

Sonia Sutcliffe, who is expected to be called as a witness, was not present in court yesterday. Sutcliffe, wearing a dove grey suit, slightly crumpled, and a blue open-necked shirt, gazed impassively at the judge, Mr Justice Boreham.

A dramatic moment came when Sir Michael told of how Sutcliffe first admitted being the Ripper. Police officers had spent hours interviewing him after his arrest with a prostitute in his car in Sheffield. She said he knew what they were leading up to.

An officer said: "Leading up to what?"

Sutcliffe: "The Yorkshire Ripper."

Police: "What about the Yorkshire Ripper?"

Sutcliffe: "Well...it is me. I am glad it is all over."

The hoax messages

An envelope containing a cassette arrived on the desk of George Oldfield, the policeman leading the hunt for the Ripper, on 18th June 1979. It was addressed in the same handwriting as two anonymous letters posted in Sunderland which had come the previous March. One of these letters was addressed to Oldfield, the other to the editor of the *Daily Mirror* in Manchester. Then almost a year later, in March 1979, Oldfield had received a third letter with the same handwriting from Sunderland. The police believed this contained information which only the killer could have known.
Two weeks after that letter arrived, Josephine Whitaker was murdered in Halifax.

The voice on the cassette said, "I'm Jack. I see you're still having no luck catching me...I reckon your boys are letting you down George. You can't be much good can ya?...I warned you in March that I woud strike again, sorry it wasn't Bradford...I'm not sure when I will strike again, but it will definitely be some time this year, maybe September or October, even sooner if I get the chance...I'm not sure where, maybe Manchester. Like it there. There's plenty of them knocking about. They never do learn do they George?...Well, it's been nice talking to you. Yours Jack the Ripper." The voice was followed by Andrew Gold's song *Thank You For Being a Friend*.

Superintendent Oldfield was convinced of the tape's authenticity. Police insistence that the Ripper was from the north east led to them discounting other suspects, including someone they had already picked up and interviewed four times, a bearded lorry driver from Bradford called Peter Sutcliffe.

George Oldfield listens to the tape recording at a June 1979 press conference

Macabre display at the Old Bailey

During the trial in Courtroom Number One at the Old Bailey, the implements Peter Sutcliffe had used in his years of terrorising women lay neatly documented on a long wooden table. It was a macabre and grisly collection. There were seven examples of his trademark weapon, the ball-pein hammer, as well as a claw hammer. There was a metal-framed hacksaw, several carving knives and eight screwdrivers of various descriptions which he had sometimes used to mutilate his victims – leaving sights which had turned the stomachs of even the most hardened detectives investigating the case. One was the rusting Phillips screwdriver Sutcliffe had sharpened to a point and which he had used to stab Josephine Whitaker through the eye. The collection also contained a wooden-handled cobbler's knife and a short piece of rope Sutcliffe employed to wrap round the throats of some of his victims to make them pass out.

The crowd gathered outside Dewsbury Magistrates' Court, at Sutcliffe's first appearance after his arrest

Got him at last

On 2nd January 1981 Sergeant Bob Ring and PC Robert Hydes started their evening shift by checking out the red light district of Melbourne Avenue in Sheffield. They spotted Olivia Reivers climbing into a Rover V8 and went to talk to the driver. He identified himself as Peter Williams and asked the officers if he could go and relieve himself in the dark by some bushes. The police agreed and then discovered the car number plates were false. They took prostitute and client to Hammerton Road police station and the man (now identified as Peter William Sutcliffe) went to the lavatory during the interview.

Sutcliffe was kept overnight in Sheffield and then transferred to Dewsbury police station. After the Ripper squad had been called in from Millgarth police station in Leeds, Sutcliffe was held for a second night.

Next day, Sergeant Ring heard that the man he'd picked up for having false plates was being interviewed by the Ripper squad and went back to the spot in Melbourne Avenue. In the bushes where Sutcliffe had gone to relieve himself he found a ball pein hammer and a knife. Later, in the cistern at the lavatory in Hammerton Road police station they found a second knife had been hidden. On the Sunday afternoon at Dewsbury, 4th January, Sutcliffe confessed he was the Ripper.

127

The Black Panther

Donald Neilson became known as The Black Panther because of the trademark black clothes and balaclava he wore on the prowl. Roger Cross examined a man with dark obsessions.

Donald Neilson had few of life's natural advantages. He was born at the maternity hospital in Morley to the west of Leeds on 1st August 1936 and home was a one up and one down terrace off the main street. His father was a lowly-paid woollen worker and the young Donald was to suffer, then and later, from his lack of physical stature. On top of all that, he was handicapped by a name that became a natural target for every local oaf and bully and even those of a more gentle disposition.

Donald Neilson was in fact born Donald Nappey, a name that was to generate the sort of teasing that only a well-rehearsed stoicism could cope with. When he was 23 his daughter was born and he took the surname Neilson to prevent her suffering the same agonies.

Neilson's mother had died from breast cancer when he was ten and by the time he left home his family had virtually split up. Exchanging one drab existence for another, he became a lodger with the mother of a schoolfriend, worked as an apprentice carpenter and didn't drink or smoke. His main pleasure seemed confined to going dancing in Bradford once a week.

He was a loner. None of his contemporaries remember him having a girlfriend other than a girl he met at a dance, Irene Tate, who became his wife in 1955. Their wedding was secret – not even her twin sister was invited. It was to set the tone of their life together.

His time as a national serviceman with the King's Own Yorkshire Light Infantry, where he became a lance corporal was to have a dramatic effect, particularly the training in physical fitness, survival and how to handle guns.

He was sent to Kenya where he was usually part of a six-man squad patrolling the rain forest. For the little man from Morley, sleeping under the stars on beds of leaves in bivouacs disguised by branches, it was a magical time.

Posted to Cyprus, he learned from the EOKA terrorists how to equip a secret hideaway. They tended to favour caves where they stored food, spare clothes, maps and guns. Some 20 years later an underground drainage shaft in Staffordshire was to resemble the hiding place of a man

"He'd insist his wife and daughter pose for photographs as he enacted increasingly complex war games. In every one he was the commanding officer and he was always the winner"

equally as ruthless as a terrorist.

The young boy who neighbours had once found shivering in shop door-ways when he played truant from school because he could not face the taunts, returned home from the army a man. The young couple lived with her mother then bought a terrace home in Grangefield Avenue, beside the busy Leeds Road leading out of

Bradford and virtually disappeared within its walls and within themselves.

Neilson tried labouring and part time taxi driving. Their daughter Kathryn was born in 1960, but the one thing neighbours – who were not allowed into the house – do remember was how the head of the household walked with a military spring in his step at all times, often seeming to move and work at the double. He took to wearing paratroopers' boots and battledress jackets and olive green trousers and started driving an ex-army jeep. People spoke of his enormous energy and the almost obsessive concentration he brought to tasks. A constant theme detected by those who came into contact with Neilson was his desire to be richer than he was and a dislike of those either better-off than him or in authority.

He would go running with a weighty pack on his back in his search for perfect fitness and began to take his wife and his daughter to some nearby woods in his battered army jeep. He'd insist they pose for photographs as he enacted increasingly complex war games. In every one he was the commanding officer and he was always the winner.

The photographs he kept in a special album. He moved it to the front attic bedroom of their home, a room which was always kept locked and where he also kept all the tools of his burgeoning trade as a criminal. It was to stay locked for several years, with him as the only visitor. By the time it was opened by police and its contents revealed, three men and a young heiress from Shropshire would be dead.

The victims of Donald Neilson

- **15th February 1974:**
  Donald Skepper, murdered at
  New Park post office, Harrogate
- **6th September 1974:**
  Derek Astin, murdered Higher
  Baxenden post office, Accrington
- **11th November 1974:**
  Sidney Grayland, murdered
  Langley post office,
  West Midlands
- **15th January 1975:**
  Gerald Smith, attempted murder
- **17th January 1975:**
  Lesley Whittle, abduction
  and murder

Neilson started out as a small time
burglar in 1965, using a carpenter's
brace and bit to break into some
400 properties. Within two years
he switched his target to sub-post
offices, robbing 19 in Yorkshire and
Lancashire by 1974. In January the
following year, hooded and armed,
he forced the 17-year-old student
Lesley Whittle from her bed in her
Midlands home – a kidnap he'd
been planning for two years – and
demanded a ransom of £50,000.
Neilson led her family on a three-
week trail of clues and then after a
series of police blunders, including
the failure to impose an effective
news blackout, he killed his victim.
Police found Lesley's body in a flood
drainage shaft system in Bathpool
Park in Staffordshire on the 7th
March 1975. He was not caught
until 11th December 1975.

Lesley Whittle, Neilson's last victim

YORKSHIRE POST

ESTAB. 1754 No. 39,731   LEEDS SATURDAY MARCH 8 1975   PRICE 6p Tel. LEEDS 32701

Lesley
Body found in park drain

CID chief tells of climb down 60 ft shaft

A MURDER HUNT was on at Kidsgrove,
Staffs., early today following the discovery
of the body of the 17-year-old kidnapped
heiress, Lesley Whittle.

She was found in a drain 60ft below ground in the

**Grim news: Lesley's body is found in a shaft in Staffordshire (below),
and (above) how the *Yorkshire Post* reported the story**

Michael Sams: wolf in sheep's clothing

Sams boasted he couldn't be caught. When he was, Robin Ackroyd and Chris Benfield reported on the train-spotter who went wrong.

Within 20 years of Donald Neilson being put away, Michael Sams murdered Julie Dart and kidnapped Birmingham estate agent Stephanie Slater. Julie, aged 18, was last seen by her family in Leeds on the evening of 9th July 1991. She was picked up on a street corner in Chapeltown about midnight by Michael Sams. Police received a letter a few days later demanding £140,000 for her life. On Friday 19th July, a farmer found Julie's naked body, wrapped in a sheet, in a field near Grantham in Lincolnshire.

Six months later, on 22nd January 1992, the 25 year-old estate agent Stephanie Slater was abducted at knife-point by Sams who was posing as a client as they made a house visit at Great Barr, Birmingham. Ransom notes and telephone calls for £175,000 led the police on a wild goose chase. Stephanie's ordeal lasted eight days before Sams released her. Like Donald Neilson, Sams was brought up in West Yorkshire – this time in Keighley – and like the jobbing carpenter Neilson he was good with his hands, running his own workshop. Both had small-time scrapes with the law, enjoyed military-style planning and regarded outwitting the police as a test of their own intellectual superiority. Sams claimed that they would never capture him.

On the surface, Michael Sams was a very ordinary man. Some neighbours did not even know he had an artificial leg. But as his clothes hid that handicap, so his mild manner hid the bitterness inside him.

He resented the police and the prison service and blamed them for the loss of his leg after a jail sentence for fraud. He resented the women who had rejected him and the vasectomy which meant he could have no more children after losing custody of the boys from his first marriage.

His third was already heading for divorce when he was arrested.

Meanwhile, he had turned to visiting prostitutes, despising both them and himself. He blamed the kidnap and murder of Julie Dart on a 'mate' who was in fact the other side of his own personality. Sams played the faithful charmer with his wives. But his alter ego wrote to the police threatening to kill another woman from a red light district in an eerie echo of the Ripper case.

His heroes were small-town pirates. Sams, the train-spotting mechanic, admired them for their swagger. But his own first venture into crime left him crippled and his dabbles in property speculation left him mired in debt.

He dreamed of revenge and financial freedom at one bold stroke, worthy of a wolf in the guise of a sheep. It is a measure of the power of obsession that Julie Dart's death simply became incorporated inside his master plan.

He was born on 11th August 1941, at the old St John's hospital in Fell Lane, Keighley, West Yorkshire. In self-pitying moments in later life, he would tell friends he had been adopted. It was true, in a sense and might have been the thing that saved Stephanie Slater's life.

The father named on his birth certificate was Ernest Sams, an army private who had married flamboyant beauty Iris Bowes in 1939 and set her up in a new two-bedroom semi in Oakbank Avenue, Exley Head.

But Ernest, known as Ted, was away when Iris became pregnant. The child was christened Michael

Benniman Sams and George Benniman was named as co-respondent when Ted Sams filed for divorce in 1950.

Another co-respondent was Sidney Walker, a smart and successful neighbour who gave piano lessons to Michael and his younger brother. Iris married him after the divorce and he took over as the boys' father.

Ted Sams re-married and rarely saw Michael again. He died shortly before his arrest. Sams senior had worked as a postman and had served a short sentence in jail for a crime involving the fraudulent use of date-stamps on postal bets.

The idea stuck with Michael Sams. One of his abandoned kidnap plans involved the use of a window envelope he had posted to himself, so it was date-stamped. He swapped the contents and put the new letter through the door of a Crewe estate agency. He was waiting in a phone box around the corner when the agency made the call he had apparently set up days in advance.

He also suggested to the police they had been fooled by the post-marks on letters in the Dart case. The killer might have dropped them in train lavatories and left it to finders to post them.

Another theme linking Sams's childhood and his crime was railways. He grew up during the last two decades of steam engines and would spend hours hanging around local stations, placing halfpennies on the rails to squash and aimlessly collecting numbers.

The obsession stuck.

He wore a train badge when he as dealing with Stephanie Slater – apparently unaware that it might be notable.

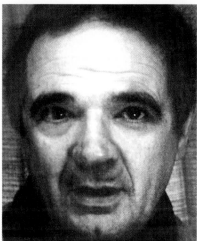

Julie Dart (top), Michael Sams and (below) Stephanie Slater, who narrowly escaped being killed

Some childhood friends were genuinely amazed to discover that quiet Michael Sams had been accused of kidnap and murder. But others recalled a destructive and bullying streak in the dark-featured little boy.

As a teenager, he got into trouble at school for letting off a bomb made from fireworks. But he was a keen member of the Scouts and collected ten O-levels and three A-levels at Eastwood Secondary Modern, Keighley Technical School and then Hull Nautical College before a spell in the merchant navy.

He married Susan Litter in 1964. She was 20 and a textile laboratory assistant. He was a handsome, 24 year old lift engineer with a sports car he had built himself. A former colleague says, "He was known as a bit of a tea leaf. He nicked everything from kettles to tiles."

Sams started his own business which went well. The couple bought a large detached house in Long Lee, Keighley. Sams prospered as a heating and glazing specialist. He knocked holes through the stairs in the cellars to set up a giant model railway for himself and their two boys, making and painting the engines and carriages himself in the evenings.

"He did everything for Susan," says a former neighbour. "She had the newest cars, the best of everything. They used to have big parties with outside caterers. He loved her more than anything. But he was easily dominated. Women could wrap him around their fingers."

His wives tell another story. All three have spoken of his outbursts of violence. Jealous and insecure, he told friends that Susan was having affairs.

They parted in 1976 and divorced in 1977. Susan went on to marry twice more and it was she and her sons who recognised Sams' voice from a police tape-recording made during the Slater case.

One reason for the divorce was Sams' slide towards disaster. Obsessed with the idea of easy money

through crime he became an accomplice to a car insurance fraud. He bought a resprayed MG which had been reported stolen. When caught, he informed on his accomplices. He was burgled, his train set was wrecked and the intruders started a fire. Sams had a troublesome right knee which he injured again in a fall while repairing the damage.

He complained about it all through his nine month sentence in Armley prison in Leeds. After he left, in 1978, doctors discovered a tumour had infected the bone and they amputated.

It was the end of Sams's social life as a runner with Bingley Harriers. Sams was 37 and infertile because of the vasectomy. Before prison, he had made contact through a lonely hearts column with a 30 year-old divorcee Jane Marks, formerly Jane Hammond who was a mature student at Leeds Polytechnic.

He married her at Silsden church with his trouser leg pinned up and a crutch under his arm, a week after his operation. He rarely drank but sometimes went missing while supposedly away on a job. When his wife challenged him he responded with a mix of lies and menace which frightened her. In 1981, she left him too.

Sams moved to Birmingham and started living with the woman who became his third wife, Teena Cooper, another divorcee. They moved to Peterborough where they married in 1988 after Teena's teenage son died suddenly.

They started a tool hire and repair shop in Peterborough then bought a house in nearby Sutton-on-Trent. Teena was mourning her son. Sams was reminded again of his own sterility. They tried to adopt, but Nottinghamshire Social Services said they were too old.

Teena lost interest in the business and moped at home. Sams was taken to court by Barclaycard. He began fraudulently claiming social security and housing benefit to meet his £700-a-month mortgage. He also began to disappear again, saying he was going train spotting.

When Stephanie Slater was trying to build a rapport with him during her time as his hostage, she told him she had been adopted as a child.

Sams told her, "You're special...someone chose you."

And he spared her life.

131

Coalfield strife

In the 20th century, Yorkshire was the major battleground for four trials of strength with the miners: 1926, 1972, 1974 and 1984.

1926 | The price of coal

In 1925 the mine-owners cut wages and Stanley Baldwin's Conservative government agreed to subsidise miners' pay for nine months while a Royal Commission investigated. The Commission took a hard line.

It rejected suggestions that the pits be nationalised and recommended the withdrawal of the government subsidy and pay reductions for miners. As if to reinforce the class divide, the Conservative MP Lady Astor, the first woman to take her seat in the House of Commons, jeered at the miners as 'earthworms'.

The mine-owners told the men bluntly: "accept new terms of employment with longer hours and pay cuts of between ten and 25 percent or be locked out from 1st May." On 1st May 1926, the TUC reacted by announcing a General Strike "in defence of miners' wages and hours" would start two days later.

Within a week the TUC – without telling the miners – met and agreed to call off the strike by 12th May. The miners held out on their own until hardship forced their hand. By the end of November that year most had reported back to work. Some were not reinstated and trudged from pit to pit for months, turned away everywhere.

Reg Dunn, then aged 25, was part of the six-strong mounted section of the West Riding Police (the only member who was not an ex-Hussar, Lancer, or Lifeguard) and took part in one of the biggest skirmishes known as the "battle of Hatfield". He recalled: "At Hatfield we were lined up in the yard of the Bluebell pub by the Chief Constable, Col. Jacynth de Coke. He liked it pronounced 'Cooke' and was horse mad. He weighed 15 stones and cut a fine figure when he rode with the Badsworth Hunt. He arrived behind the Blue Bell in his chauffeur-driven police car wearing plus fours. His instructions were simple: "Right chaps, get into the devils." Me and Jimmy Allen were to scatter the pickets with the horses and the foot men would pick them off and arrest them. I was paid what was regarded as a top wage then, £3 10s a week compared with £1 12s. a week for the miners, who were doing the dirtiest, most dangerous job in the world. But it was working-class man against working-class man.

At the height of the troubles we were expected to draw our batons and crack a few skulls if necessary, but I couldn't bring myself to do it. I settled for a few whacks across broad shoulders." There were more than 80 arrests at Hatfield that day, including one old miner well over 70 who had brought along his ferrets.

1972   The price of coal

On 9th January 1972 miners voted to strike again and a month later Conservative Prime Minister Ted Heath declared a state of emergency. Britain was blacked out for the first time since the Blitz. Power supplies were crippled and the three-day week was brought in to save electricity.

The strike followed demands at the 1971 National Union of Mineworkers' annual conference for a 43 per cent pay rise (an offer of seven to eight per cent was on the table).

The memories of 1926 played a part in creating an emotionally-charged atmosphere. We reported from Dodworth (pop 4,400), near Barnsley, which then had about 1,400 in the pits – 1,100 working underground. The seven public houses and one of the two clubs in Dodworth were feeling the pinch. The other club – the Gilroyd Social Club – had reduced the price of beer by one and a half pence to 10p a pint, and fish and chips shops dropped their prices by one penny. William Brown, then aged 32, who worked on the coal face at Wentworth Silkstone Colliery, said: "We expected hardship and we're getting it. We shan't go back until we get what we want."

He went down the pit straight from school when he was 16 and was earning just over £29.60 gross – taking home about £22· weekly. Kathleen, Mr Brown's wife, did not go out to work.

They had two children, aged 11 and 10. They were buying their house with a mortgage of £2,000. The family were living on £11.30 social security, and the money which they were saving for their next summer holiday had been spent since the strike began.

The strike's outcome marked a personal triumph for an upcoming union firebrand called Arthur Scargill, the spokesman for the Barnsley Strike Committee, and picket organiser for the Yorkshire miners. At first the miners had picketed coal-fired power stations, then changed the point of attack and employed "flying pickets" – first used to spread an unofficial strike in Yorkshire – to target all

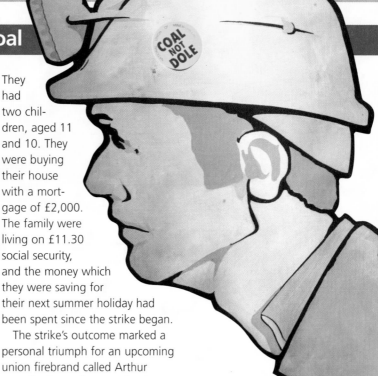

An illustration from the Rossington miners' banner

"We expected hardship and we're getting it. We shan't go back until we get what we want"

power stations, steelworks, ports and coal depots. Scargill personally coordinated the Battle of Saltley Gates at the Saltley Coke Depot in Birmingham – often considered to be the turning point in breaking the Government's will to resist.

Some 1.2 million workers were laid off. The miners did not go back until the end of the month after getting a pay package worth an annual increase of 21 per cent and costing £95m. It was a bad defeat for Ted Heath. It gave Arthur Scargill a national profile. In the following summer of 1973, he was elected president of the Yorkshire NUM.

1974   The price of coal

The situation in the coalfields had deteriorated again and miners voted in late 1973 to take action unless things improved. On 9th February a national strike was called which lasted four weeks. Picketing and campaigning were low-ley compared with 1972 but the country suffered again as another state of emergency brought in a three-day working week. Prime Minister Ted Heath called a General

Election and the issue "who governs Britain?" was prominent. The Conservatives were defeated and the new Labour government reached a deal with the miners shortly afterwards. The next ten years saw the coal industry in decline. In 1981, 66,000 members of the Yorkshire Area NUM voted to take strike action against any closures unless a pit's reserves were exhausted. This was a key factor in the 1984 dispute.

1984   The price of coal...

The National Coal Board wanted 20 pits closed, with 20,000 job losses. Militancy was in the air. Margaret Thatcher made sure coal was stockpiled at power stations and depicted miners as "the enemy within".

Clashes at Allerton Bywater Colliery near Castleford and (top) police in action against miners at Orgreave in South Yorkshire on 29th May 1984

News that Cortonwood colliery in West Yorkshire was to shut was the flashpoint. Pickets were mounted at Cortonwood on 5th March and within six days of the Yorkshire miners coming out, the strike had spread nationally. In April Arthur Scargill vetoed a national strike ballot of his members.

Revenge for the Tories' humiliation at the hands of the miners at Saltley Gates in 1972 came at the British Steel coking plant at Orgreave in South Yorkshire. On 18th June the NUM organised a mass picket with 5-6,000 men converging on Orgreave from all over the country. Police from ten counties deployed in 181 Police Support Units – at least 4,200 officers, although some accounts claim up to 8,000 – faced the miners. With between 42 and 50 mounted police on hand, the mass picket was coralled and fizzled out.

After twelve months of hardship the miners drifted back to work. An NUM delegate conference voted to call off the strike without a settlement on 3rd March 1985. Mrs Thatcher's stock went up. The cock of the walk, Arthur Scargill, was reduced to a feather duster.

...and the man who knew the cost to both sides

John Woodcock talked to John Chambers (left) on the twentieth anniversary of the strike.

"It was night and the police van came under a hail of bricks. We got out just in time because the mood among the strikers was vicious, an intent 'to get' a bobby. There were times when you wondered if you'd get out alive. I didn't condone the violence, but it was becoming like

wrong of me to criticise overall police tactics. We had to try and keep the peace, and had a tough job to do. I accepted that as much as anyone, but the whole situation saddened me. You couldn't come from Barnsley and not see it from both sides.

To understand, you would have had to live in such a community and appreciate its values. It was an extended family. I was 13 before I saw a house key. Try and imagine that nowadays." During his police training he was twice taken down a pit. "My reaction

their families, raising money and the like. My parents had no problem with me being a bobby, they were proud of the fact, but it wasn't spoken about when I visited.

"Families are still split by what happened. The strike was about men, but it was the women and children who suffered most. Now you look around and the pits are gone. Whatever you say about it as a way of life, it brought people close, and that close- ness has gone too."

"There were times when you wondered if you'd get out alive. I didn't condone the violence, but it was becoming like a war"

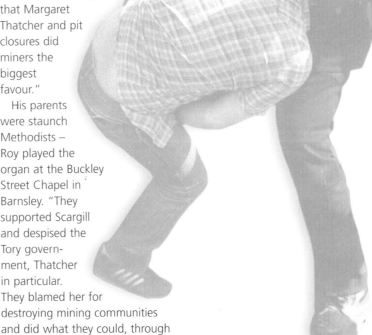

a war. What appalled me was that both sides were describing it in those terms. During briefings at the station for those being sent to the pits, senior officers would describe confronting the 'enemy'. The 'enemy'? That was my father and wider family they were refer- ring to.

It was the talk of people who didn't understand mining commu- nities and the social consequences of the strike, and it upset those of us who did. I spoke out. Not only were the miners divided. What was being said and done created animosity within the police too. Overall I loved my job but on those occasions I hated it."

John Chambers' father Roy had worked 46 years in the pit and when the strike began he was a pit deputy at Redbrook colliery on the outskirts of Barnsley. Five of John Chambers' mother's brothers had gone down the pit and died prematurely because of their working conditions. "It would be

was 'my God, dad comes into a place like this for eight hours every working day'. I don't know how he did it. It was a kind of hell. Looking back, I can't help thinking that Margaret Thatcher and pit closures did miners the biggest favour."

His parents were staunch Methodists – Roy played the organ at the Buckley Street Chapel in Barnsley. "They supported Scargill and despised the Tory govern- ment, Thatcher in particular. They blamed her for destroying mining communities and did what they could, through the chapel, to help strikers and

"Did you know the Minster's on fire?"

Shortly after two o'clock in the morning of 9th July, York Minster caught fire and 150 fire-fighters raced to tackle the blaze concentrated in the 13th century South Transept. John Scott was the first reporter on the scene.

Flames leapt hundreds of feet into the night sky before the roof of the south transept came crashing down. The southern 'arm' of the great cathedral was left a smoking ruin open to the sky. And I thought it was a hoax when there was a telephone call in the middle of the night and a strange voice said: "Did you know the Minster is on fire?"

As the Chief Reporter for the *Yorkshire Post* in York at that time it was my job to find out and when I arrived in Deangate a few minutes later it was clearly no hoax. The transept roof had just fallen and wisps of smoke were still rising. Although I was the first reporter on the scene I was not alone. The then Archbishop of York, Dr John Habgood, was also in the street with his lay chaplain, David Blunt. Mr Blunt had got dressed so quickly he was still wearing his pyjama top. Both of them were as shocked and amazed as I was.

The Archbishop had been anxious to see if he still had a cathedral before he left for a church meeting in Geneva and had rushed to Deangate by car. Fire chiefs were able to reassure him that the fire was out and the Minster had been saved. When he was invited inside to have a look for himself I followed along behind and it was an eerie never-to-be-forgotten journey.

The nave was awash with water from the firemen's hoses and smoke was clinging along the nave roof like a sinister bank of fog. When we reached the south transept on the floor was a

tangled pile of charred and blackened roof timbers still wet and gently steaming. And instead of a ceiling there was a clear blue summer sky.

The stone gable end of the transept was still standing and miraculously the Rose Window with its priceless stained glass was intact. The early morning sun was beginning to shine through the glass. Looking in awe at the damage was a member of the Minster staff repeatedly muttering to himself: "A moment of history." Which of course it was.

The Archbishop's comment was more down to earth: "We must be grateful it is not worse but it is certainly terrible." Details of what had happened at the height of the fire then began to emerge and had to be quickly gathered in. Those were the days when 'stories' were scribbled in notebooks and dictated down telephones to copy girls at head office miles away. There were no laptop computers and instant electronic communication. And what stories they were...Clergy living near the cathedral had rushed into the church to try and save its treasures as the huge building filled with smoke.

The Dean, Dr Ronald Jasper, led the rescue and saw the fire spreading along the transept roof in seconds. The candlesticks, crosses and altar cloths from the high altar were saved with police joining in the rush to scramble them to safety. Then the fire brigade ordered everyone out of the building.

It had started 'raining' inside only the

drops were not water but molten lead from the roof. Other stories too emerged – of the American couple staying at a nearby hotel who had slept fitfully through the night and then complained to the manager over breakfast about all the noise.

By way of explanation the manager was said to have opened the curtains and just pointed. Other more wide-awake guests, however, had a ringside seat and watched the fire fighting from their bedroom windows. But the question on everyone's lips was: how did the fire start?

Was it an accident? Was it arson? One theory was soon rapidly doing the rounds: had it been an act of God, but one with a specific purpose? Only three days before the fire, the controversial cleric, David Jenkins had been consecrated as Bishop of Durham in the Minster.

Professor Jenkins had challenged some of the fundamentals of church doctrine – he had denied the Virgin Birth and questioned the Resurrection – with the result that protestors made their presence felt outside the Minster before the consecration and twice interrupted the service itself. One of them was the Rev John Mowll, from Congleton who was escorted out of the Minster. After the fire he was quoted as saying: "I would not rule out the possibility of divine intervention. The God I believe in is a supernatural God and He does intervene in human affairs from time to time." He did add, however,

that he had been horrified at the damage.

So had the good Lord intervened Himself in the dispute and sent a thunderbolt to show his displeasure? The 'inquest' into the cause of the fire settled on it having been an act of God. This had apparently taken the form of a lightning strike but no evidence was ever forthcoming about the motive – whether it was just a randomly discharged blast from above or if it had had the benefit of a divine guidance system.

Looking back to the day after the fire I remember the sense of shock that it caused in York. The whole city was subdued, particularly when it was realised just how close the cathedral had come to being destroyed completely. But the reaction to the disaster from those in authority was immediate and determined. It was summed up by Dr Robert Runcie the

Archbishop of Canterbury when he paid a visit and stood among the ruins a few days later. "It will rise again," he said and, of course, it did.

Yorkshire country estates gave up prime oak trees to make the huge 'A' frame trusses to support the new roof and craftsmen every bit as skilled as the original builders put everything back together again. For journalists like myself the repairs became an ongoing saga and the work kept the cathedral and the burgeoning tourist city of York in the public eye for the next five years. Since then the fire of 1984 has indeed become just another moment in the long history of York Minster but visitors still look at the 'new' south transept in amazement and wonder.

The fire happened in the middle of a spell of hot cloudless weather and North Yorkshire Fire Brigade's report to the Home Office confirmed that lightning was the most likely cause. There

was criticism of the placement of smoke detectors and afterwards £350,000 was raised to install modern fire protection systems. It was agreed that the roof should be repaired using the traditional structure and materials of the medieval builders wherever possible with 62 new bosses carved with figures and scenes. Six were of modern events chosen by competition from designs submitted by children. The 16th century Rose window, fragmented into 40,000 pieces by the intense heat, had stayed in place thanks to the re-leading which had been done only 12 years before. It was restored with additional reinforcement.

The basic cost of restoration was in the region of £2.25m. Hundreds of people gave their support, which ranged from cash donations to oak trees. It took four years to complete repairs and the Minster was finally re-dedicated in a service attended by the Queen in November 1988.

JULY 2001

Despatch from the front

On the weekend of 7th-8th July 2001, Bradford was the scene of some of the worst violence in mainland Britain for 20 years. Will Stewart reported.

It all began so quietly. At 11am the only sign of the trouble to come was a lone skinhead sitting in a Bradford city centre bus shelter. With a 1970s throwback bomber jacket, complete with sewn-on Union flag badge, he looked more comical than threatening. At noon, as Anti-Nazi League demonstrators set up their trestle table in a hot and sticky Centenary Square, the atmosphere felt more like a fete. More protesters arrived but for now they were easily outnumbered by the massed ranks of the national media.

A fish and chip shop on the edge of Centenary Square was one of several that had decided to board up its windows, in case of any trouble. The mood was upbeat. White, black and Asian Bradfordians mingled, ready to show the National Front that their threatened protest was not welcome.

At 1.50pm a group of burly-looking young white men strode into the square, several sporting very short hair cuts. Immediately they were surrounded by Asian youths, cries going out of, "let's sort them out".

It took a few tense seconds before the intruders could explain they were Anti-Nazi campaigners. The National Front was expected in Bradford at 3pm. By 2.40pm police began to seal off the streets surrounding Centenary Square, penning in the crowd. The waiting began. But nothing happened. By 4pm police announced they were to reopen the roads. Cheers

went up, the National Front had "bottled it", the day was won and everyone could go home.

Meanwhile, just yards away, Kasel Altaf, a 21 year-old from the Toller Lane area, was walking through Ivegate, on a shopping trip. As he passed Addisons Bar, he was confronted by a group of between ten to 15 white men. "They called me Paki," he said. "Then they just grabbed me, and put me on the floor and started punching and kicking me."

The fuse was lit. It may have been a mobile phone call, or it could just have been the sight of police rushing to attend the incident. But somehow word got back to the crowd in the square, and at 4.20pm, with no police lines left to stop them, scores of Asian youths charged up Ivegate to confront the attackers.

The angry crowd poured out of the square, and up Sunbridge Road. Violence was breaking out all over the city centre. At about 5pm on Southgate, off Thornton Road, the first of two stabbings took place. An eyewitness said: "There were about 12 Asian youths and a white guy. I don't know how it started, but basically they corralled him in Southgate. He was punching them, trying to escape, but they tripped him, and in the melee he was stabbed. Suddenly there was a hole in his back, with blood coming out."

By 6pm, riot police had begun to

clear the city centre, forcing the crowds out towards Westgate. The police tactic appeared to be to drive them into Manningham, in the hope that the youths would not want to destroy the area's Asian businesses.

Within half an hour, White Abbey Road resembled a war zone. Makeshift barricades burned in the middle of a road strewn with rocks, that had been hurled at the advancing police. Rows of officers slowly pushed the troublemakers up the hill, their riot suits resembling a scene from a *Star Wars* film.

Further up the road, a white Cavalier car had been torched. Every so often 18 police horses, ridden by officers with batons drawn, charged up the street, to drive back rioters. Minutes later they would return and re-group, before starting again.

For the next three to four hours the rioting settled down to a steady destructive rhythm. The frontline would ebb and flow within a space of about 100 yards, but neither side was gaining much ground. The evening was hot and sultry – "perfect rioting weather" one bystander commented drily. You could almost feel the adrenaline in the air and the non-stop pace of events began to make it feel as if time had slowed to a crawl.

By 7.55pm, petrol bombs began to fall on police lines. As the flames flew through the air, cheers went up from the rioters, who, by now were on the higher ground of Whetley Hill.

Injured police officer in White Abbey Road, and (below) conflagration at Whetley Hill

Bruce Rollinson

There was a constant cacophony, with the police helicopter buzzing above, the clunk of rocks hitting riot shields, and shouts of "get back" from the officers carrying them.

Behind the police lines, crowds of mainly Asian local residents stood outside their homes and watched in disbelief. Ibrah Ahmed, a community worker from Heaton, said: "As Asians, we are not proud of this. It is appalling. But all the police have

Bruce Rollinson

got to do is back off, and it would calm down. The National Front will be proud of themselves. They have caused the trouble between the community and the police, this is an achievement for them."

White Abbey Road became a makeshift police base. At least 30 vans were parked up, police horses grazed on the verges and resting officers sprawled on the pavement, gulping down water before the next onslaught.

By 10.15pm the first building had been set alight. Several attempts to mediate with the estimated core of 40 or 50 youths causing the trouble had failed.

Half an hour later, the violence stepped up a gear. Missiles increased in intensity. For a solid ten minutes, an avalanche of bricks, planks and rocks fell, knocking officers down like ninepins. By 11pm there were reports of stolen cars being driven at police lines.

Then, just as quickly, boosted by reinforcements, the police regained

the upper hand. Alsatian dogs were used to clear away onlookers, and by 12.30am the frontline had been pushed all the way up Whetley Hill, to the crossroads with Carlisle Road, Toller Lane and Whetley Lane.

There police were met with the sight of The Upper Globe pub fully ablaze. To the left of it, just across the road, Manningham Ward Labour Club was beginning to smoke. Around 25 terrified customers told of being trapped inside, as rioters broke windows, before finding refuge in a cellar.

By 1am rioters were dispersing to other areas of Manningham. It was another four hours before the police could declare that the worst British riots in 20 years were finally over.

All night a single Anti-Nazi protester had been marching around behind police lines, his fist proudly clenched around a placard that declared "Smash the NF". But it was too late.

The National Front weren't there anymore. They were at home laughing themselves to sleep.

MAY 1985

City on fire

A bumper 11,000 crowd at Valley Parade came to cheer Bradford City, the new Third Division champions, against Lincoln on 11th May. Two of the fans were Bill Bridge, then *Yorkshire Post* Sports Editor, and his young son.

Two minutes before half-time the chap in front clambered over the bright yellow wooden fence into the gangway, aiming to beat the rush to the gents. One unbelievable minute later his two sons leapt in pursuit to save his life. That was the speed, the killing speed, at which Bradford City's day of celebration was transformed into an afternoon of death.

The all-wood old-fashioned stand was full, all tickets sold on Friday for the match which would bring to a triumphant conclusion Bradford City's great season. They were to be presented with the Third Division championship trophy. The manager Trevor Cherry received a gallon of whisky as manager of the month, Dave Evans took the player-of-the-year award. And the majorettes from Thornhill twirled on.

It was to be a fun day – that was why my son Richard had asked on Monday evening if he could go to Valley Parade to see City get the trophy. "Only if we can buy seats in the stand," I told him. "We're not going to stand up, it's too dangerous among all those tearaways."

So we had seats, Grandstand Block B, Row L, seats 43-44. The match started, was interrupted by a Lincoln player being taken off by stretcher, two lugubrious First Aid gentlemen being chastised by City's assistant Terry Yorath for their lack of urgency, and was meandering peacefully to its interval.

"Look, smoke over there," said someone. At the far end of the stand there it was, easing up to the roof,

billowing out. No problem. Eyes returned to the football. But not Richard's. "Dad, there's a fire down there," he murmured. The personal call moved the man, suddenly smoke stabbed into Richard's throat and movement was urgent.

Flames were within 25 yards. The heat exploded, the whole tinderbox was conceding to the wind-swept inferno without a struggle. The exits – one-man-wide passages connected by a narrow corridor – were suddenly choking with people anxious not to panic but fully conscious that something awful was happening.

Jim Moran

Flowers laid for the victims of the fire in Bradford City Square

The pitch was the lifeboat in the sea of smoke and fast-moving flames. Sideways we edged, then down over a fence, over another, an elderly woman being shepherded by her husband imploring, weeping, "Don't panic". No one did, at least in our little, rapidly shrinking, coughing avenue to safety.

The wall to the pitch was taken with relief of a strange new kind. Fear is strange. Until you can see, smell, breathe and almost touch the flames anything that went before was not fear.

The relief was also communal. Young men with strange-coloured hair joined with men who had watched City from their long-gone youth. We were glad to be out.

Policemen, straining, glaring, some even cursing, were everywhere, urging us to the far side of the pitch – then racing forward to pull clear a man, a boy or even a fellow constable as the tinderbox became a deathtrap.

Players were among the flock, sweat-stained, puzzled, lost and frightened. Still the smoke poured, the flames by now running the whole length of the ancient, timber-rigged shelter that had witnessed so many sad days for City but none nearly so horrific.

"Don't panic," was still on every lip. But across the pitch from the conflagration the only thought in certainly our two minds was to get out of the ground. Others obviously thought the same and, with athleticism developed to new dimensions, 10-foot fences were a minor obstacle.

The main stand at Valley Parade ablaze

With the willing advice and support of two burly sharp-thinking constables, a whole stretch of plyboard fencing was ripped from its frame. Another door was open.

Yet still the panic was bubbling on the inside. The urge to push, heave and get out was not lessened by the distance, by now 70 yards but still too hot for sanity, from those seats we had filled just three minutes ago.

Another elderly lady was calmly walking down the long, narrow lane of steps to Midland Road; she was helped by a gentle, insistent gathering of lads in denim jackets who looked more the types to steal her purse and run. But looks were nothing and nobody was running.

Out on to the blessed near-calm of the Midland Road, cars starting, stalling, bumping, sirens wailing and the realisation of space was marvellous. A can of fizzy orange juice bought in the stand to gurgle at half-time was opened.

Richard could still taste the smoke and he needed a mouthwash. But neither he nor I could hold the can still.

A walk to town, up a street of puzzled, silent people, the cloud of smoke blowing downwind into the shopping centre, the pandemonium and the tension dripping slowly away. Down Manningham Lane, into Rawson Place, people shopping, talking, smiling, arguing. Nothing had happened. A reassuring phone call to granddad – who had not heard yet of the disaster – an earlier meeting than planned with the rest of the family

and home via Haworth Road. The sky was clear, the taste of smoke had gone.

The worst fire disaster in British football probably started with the accidental dropping of a match, or a cigarette stubbed out in a polystyrene cup. The flames, fuelled by rubbish underneath the wooden stand, eventually claimed the lives of 56 supporters and about 265 were injured. There could have been more deaths but for the courage of police officers and 22 spectators who later received bravery awards. Sir Oliver Popplewell was appointed to chair an inquiry whose 1986 report resulted in new legislation governing safety at sports grounds across the country. A Bradford Disaster Appeal Fund raised £3.5m for the victims and their families.

141

The end of the terrace

The Leppings Lane End, Hillsborough: English football would never be the same again.

The match on 15th April was to be one of football's set-piece occasions on a sunny spring day: Nottingham Forest were playing Liverpool in the FA Cup semi-final on neutral territory at Sheffield Wednesday's ground, Hillsborough.

It was soon apparent something was terribly wrong in the packed crowd at the Leppings Lane End. As the awful events unfolded the truth became hard to contemplate: 96 Liverpool fans had been crushed to death. It was the worst disaster ever to strike the national game. Senior officers of the South Yorkshire force left a press conference refusing to answer questions on what went wrong. Their part in the tragedy was to be investigated by West Midlands police. The Prime Minister, after visiting survivors and touring the ground, announced a public inquiry.

When the West Midlands police inquiries were completed, the Director of Public Prosecutions decided there was insufficient evidence to bring about a prosecution. A verdict of accidental death

was passed on all who died.

In June 2000 at Leeds Crown Court, a private prosecution began against David Duckenfield who had been the chief superintendent in charge of policing on the day at Hillsborough and against his deputy superintendent Bernard Murray – the officer who had been in charge of the police control room at the ground.

The trial was brought by the Hillsborough Family Support Group and had taken two years to go through the courts. The prosecution alleged that the two officers were responsible for the deaths because they ordered the opening of an exit gate to relieve the crush of supporters at the turnstiles without blocking off a tunnel leading to overcrowded terraces.

On Wednesday 26th July 2000, the judge at Leeds, Justice Hooper, stayed two charges of manslaughter against David Duckenfield after jurors failed to reach a verdict on two others. They had done the same with Bernard Murray the previous week. The Hillsborough Family Support Group urged that

the officers be re-tried. Justice Hooper ruled that the men would not receive a fair retrial on manslaughter charges. He decided that forcing Mr Duckenfield to undergo another trial would constitute "clear oppression". He said the six-week trial had been very public and the defendants had faced the public humiliation that accompanied it.

The Home Office set up an inquiry under Lord Justice Taylor immediately after the disaster and an interim report on Hillsborough was published in August 1989 with 43 immediate practical recommendations for League clubs to improve safety.

In his final report in January 1990, Lord Justice Taylor praised the football clubs for their positive attitude in implementing them.

One of the most important of his final 76 recommendations was the progressive replacement of terraces with seated areas. All First and Second Division stadia had to be all-seater by the start of the 1994-5 season and all Third and Fourth Division by 1999-2000.

SPRING 2001

The driver who woke up to a nightmare

How Gary Hart's mistake on the road brought catastrophe on the railway.

At 12 minutes after six o'clock in the morning of 28th February 2001, Gary Hart was heading west in his Land Rover along the M62 at Great Heck between Goole and Selby in North Yorkshire.

Having left home at Strubby in Lincolnshire, Gary Hart was bound for Wigan towing a trailer. When he fell asleep at the wheel, his Land Rover left the road and slid down a railway embankment, coming to rest on the rails of the East Coast main line.

As Hart called the emergency services, the south-bound GNER InterCity 225 express travelling at about 120mph hit the Land Rover, and was derailed. The express was then hit by a northbound freight train travelling at 70mph carrying more than 1,000 tonnes of coal to Ferrybridge. The impact of the collision threw one of the GNER carriages 100 yards into a field. Ten people, three railway workers and seven passengers were killed and many more injured. The whole catastrophic series of events had only taken a few minutes to unfold.

Gary Hart drove hundreds of miles each day, would sometimes go without sleep between journeys and could stay up for 36 hours at a time. On the night prior to the Selby rail crash, Hart had been talking to a new girlfriend on the telephone for up to five hours. He pleaded not guilty to causing 10 deaths by dangerous driving. When found guilty the judge said he was responsible for the "worst driving-related incident in the UK in recent years". He was released from prison on 12th July 2004 after serving half his five year sentence.

Gary Longbottom

Rescue services at the crash scene and (right) Gary Hart outside court

Mike Cowling

OCTOBER/NOVEMBER 2000

The waterlogged
Knavesmire,
York racecourse
Simon Hulme

After the deluge

Jo Makel reported on how Yorkshire coped with record autumn rainfall.

There has not been a downpour like it since records began in 1727, with more than 18 inches of rain falling on the country in the last three months – 77 per cent more than average and beating the last rainfall record set in 1852. Forecasters look to the sky and gloomily warn it's not over yet. They say there is more wet weather on its way and rainfall levels will exceed all record-breaking predictions.

At the end of October and early November large parts of Yorkshire came to a virtual standstill through heavy rain and snow which also brought chaos to the region's roads and rail services.

Some people were lucky to escape with their lives as gale-force winds brought trees crashing to the ground.

At York, Selby and elsewhere the army was brought in to strengthen flood defences with sandbags. Even so, at York it was touch-and-go. An earth barrier on Clifton Ings just up stream from the city which holds back immense amounts of water on a flood plain was within inches of being over-whelmed and some of the extra sand-bagging was swept away. At danger point, police closed Clifton Bridge. If the barrier had failed the destruction caused to York by a wall of water sweeping down river would have been incalculable.

According to the Environment

Agency, there was twice the expected monthly total rainfall in Yorkshire in September and reservoirs were full by mid-October, three months earlier than usual.

The agency will take a new look at the way it forecasts flooding. More telemetry stations in the region's rivers will monitor quick changes in the water levels by taking readings every few minutes. The data collated over the last three months has rewritten history: the rainfall measurements, the river measurements – much of which broke all previous records – and photographic and video evidence will now help the agency plan for the future.

JULY 1997

Donnygate: how the Yorkshire Post exposed the shocking truth

Revelations about the culture of corruption in Doncaster council marked the climax of a series of major inquiries which established the *Yorkshire Post* as one of the leading investigative newspapers in Britain. Rob Waugh reports.

There had been whispers for years that something was very wrong in Doncaster – and it took a lengthy investigation by the *Yorkshire Post* to uncover the truth. Our inquiries began in January 1997, after a report by District Auditor Gordon Sutton highlighted abuses of foreign trips, expenses, hospitality and free gifts. But there was more to be discovered. With the help of public-spirited council insiders who will never be named, and with countless hours of meticulous searching through records and planning applications, we slowly pieced together evidence of local government corruption on a scale not seen since the Poulson affair in the early Seventies (Wakefield architect John Poulson, a senior civil servant called George Pottinger and a clutch of local politicians and officials were found at the heart of a bribery scandal).

In July 1997 we published what we described as the "real Donnygate scandal". Our team's investigation of councillors and officers led directly to the suspension of five senior councillors from the authority's Labour group and the suspension of the entire Doncaster District Labour Party. It also led to the suspension and subsequent dismissal of the council's director of planning.

We revealed the shocking scale of what was really going on in Britain's most rotten borough - and how the revelations came as a huge embarrassment to a Labour Party elected on a trust ticket. We told how the council was dominated by a caucus of immensely powerful members, the Mining Community Group, which met secretly to decide council policy.

We discovered that the scandal reached back at least to 1992, when the 10-year planning blueprint for Doncaster went out to public consultation. Officers were horrified to discover that some councillors were lobbying for housing to be built on agricultural and green-belt land specifically excluded from the development plan. The effect was to increase the number of projected new homes by almost 30 per cent, from a recommended target of 14,600 houses to more than 20,000, even though such an increase could not be justified by population growth, while land values in the affected areas stood to increase by up to £58m. *Yorkshire Post* reporters spent many hours scrutinising the development plan and studying individual planning applications.

We obtained a confidential memo revealing how officers tried to object, only to have their concerns brushed aside. Dedicated professionals had been ordered to find a way of getting the corrupt councillors' version past the scrutiny of Government inspectors. The instruction was backed by veiled threats that their careers would be at risk if they did not comply.

In the 1998 *Press Gazette* Regional Press Awards our team of reporters – Andrew Norfolk, Simon Glover, Angela Spencer and Nicola Megson – won the Campaign of the Year section. The judges called it: "Historic stuff that won't be forgotten: an outstanding example of uncovering a major scandal of both local and national significance."

To the frustration of Mick Burdis, the former head of South Yorkshire CID, who had overall responsibility for Operation Danum, one of the biggest ever police inquiries into municipal crime, the real level of corruption ran deeper still. There could and perhaps should have been more people in the dock. But when push came to shove, the protection of careers and livelihoods, for some, took precedence over naming the guilty.

On 19th March 2004, a former council official and three builders admitted corruption, bringing the final number of people convicted during the Donnygate scandal to 35. Operation Danum began in 1997 and of the 35 people found guilty, 25 were Labour councillors mostly convicted of fiddling expenses, while former Tory group leader John Dainty was convicted of corruption. The most severe sentences were handed down at the landmark Donnygate trial in March 2002.

13 A new home

Newspapers have always adapted to what they think their readers want and to the technology for delivering it. The Sixties were a watershed when tastes, fashion and attitudes to authority were being turned upside down. The *Yorkshire Post* needed to make a step-change to adjust. While Linton Andrews was still in the chair, Viscount Ingilby, then a director of the *Yorkshire Post,* approached a former editor turned assistant managing director of the *Sheffield Telegraph,* Gordon Linacre (later Sir Gordon). They wanted him in Leeds as the *Yorkshire Post's* managing director. The newspaper had never had one before. For historical and family reasons it was still run by the chairman Rupert Beckett, also chairman of Westminster Bank, who gave little information to the board.

Goodbye to
Albion Street,
Leeds

Linacre met the board and privately took the view that they were excellent people but relatively clueless about publishing newspapers. Post-war newsprint rationing had ruled out printing bigger papers and now that the restrictions were lifted, some newspapers were already expanding. While prospects were good, most papers were not in a position to exploit it: they did not have the equipment to produce bigger and more profitable, papers. They were hamstrung by the fact that they were often situated in the middle of towns where getting the required new presses installed was tricky.

The *Yorkshire Post's* old presses were clapped out. Linacre's initial impression was that everything about the place was a museum piece. He could see a technical revolution was coming – in photo composition and web-offset printing – and the *Yorkshire Post* needed to be brought fairly swiftly into the second half of the 20th century.

Linacre's priority was to get the paper out of its jumble of buildings in Albion Street in the centre of Leeds. Another site for a purpose-built headquarters was earmarked on the west of the city. New presses were purchased and in a shake-up of management, the *Yorkshire Post's* editor was brought onto the company board for the first time.

Linacre went to the Westminster Bank – Beckett's Bank was now part of it – who agreed to bankroll the re-building and re-equipping with an overdraft of £2m. This was a staggering sum in the early Sixties. In the event, the company did not need to draw on anything like the money available since it started to do quite well. Advertising went up and the classified (small ads) department grew into the biggest money-spinning classified department in Britain.

When the parent company bought the *Doncaster Evening Post* a request was made for a royal personage to conduct an official opening. The Earl of Scarborough, who fixed these things, shook his head: he couldn't possibly go to the royal family with this because they had to be careful not to be too involved politically. But surely there were other companies, equally as Conservative as this one, where the royals were happy to do the honours? He replied that was so. But they did not call themselves Conservative.

It was too late to do anything about Doncaster. A dyed-in-the-wool trades unionist and Labour government minister, Ray Gunter, came to cut the ribbon.

In 1967, as the new *Yorkshire Post* building began taking shape, thoughts turned to the kind of ceremony that was needed to mark the most significant single step forward in the company's history. This time, a royal presence was a must. The simplest way to achieve that was to bow to the inevitable. If having Conservative in the company's title guaranteed refusal, then change it. Yorkshire Conservative Newspapers was turned into Yorkshire Post Newspapers. When it became part of United Newspapers towards the end of the Sixties, it maintained its autonomy and kept its bankers, lawyers and accountants.

On the evening of Saturday 26th September 1970, after the last football edition had been printed in Albion Street, the paper upped sticks and moved to its new headquarters at Bean Ings. It was here in the 1790s that Benjamin Gott had built a factory which brought all the processes of wool manufacture under one roof for the first time. It had pushed Leeds to the forefront of the Industrial Revolution. The new YPN building placed Leeds at the front of newspaper production.

It was a seamless transition. In a remarkable feat of pre-planning, the day after the Saturday move from Albion Street the presses started rolling to print the first editions of Monday's *Yorkshire Post*.

The Zen Buddhist garden was more problematic. The idea of creating one on the first-floor concourse open to the sky came from the architect. Gordon Linacre, recently back from Japan, liked it. Polished stones were set out on sand that had been carefully prepared and raked to induce the correct meditative and tranquil state. Arriving for a board meeting on the building's first morning, the vice chairman Colin Forbes Adam spotted the garden and, not in touch with the finer points of Zen, walked straight across the sand, leaving large boot prints. That night, a breeze got up. An increasing wind created a funneling effect in the concourse and next morning most of the Zen Buddhist garden was found on the roof. The change of company name did work as desired. Prince Charles accepted an invitation to open the new building that December.

Editor Linton Andrews had been followed by another Yorkshireman, Kenneth Young, who came from near Wakefield. He was succeeded by Ted Crossley who died suddenly at a hotel in London.

John Edwards had begun as a news

ANTHONY BURGESS SACKED

Linton Andrews' successor, Kenneth Young, came from the *Daily Telegraph* and devised the Literary Luncheons to raise the newspaper's profile. Yorkshire's biggest literary lion, JB Priestley, came to growl at the first one in 1961. Young was also determined to improve the books pages and one of the top-line fiction reviewers he took on in January 1961 was the novelist Anthony Burgess.

Burgess wrote a fortnightly column for the paper on new novels until May 1963. On 16th May 1963, Burgess's review column gave pride of place to a novel called *Inside Mr Enderby* by a writer called Joseph Kell. Burgess gave this more space in his column than his reviews of two other novels put together and Burgess remarked, *"how thin and under-savoury everything else seems after Enderby's gross richness."* In fact, Burgess and Kell were the same person.

Burgess later claimed that when Kenneth Young had sent him the novel for review he thought he was playing a practical joke (there's some foundation for this: apart from Joseph Kell, Burgess regularly used a number of aliases, including Mohamed Ali).

Kenneth Young had not been joking. He accused Burgess of "log-rolling" to get his new book noticed; there was even a denunciation on local television. An apology appeared in the *Yorkshire Post* the following week, making it clear Anthony Burgess was now a former reviewer of the paper.

The *Yorkshire Post's* premises on Wellington Street

Clockwise from top left: Sir Gordon Linacre;
John Edwards; Rachael Campey; Tony Watson

sub-editor on the *Yorkshire Post* before moving to Fleet Street. He had returned and had already radically overhauled the paper's business coverage when he was offered the editor's chair in the spring of 1969. Edwards relished the swashbuckling side of the job and made the newspaper more exciting and responsive. It was on John Edwards' watch that Yorkshire became the focus for some of the country's most sensational murder hunts and he ensured that despite a refusal to engage in cheque-book journalism, the newspaper's coverage set the pace for the national pack, especially with the Yorkshire Ripper.

Campaigns were on the agenda. In the early Seventies, well before the environment became an area of fashionable concern, Geoffrey Lean investigated the state of Yorkshire's rivers and won several awards. Roger Ratcliffe's investigations into the pernicious effect on children's health of lead additives in petrol made many people think seriously about green issues for the first time.

Another reporter John Edwards set loose on investigations, particularly into the burgeoning drugs scene, was a 29 year-old who joined from the Darlington evening paper in 1984, Tony Watson. Watson's work was so fruitful, *World In Action* asked him to come and do the same for them on television. Watson left the programme in February 1988 to return to Leeds as deputy to John Edwards. The editor was ailing and for the ten months up to his death in March 1989, Watson ran the paper.

The editorship was thrown open to outside candidates, including big-hitters from Fleet

Street. Two days before his 34th birthday, Tony Watson heard that he was the former first staff reporter to make the step to editor.

He was conscious that his new charge was conservative in outlook as well as politics. Even so, he burnt his fingers early on over an issue of major concern for the readership: the Births Marriages and Deaths column. Traditionally it had appeared on page three. Sometimes these notices took up an extravagant amount of space on what was the prime inside news page. So the column was moved. Watson was deluged with letters of protest, a volume greater than for any other single issue during his editorship. He took it as a practical exercise in reader research and a compromise was reached. The BMDs column was placed on page four and harmony was restored.

Campaigns became sharper-edged with Donnygate the biggest triumph. Other campaigns, not so hard-nosed, registered results. A conversation one day around the editorial conference table, bemoaning the state of Yorkshire cricket and the national game, led to the setting up of an annual schools cricket competition. It is now fixed in the calendar of schools throughout Yorkshire. For the Final, the children play on the hallowed turf at Headingley.

When historic stories like the fall of the Berlin Wall broke, there was now usually someone from the *Yorkshire Post* to cover it on the spot. As the *Leeds Intelligencer* had first discovered with the Peterloo massacre, sharp, first-hand colour writing enriches a paper's coverage of momentous occasions. Two reporters were ordered to New York on 9/11, a difficult proposition on a tight budget but it was reckoned to be essential for the paper to have its own take on the aftermath.

The wind of change blew steadily during the Watson years. The masthead was redesigned, along with the rest of the paper. Sport was no longer a Cinderella and appeared on the back page for the first time. A separate Monday sports section was introduced. The newspaper's approach to its female readers was re-thought and the Women's Post supplement expanded. An entertainment and listings magazine for Fridays and a Saturday magazine were added. Business coverage grew and a Business Week section started.

An evolving editorial culture led to a new sharpness and focus to the writing, more visual drama in page design and in the presentation of photographs. This was acknowledged by the judges of the Regional Press Awards in July 2002 when they voted the *Yorkshire Post* Newspaper of the Year for the first time.

Ownership of the paper passed in 1998 from United to Regional Independent Media and then again in April 2002 to Johnston Press who bought RIM for £560m.

When Tony Watson moved on, the choice of his successor in 2003 marked another first in the long history of the newspaper. Rachael Campey, from *The Times,* became the first woman editor of the *Yorkshire Post*. She set about re-creating the paper again to meet the latest set of challenges.

Over 250 years, the history of this paper has been the history of the people of the region. Like them, it has adapted to new circumstances while remaining Yorkshire through-and-through. The relationship has always been based on mutual affection and respect and nothing will change that.

Looking back to the beginning of our story is a dizzying prospect. Ten monarchs have ruled since the first *Leedes Intelligencer* was sold on 2nd July 1754. Our back numbers stand in rows of heavy, bound volumes in our archives. They appear monumental, testifying to an unbroken past. But continuity for a newspaper is never a certain process. There have been times when rivals seemed better placed to succeed. The *Leeds Mercury* during half of the 19th century seemed unstoppable. Yet it faded away and it was the *Yorkshire Post* which saw off the competition.

In the half century since the *Yorkshire Post's* last big anniversary in 1954, seismic changes have transfigured the political and demographic landscape. Another information revolution has fundamentally altered how we receive news and there were confident predictions this would bring about the death of newspapers. That has not happened, although it has affected what readers expect newspapers to provide and how they present it.

Underneath the restlessness and the search for the new, people's values have probably not altered all that much since young Griffith Wright set up in type the "freshest advices" newly arrived on the London mail coach.

The *Yorkshire Post* will continue to sustain and voice those straight-forward values – a prospect which lends at least some degree of certainty to what looks like an unsettled future.

149

Index

Bibliography

Anthony Eden: Robert Rhodes James. McGraw Hill

The Autobiography of a Journalist: Sir William Linton Andrews. Ernest Benn

Blunt: John Peart-Binns. The Mountain Press.

British Newspapers: A History and Guide for Collectors: Brian Lake. Sheppard Press

The Development of the Provincial Newspaper 1700-1760: GA Cranfield. Oxford University Press

The English Newspaper: An Illustrated History to 1900: Keith Williams. Springwood Books

Freshest Advices: Early Provincial Newspapers in England: RM Wiles. Columbus, Ohio, 1965

Leeds: The Story of a City: David Thornton. Fort Publishing

The Memoirs of Sir Anthony Eden. Cassell

The Newspapers Press in Britain: an annotated bibliography: Editors David Linton and Ray Boston

Nowt So Queer As Folk: Derrick Boothroyd. Watmoughs, Bradford

Our Mutual Friend: Charles Dickens. Penguin

Oxford Companion to the Brontes: Christine Alexander and Margaret Smith. Oxford University Press

The Press and the People: Donald Read. Severn House Publishers

Print and the People: 1819-1851: Louis James. Allen Lane

Printing in York from the 1490s to the Present Day: William K and E Margaret Sessions. William Sessions, York

Printing Presses. History and Development from the 15th Century to Modern Times: James Moran. Faber and Faber

The Romance of Old Leeds: Alfred Mattison and Walter Meakin. Reprinted from the Yorkshire Daily Observer

Tickle the Public: One Hundred Years of the Popular Press. Matthew Engel. Victor Gollancz

Time and Chance: an autobiography: Peter Townsend. Methuen USA (all attempts have been made to locate the copyright holder/administrator for permission to use the quotations on page 88)

The Yorkshire Post: two centuries. Mildred A Gibb and Frank Beckwith. Yorkshire Conservative Newspapers

Acknowledgements

Michael Hickling thanks:

Robin Turton, whose designing skill and commitment made the presentational ideas for this book a reality.
Leeds historian Dr David Thornton, for early guidance and practical advice and for reading the proofs of the early chapters.
Geoffrey Forster, Librarian of the Leeds Library for his kind suggestions and help.
Retired printer Brian Aldred.
Janet Bowes at the Yorkshire Farming Museum, Murton, York.
The library and picture operations staff at the *Yorkshire Post*, for their patience and helpfulness.

Text credits

The writers of the feature articles in this book whose titles are not given are present or past *Yorkshire Post* staff writers: Robin Ackroyd, Malcolm Barker, Chris Benfield, Reginald Brace, Terry Brindle, Richard Dodd, Alec Donaldson, Stephen McClarence, Jo Makel, Frederick Manby, Will Stewart, Paul Vallely, Rob Waugh, Geoffrey Winter and John Woodcock. Roger Cross was latterly an assistant editor. Malcolm Barker is a former deputy editor of the *Yorkshire Post* and also a former editor of the *Yorkshire Evening Post*.
Barbara Taylor-Bradford interview by Sheena Hastings. Apologies to colleagues whose work also deserved a place and was omitted solely through of shortage of time.

Picture credits

Cover photograph of Peter Sutcliffe and photographs on pages 120, 126-127, 132, 134, 135, 141, courtesy the Press Association.
Cover photograph of Lynda Logan, courtesy Terry Logan.
Printing shop print, page 2, courtesy Brian Aldred
Photograph of Alfred Wight, page 20, courtesy The World of James Herriot, Thirsk
Illustration of recruiting sergeant page 36, from The Costume of Yorkshire by George Walker, courtesy The Leeds Library.
Painting of Salts Mill page 41, copyright David Hockney 1997, courtesy Salt's Mill.
Painting of Charlotte Brontë, back cover and page 47, courtesy Brontë Society.
Painting of the charge of the 13th Light Dragoons at Balaklava page 58, courtesy The Light Dragoons.
Photograph of Frank Meadow Sutcliffe, page 73, courtesy The Sutcliffe Gallery, Whitby.
World War I recruitment advertisements, pages 76 and 78, courtesy the Liddle Collection, Leeds University.
Photograph of *Yorkshire Post* sign by HL Mann page 87, courtesy HL Mann estate.
Photograph of Amy Johnson page 97, by John Capstack. Copyright Capstack Portrait Archive.

Every effort has been made to trace copyright holders and obtain permission.
Any omission brought to our attention will be remedied in future editions.

Enquiries to purchase photographs in this book: contact our photosales department, telephone 0113 243 2701, extension 1360. View and buy the full range of pictures taken by our photographers by visiting *www.yorkshireposttoday.co.uk*

* Note: A sum of money before decimalisation in 1971 would be written in Pounds, Shillings and Pence (£sd). Four farthings or two halfpennies made a penny; twelve pence made a shilling; twelve shillings (240 pence) made one pound. A guinea was one pound one shilling, or 21 shillings. Shillings could be expressed thus: 40/-.

Style: most original spellings and constructions have been retained.
Some have been modernised for clarity.

Subscribers

Mr John Abbott
Paul Abraham
Albert Acaster
Mrs B Acres
Barbara Adams
Ian Duthie Adams
Michael Adams
Rebecca Addis
Avril & David Ainscough
John Richard Ainsworth
Brian Aldred
M & K Allen
Richard Allison
Shawn Allison
Alan & Jean P Allsopp
Mrs Margaret Alnwick
Robert Appleyard
Barbara Allwood & Jean
Buckley
David C Almond
Colin Alston
Dr John Alwyn
Margaret L Ambler
Robert D Ambler
Mrs Audrey Anderson
John Aylmer Anderson
D Anderson
Penny Anderson
Bruce Anderton
Mrs Ruth Andrew
Margaret Ansell
Colin Appleby
Vivienne Applequist
Robert Appleyard
Pat Apps
Mr James Archer
Philip D Ardron
R C Arminson
David W Armitage
J O & E Armstrong
Leslie Arnall
Peter Roy Arrand
Marjorie Arundel
Mrs Patricia Arundel
Michael Ash
Robert James Ashall
Stuart W Ashton
Mr P C L Ashworth
R G Ashworth
Thelma Rose Askwith
Jo-Anne & Richard Aspinall
William Kitson Asquith
David L Astley
Keith A Atkin
Mr Alan Atkinson
Mrs B E Atkinson
J D & F K Atkinson
Margaret & John Atkinson
Neville Atkinson
Peter Atkinson
Robert Atkinson
Roger Atkinson
Margaret Attwood

W B Austin
Douglas Ayre
Malcolm Ayre
Mrs Anne Ayton
Dr Richard W Backhouse
Philip Bacon
Mr Alan S Bagot
David H Baguley
Pamela Baguley
Rowley Bailey
Jack Baines
Mrs Jessie Baker
J W Baker
Margaret E Baker
Mrs P M Baker
Ray Baker
Mike Baldridge
Thomas Baldwin
Mr D H Ball
Ruth Ball
Donald Walker Bamforth
Harry Bannister
Ron & Joy Bannister
Julie Barber
Jamie Barbor
Judith Barden
Peter B Baren
Mr & Mrs G L Bargh
Andrew Barker
Mr Colin Barker
Cyd Barker
David Barker
Mr & Mrs H & J Barker
Hugh Richard Barker
M Barker
Malcolm G Barker
Mrs Sylvia Barker
Mrs Karen Barkley
E B Barmby
Raymond & Edna Barnard
John Barnes
Marjorie A Barnes
T Barnes-Warden
M Deirdre Barr
Mike Barr
Mr John M Barraclough
Margaret Barraclough
Mr G Barron
Ray Bartlett
Charlotte Louise Barton
Sarah Barton
John Barwick
Nigel R Baseley
Geoffrey Bass
Mrs R G Bate
Mr & Mrs D J Bate
Jill Bateman
Vincent Batty
Roger Baumeister
Alan T Baxter
Polly Baxter
Valerie Beadman
Charles R Beardsley

J M Beasley
Pauline & Paul Beasley
Margaret Beaumont
Ronald Edward Beckett
Carolyne Beckwith
Mr & Mrs E W Beckwith
Pamela Bedford
John Pickard Beesley
Colin & Patricia Belford
W B Bell (East Riding)
Mrs P A Bellchambers
D Benn
Arthur Bennett
Ben Bennett
Mrs A Benson
D M Benson
Brian Bentley
Joan Bentley
Miss M Bentley
Brian Berridge
Joan Berriman
Dorothy Jean Berry
Jack Berry
Thomas Best
Mrs P Bevan
R Bewell
Alwyn Bibb
John Bibey
F Bickerdike
Mrs Joyce M Billington
Emily Bilton
Brian Bingley
John R Binks
John Binns
J S Binns
Leonard Birch
Sir James Birrell
Mr Edward Black
John Black
Martin Black
Simon Black
Alan D Blackburn
James L Blackburn
Jean Blackburn
John Blackburn
Burton Blacker
Peter Blacker
Trudy Blacker
Pamela B Blagden
Barbara Blakeney
Dorothy Blakeway
Joan Blakey
Ms Minnie Bland
Mrs Mavis Blandamour
Mr D G Blankley
Leonie May Wallace Blow
John Blundell
(60 years old 2/7/04)
Mrs Audrey Blunt
(nee Priestley)
J Bobek
Henry Bolland
Lawrence Bollingham

Paul Bolton
P C Bolton
Mrs Terry Bond
Stephen John Boom
Derek Boorman
Mrs Kathleen Booth
L J Booth
Mrs Sylvia Booth
S M Boothman
Kathy & John Bostwick
John Bowcott
N W Bowen
David P Bower
John Francis Bowes
Walter Boyce
M G Boycott
Rosanna Alice Boyes
Sheila Boyes
Brian & Barbara Bradbury
Ralph C Bradbury
Doreen Bradford
Betty Bradley
Mr J R Bradley
Patricia Ann Bradley
W H & P Bradley
J P Brady
Beatrice M Braithwaite
Patricia Braithwaite
Ed & Jan Bramlett, Texas, USA
J D Bramley
Mary Bramley
Sue Bramley
Barbara Brear
Charles W Brear
John R Breare
David Brearley
H Melvyn Brearley
T M & J Brears
Peter H Breckin
Alec Brennand
Alfred Samuel Bretherick
David Brewer
E Brierley
Mr D Briggs
Robert Briggs
Paul Bright
Mr D J Britton
Colin Broadbent
Sheila Jo Broadbent
Mrs K Broadbent
Arthur Broadhead
Michael Broadhead
Mr Walter Brock
Peter W Broderick
Geoff Brogden
Anne C Brook
Carol Brook
Denis & Laura Brook
Mr J C Brook
Mr & Mrs K Brook
Kevin J Brook
Esther Brookfield
Denis Brooks

153

Jill Brooks
Michael J P Brooks
Rebecca Brooks
Barrie Brotherton
Mrs D Broughton
Anthony Brown
D Brown
Mrs Dinah C M Brown
Florence Brown
George Dennis Brown
John Brown
Pauline Brown
W A Brownlow
Terence Brumfitt
Frank & Patricia Brunt
June M Brunt
Mrs Connie Brunyee
Mr Peter G Buckland
Ian Buckley
Jacqueline Buckley
Patricia & Andrew Bugler
Thelma Bull
Ann & Michael Bunn
Mrs W W Burbridge
J A Burgess
Kenneth L Burnett
Marjorie Burnett
Tony Burnett
Alan T Burnhill
A Burns
Andrew R Burns
Mick Burns
Mrs Kathleen Margaret
Burrells
Dennis Burrow
Gwen A Burrows
Philip Burrows
Colin Bursell
F J Burton
J H & M Burton
John Burton
Ray Burton
Rose Burton
Nigel & Diane Burton
David Busfield
Alan Keith Butler
In Memory of Harry Butler
Ian Butler
Mrs B A Butler-Smith
John Butterfield
Norman Butterfield
W P Butterfield
Alice Butterworth
Anne & Victor Byrom
Roy Cairns
Glenise Calladine
B Callicot
L Jane Calverley
Mr C Calvert
Philip G Calvert
William Calvert
Alexis Campbell
E I Cansfield
Mr Kenneth Cant
Frederick Canty
Mrs C J Cardus
David Carlin
Monica Carlton
Geoffrey Carr

Mrs Irene Carr
The Carter Family
Dr & Mrs R F Carter
Robert A Carter (Kirkburton)
Thomas Terrance Carter
Mrs H M Cartwright
Derek Cash
Hazel Cassidy (Australia)
Margaret Casson
Joanne Catlow
Miss L Catterick
Herbert Jack Cawood
Patricia Cawthorn
Colin Cawthray
R W Cawthron
Joan Cazaux
Carl Chambers
David A Chambers
Anne Chapman
Mr John Chapman
Mr Thonas Brian Chapman
Mr & Mrs K F Charge
Albert Edward Charlesworth
Mr Joe Charlesworth
James Cheetham
Susan Helen Child
Barbara Chippindale
Anthony Chisenhale-Marsh D L
Mary J Chorlton
Mr Ian Christie
Janet Church
Janet Clark
Mr J D Clark
J Keith Clark
Norman R Clark
Francis W Clarke
Terry Clarke
C L Clarkson
David & Mary Clarkson
T H Clarkson
John Fairclough Claxton
Mrs Joan Clay
Harry Clayden
Mavis Clayden
Tony Clayton
Jean Clegg
Paul Clegg
Mr Dennis Clements
Mrs Jean Cliff
Michael A Cliff
Shirley Clifford
Trevor & Doreen Clough
Joyce M Cochrane
Kenneth Cockcroft
Margaret Codling
Mr M Colbeck
Douglas Colby
Miss E Coldwell
Mrs Iris Cole
Dennis Collett
Pamela Collison
John E Colton
George F Connelly
Mrs Susan Conyers
Joseph Neil Cook
R & B Cook
J R Cooke
Patricia Cooke
Raymond Cooke

Stephen Charles Cooke
W T Cooke
Neill Stewart Cooney
Mrs Cynthia M Copeland
James E Corden
Mrs Joyce M Cordingley
Elizabeth Corner
Oliver & Heather Cornish
Rita Corrigan
Jack Costello
A Cother
Mr Tony Cother
John Granville Coulson
J I Coupe
Peter W Cowgill
W G I Cox
Colin & Betsy Crabtree
Hadrian Peter Cracknell
Mr H Crane
Claire Craven
Jane & David Craven
Mr Michael E Craven
R E Crawford
H Crockett
Brian Croft
Lynne Croker
G B Crompton
Peter Crooks
Julie Crookes
Elizabeth Helen Crosier
Peter & Marilyn Cross
Brian S Crossland
Dean Crossland
Holly MacGregor Crossland
Michael Crossland
Arthur Crow
Annie Crowther
Hazel Crowther
Mrs June Crowther
John Cullen
Halton Curry
J P Curry
P D Curry
Graham Curtis
Malcolm Cushworth
Jim & Audrey Cussons
Margot & John Cutt
Stephen P Cuttle
A D Dakeyne
Philip Dalby
Victoria Dalby
George G Dale
R Dale
Rhoda Dale
John Dales
Mrs Audrey Daley
Mr Andrew L Danes
Jessie Darnbrough
Mrs Lois Darnley
William Davey
Miss Beryl Davies
John Davies
Olwen Davies
Paul R Davies
J Davis
Roger Davis
Mark and Suzanne Davy
Cyril Dawson
Mr Eric Dawson

Albert Edward Day
Dorothy Day
Peter Dealtry
Eric Dean
Jean & Ben Dean
Margaret & Harold Dean
Charles E Deighton
K A Delaney
Kathleen Denison
Alan Dennison
Andrew & Jana Dennison
Jean M Denton
E Brian Derrington
Pamela Dibb
Alan John Dickin
A M W Dickinson
Edward Smart Dickinson
Mavis Dickson
Elaine Dinsdale
Sylvia Dinsdale
Andrew Dixon
Mr F S Dixon
Ken Dixon
Raymond & June Dixon
Hannah Dobson
Stephen Barrie Dobson
Mr John Dodds
Barbara Dodsworth
Ian K Dodsworth
Dr G Donaldson
Janet Donaldson
Dr Roger Donaldson
Alan Donlan
Mr Donnelly
Stephen Donohue
Mrs Eileen Dooks
B & R Doonan
Judith A Dorman
Mr V J Double
Mr D S Douglas
Harry Douglas
Mr & Mrs J L Douglas
R Martin Downs
Gay Doyle
Jack Doyle
Clifford Drake
Elsie Drake
Mr P R Drewery
Cynthia Mary Drinkall
Christopher Dronsfield
Alison M Drury
Tom Drury
Susan Valerie Duchatel
John H Duff
Susan Margaret Duffin
John Gibson Dufton
W Duggleby
David Duncan
George Duke
William Clifford Anthony Duke
Mr & Mrs J M Duncalf
Sam Dunderdale
Barbara Dunks
T S Dunn
Clive Dunnill
Stephen Dunning
D Enid Dunsby
Granville Dunstan
Paul Durkin

David Durrans
Neil Duthie
Rodney Dyke
Hilary Dyson
Mr John B Dyson
Kenneth M Dyson
P G Dyson
Sarah Anne Dyson
John Earless
Alan Easter
Joan Easter
David Eastwood
Jennifer M Eastwood
Mrs B M Ebdon
Dennis Eddon
Peter Edmunds
Peter Edwards
Martin and Judy Eland
Mr H Lesley Ellarby
James Ellin
P M Elliot
Rosemary & Richard Elliot
Royce Elliot
Carole & Bernard Ellis
George Ellis
Peter Ellway
Mrs L G Ellwood
John Rowland Emmott
K England Esq
Joyce M English
Anne & Martin Ensor
C P Ensor
Mr & Mrs J Entwistle
(Sydney, Australia)
I B Epstein
B E Evans
Geoffrey Edward Evans
Janita Evans
John Evans
Miss P Evans
Eric Evers
W Raymond Ewbank
John & Elaine Fairfax
Janet & Peter Fairs
Ann Falconer
John Farling
Paul Barrie Farnell
Miss Edith Farrar
Mrs Janet Farrar
Mark Farrar
P J Farrar
Maurice E Farrand
Mrs Anne Faulding
C M Fawcett
Michael Fearnley
Kenneth A J Fenwick
Stuart Ferguson
Mrs M Fethney
D Fieldhouse
Leon Finsbury
Allan Firth
Debbie & Robert Firth
Jean & Michael Firth
John Firth
Leslie M Firth
Michael Firth
Rob Firth
Miss W M Firth
Harry Fish

Elizabeth & Robin Fisher
Rebecca Fisher
Mr John Fitzgerald
Paul Flaherty
Brian Flanagan
Elizabeth Flathers
John & Jean Fleming
Wendy J Fleming
Gloria Fletcher
J K Fletcher
S G Fletcher
Arthur Flint
Alan Flintham
Ian M Forbes
Don Foster
John Forster
Christine Foster
Jack & Betty Foster
Richard Foster
Stanley Foster
P B Fowler
Cynthia Fox
Maurice Fox
T W Fox
Tim Frampton
J R France
Mr Thomas Frank
Michael G Free
Mrs E Freeman
John Freeman
Nancy Freeman
Peter Fretwell
Caroline Frisby-Shaw
Ernest Froggatt
Jean Froggett
The Frost Family
Mr Gordon Frost
Mr Melvyn Frost
M Frot
Connie & John Frudd
Clare Fry
Valerie Jean Full
Helen Fuller
John Furniss
Poppy Patricia Fyfe
Marjorie Gaimster
Jane Charlotte Anne Gair
John Gallagher
Ken Galletly
W H Galleway
Peter Joseph Gallivan
J Gambold
J M C Garbutt
Andrew Gardner
Margaret Garner
J N Gaunt
Sheila Gaunt
Kenneth Gavins
Terry George
John Gibbs
Mrs P Y Gibbs
A & M Gibson
Eileen Gibson
Geoffrey Gibson
Patricia Gibson
Thomas R Gibson
Mrs Jean M Gidman
Patricia Mary Gilfoy
Colin Gilks

Colin Michael Gill
Lucy Victoria Gill
Mr Edward J Gillard
Robert G Gillard
John Gilleghan M.B.E
Mr & Mrs J B Gisburn
Colin Glass
Mr David Gledhill
Ronald Gledhill
Peter Glossop
J & H Goddard
Carole Godfrey
A G Goldsbrough
Peter L Goldsmith
Chris Gooch
C Goodwill
Geoff & Anne Goodwill
John Goody
Richard Goodyear
Chris & Patricia Googe
Ann C Gordon
Jim Gordon
P D Gosden
Misses L & C Gosney
Margaret & Harvey Gothelf
Adrian Gough
Timothy J Grace
Kevin Grady
Rev. J Neil Graham
Miss W J Graham
Angela Gray
Anne & Quentin Gray
Robert Grayson
Michael T Greaves
Stephen Greaves
Andrew Green
Andrew N Green
Beatrice Mary Green
Mrs Dorothy Green
Graham J Green
Mrs Jean Green
Joan V Green
Dr & Mrs K R Green
Richard Green
Daniel Hugh Maurice
Greenwood
Harold Greenwood
Kenneth Lindsay Greenwood
Marie Greenwood
Mr & Mrs H H Gregg
Mr John Malcolm Gregory
Dr C J Griffiths
Alfred Grimes
Louise & Steve Grimes
Mrs W E Groves
John G Guest
John Gunnell
C R Guthrie
F S Hague
Alastair J Haigh
Anne Haigh
Doug Haigh
Gordon Haigh
Jane Haigh
Marjorie Haigh
Norman D Hainsworth
Peter & Jenifer Hainsworth
Sheila Hainsworth
Mark Irwin Hale

George Haley
Garry J Hall
Geoff Hall
Marjorie Hall
Richard & Margaret Hall
Terry Hall
W Martin Hall
Geoff Hallas
Harry Hallas
Moira Halloways
Brenda Halls
L A Halpern
Peter Halsall
Dennis Halstead
Duncan Hamilton
Kenneth Phipps Hammill
Henry Kit Hampshaw
Christopher Hampstead
Donald Hancock
Paul Hancock
In memory of Stephen John
Haney
Michael J Hankinson
Mrs Kathleen Hanlon
Peter Hanneman
J A Hanslow
Brian Hanson
Mr Charles Kenneth Hanson
Mrs Sheila M Hanson
Mrs Janet E Hardaker
Mr Thomas William Hardcastle
Frank Hardgrave
Leslie Harding
Mrs R W Hardman
Pat Hargreaves
R C W Hargreaves
Terrance Hargreaves
Lavinia J Harmson
Jason Richard Harpham
Mr Peter Harpham
Mr Peter Mark Harpham
Malcolm Harpin
Mrs P J Harpin
J & N Harran
A H & B Harrison
Mrs B Harrison
David Harrison
Jan Christine Harrison
John William Harrison
Paul Harrison
Mr & Mrs K Harrop
Joan Hart
Mr John Hart
Denis Hartley
Keith Hartley
Fred Haughey
Debbie Havercroft
Christopher Hawley
Gilian Haxby
Brian & Denise Hebblethwaite
Mr J Hebblethwaite
John & Pamela Hebblethwaite
William Robin Hebblethwaite
M D Hellawell
Mrs Joan Y Helm
Forrest Dwayne Helton
G H Hepworth
J B Herbert
Olivia Herbert

Derek Hercock
D D Herd
Keith Herd
Ronald B Hesselden
Daisy Heywood
Gary & Gill Hibberd
David Hickes
Tony Hickson
Derek M Higgins
John Higgott
Brian Higgs
Anne Hildred
Bernard Hill
Mrs D Hill SRN, SS Ord. St John
Harry A Hill F.R.I.C.S
Jean Hill
Mrs Marjorie Hill
Mr Peter Hill
Richard Hill
Wiliam Hill
Mr E R Hinckley
Irene Hinds
Miss B Hinton
Mrs Alice Hird
Barbara M Hird
John Bryan Hirst
John H Hirst
Mrs Pamela Hirst
Robert Hirst
Mrs Lily Hitchenor
Mr & Mrs P Hobson
Brian Hodge
Carl Hodges
Brian Hodgkinson
Mrs Beatrice Hodgson
Kathleen N Hodgson
Monica Holbrook
Derek Holden
Gordon D Holderness
J Holdsworth
Margaret Holdsworth
Mr Nigel E Holdsworth
John Holland
Francis Holleran
Joan Holliday
Andrew Holmes
Dennis Holmes
John A Holmes
Judith M Holmes
June V Holstead
Jesse D Holt
Mr William Holt
Ann M Holubecki
Jack Hood
Gwen Hopkins
Joan E Hopkinson
Clarice Hopper
Philip Hopper
Terence Hopper
David G Horner
Mr & Mrs A T Hornsby
Jim & Margaret Horrox
D B Horsley Esq
Malcolm Horsley
Kathleen Horspool
M Houghton
Mrs Nancy Houlgate
Graham John Hoult
Andrew Howard

Donald Howden
Edward (Ted) Howell
Allan Charles Howes
Paul Howley
David Howram
C Howse
Nanette Hoyland
Rev`d A G & Mrs M E Hudson
Gill Hudson
James Neil Hudson
J Hughes
Ruth Margaret Hughes
Cyril Hulley
John Hume
Geoffrey W Hunn
Adam Firth Hunt
Ian Ryder Hunter
Mr W R Hunter
Ian Hutchinson
John V Hutchinson
Margaret Hutchinson
Mr R & Mrs G S Hutchinson
W N Hutchinson
Mr & Mrs J R Hutton
Richard & Janice Hutton
Harold Hyatt
Margaret and John Ibbeson
David & Madeleine Ibbitson
Peter & Gaye Ibbitson
Robert Ibbitson
John & Caroline Ibbotson
Ann Frances Ikoku
Joyce Illingworth
Susan R Ingham
Paul Ingwell
Sheila Ireland & Terry Phillips
Mr & Mrs A Irwin
Gill Irwin
Mrs Freda Jackson
Mr H B Jackson
John David Jackson
John Ian Jackson
J Philip Jackson
Judith Jackson
Mary Jackson
Mervyn Jackson
P T Jackson
Richard Jackson
Robert R Jackson
Sheila Jackson
Simon T Jackson
Kevin Jacques
Mrs Betty Jagger
Mike James
Malcolm & Lesley Jameson
Ann Jamieson
Michael Jay
Dr J B Jennings
Geoffrey Jennings
John Gordon Jephcott
Brian Jerome
Pamela Jessop
Rosemary Jessup
Ron Jevons
Neil Jewsbury
Mr Albert G Jibson
Dean Jobson
Antony Johns
Andrew Alan Johnson

Elaine Johnson
Keith Johnson
Peggy Johnson
Robin Johnson
Steve Johnson
Valerie Johnson
M E Johnston
Alan R Jones
Brian A Jones
Edith Rose Jones
E E Jones
Mr G L & Mrs P Jones
Jim Jones
Keith Jones
M F Jones
Milson Peter Jones
Terry Jones
Andrew D de Jong
John H Jose
Richard Jowett
Nancy Jubb
Z Kaja
Martin Kavanagh
William Kay
Derek Kaye
John S Kaye
Mr Keith M Kaye
William D Kaye
J M Keenan
Richard Keith
Mrs Valerie Kellett
Brian Kelly
David Kenington
Paul Kenington
Chris Kenny
Dorothy Kent (Ripon)
James A Kent
Mr & Mrs Michael Kent
J L Kenyon
Mr L Keough
Mr M Keough
Paul B Kershaw
Ronald Kershaw
Roger Ketteringham
Jeremy Kettlestring
Peter Kew
David Kidd
Gordon D Kilburn
Mrs J M Kilburn
Brian Kilner
Kenneth Kilner
Mrs B E King
Mr David King
Isabel M King
Margaret King
Mr Arthur Kinghorn
Dorinda Kinghorn
Christine Kinloch
John R Kirby
D J Kirk
O M Kirkby
C G Kirkwood
Trevor Kitchen
Helen Krushniak
A J Lalley
Mr P W Lambert & Family
Audrey Lancashire
Adrian Pearson Lane
Julian Peter Lane

Susan Lane
K Lang
Miss Catherine Mary Langan
Dr Rachel Langford
Thomas Lannen
Mrs D Lapish
Renee Lapworth
Geoff Large
Peter Larkin
Sylvia Laverick
Steven Lavin
Joyce Lawson
Mark Alexander Lawson
David John Lawton
Brian Geoffrey Layton
Mary Lea
Freda Leadley
Mrs Jean Learoyd
Jim Leason
Mr C M Leather
Andrew Ledger
Catherine Lee
Derrick Lee
Graeme M Lee
H Trevor Lee
Roy Lee
Anthony John Leedal
Patricia Anne Leggott
(Grimsby)
Mr C Lemmon
Regina Kathleen Le Page
Mr Roy Lester
The Levin Family
Ashley Lewis
Jane Lewis
A G & C A Liddle
Mr & Mrs P L Lightfoot
Tracy Lightfoot
Edith Mary Lill
Anne Lindley
Richard Ling
Brenda Linley
Christopher Linley
Marjorie Lister
Gwen Littlewood
E Liversidge
Barbara A Lloyd
M E Lloyd
Sue Lobley
Alan Howard Lockwood
Mrs Christine Lockwood
Morris Lockwood
R Lockwood
John Shenton Lodge
Denis Lofthouse
K S Longbottom
Sheila M Longbottom
M Glen Longman
Mrs B H Longstaff
D A Longstaff
Paul Longstaff
Bryan Longworth
C W Loughton
Margaret Lound
Mr Fred Lovell
Donald Low
Gerald Lowe
Anne & Philip Lowery
Raymond Lowther

Charles David Lumb
Christopher Lumb
Ray Lumb, Cleckheaton
David H Lund
Mr Gordon Lunn
Mrs Pat Lupton
S & W Lupton
Janet E Lute
Robert Lyons
Gordon Lythgoe
Yvonne Joyce Alice Mace
Margaret Macgill
Dr F B Maclaren
John Gordon (Mac) Macleod
Ritchie Macpherson
Tom Madden
Karen Maddocks
Ann Madeley
David Main
Linda Main
Michael C Makey
Alan Makin
Constance Makings
Jo Malcolm-O'Neill
Graham Mallinson
Janet Mallinson
Mr & Mrs J E Mallinson
James Malone
Michael G Malone
Jean M Mann
Stephen J Mann
J C Mansfield
R L & S P Mansfield
Stewart Manyweathers
Diana Marcus
G S Markham
Nigel Marks
Sheila M Marsay
Derrick Marsden
Donald Marsden
George Marsden
Jonathan D Marsden
Maureen Marsden
Roger Marsden
William Marsden
Graham Marsh
Christopher A Marshall
John Marshall
John W Marshall
Tom Marshall
Mr Peter Marsland
Arthur Marson
Mr Gerald A Martin
Peter Martin
Sandra Martin
R T Martinson
Alan & Irene Marwood
Sheena Marx
Pauline Mason-Brown
L G W Mathews
Michael Matthews
Graham Maud
John H Maud
Mrs M E Maud
Neville S Maw
Mr Bryan J Mawson
Charles F Mawson
Mr Reginald McAllister
Paul & Janine McAndrew

Mrs Marie McAvoy
Winifred McCarthy
The McDermott Family (Leeds)
Richard & Anita McDonald
Peter McGarry
Elsie McKeating
Diane M McKechnie
John A McLeod
Mr Gordon McMaster
Lena Meadowcroft
Mr Tony Medlicott
Ronald Megginson
Sheila Meiklejohn
F & W Melia
M F Melia
Alan G Mellon
Raymond Mellor
Jack Meltham
David & Jennifer Meredith
Barry Merrick
Mrs C Metcalfe
Cyril Metcalfe
John Metcalfe
Judith & John Micklethwaite
Mr Keith Middleton
Pauline Milbourn
Mrs P R Milburn
Mark Anthony Millard
A J Miller
Doris Miller
Mrs W Miller
Howard Milner
Alexander Milnes
Kenneth Tweed Milnes
Les Milnes
Allan S Mirfield
Austin Mitchell
G F B Mitchell
Mr Terence Mitchell
Charlotte Mitton
Francis Moll
Mr & Mrs M Molloy
Jon Monkman-Pountney
Jean Moody
Andrew Moon
Allen Moore
E Moore Esq
Mr J S Moore
Mr Nicholas Moore
Peter Moore
James Moran
Dr Gareth Morgan
Frank Andrew Morley
Timothy Morley
Paul Anthony Morrell
Bernard Morris
John W Morris
Richard Morrish
Ronnie Morrison
Mr Arthur Morton
Perry Morton
Mrs Anne Moscrop
D Mountain
Doris Moxon
Richard Moy
Evelyn Olive Moyse
Christine & Raymond Mudd
Mary Muff
Brian Muffitt

J Muggeridge
Cath Muldowney
Kenneth Mullins
Barbara Mungovin
Will D Murgatroyd
John Murray
Dave & Janet Myers
Gerald W Myers
Ken Myers
N B & J D Myers
P B & C A Myers
Geoffrey Nalton
Councillor Bob Nash
James Naylor
Mrs K Neal
Michael Fitzgerald Neal
Sam Neave
Michael Needham
Moira Alma Needham
Nudger Needham
Kenneth Nellar
Jacqueline Nelson
Pam Nelson
S C Nesom
Brian Nettleton
Doreen Neville
Michael Neville
Bernard Newington
M Newsome
June Dorothy Newton
Audrey Nicholson
E S Nicholson
Gordon Nicholson
Mr Lawrence R Nicholson
John R Noble
Mr Neil Noble
Simon D Noble
Steven Peter Noble
Brian Norfolk
David Ian North
Harold North
Michael G North
Mr William Lionel North
P G Nottingham
David L Nunn
Iain Alan Nutt
Colin Oakey
Donald S Oates
George T J O'Connor
Mary V Oddie
Pip Oldroyd
James Alan Oliver
Norman O'Riley
Robert Michael Ormondroyd
Kathleen R O'Shea
R W Osler
Rob Outhwaite
Ms D Page
Penny & Rick Painter
Mrs Dorothy Palmer (Dacre Banks)
J Brian Palmer
R E Palmer
Dave & Christine Panting
John Parish
Mr Neil M Park
Stephen S Park
Trevor & Diane Park
Mr Andrew Philip Parker

Brian Parker
Graham Parker
John Malcolm Francis Parker
Rev J R Parker
Mrs M R Parker
Margaret Parkin
Dr Roger Downend Parkin
Ann & Nevil Parkinson
Adrian Parr
C T Partridge
James Passmore
Marion Patchett
Andrew Patching
Ian Patterson
Mr John Pattison-Sharp
Pam Peace
The Peaches
Ada Pearson
Mr D N Pearson
Peggy Pearson
Cyril E Pease
Jack Peat
Barbara Peate of Yeadon & Scarborough
D Peel
Gerry Peel (Horsforth)
John & Barbara Peel
Christopher Andrew Peet
Mr Christopher Edward Peever
Alan Pell
Dorothy Penso
Beryl Percival
Timothy Percival
Mr & Mrs R W Perkin
G J Perry
Valerie Pettifer
Harold Petyt
Freda Phalp
L Phillips
Lilian & Eric Phillips
Leslie A Philpott
Robert B Pick
Jill Pickering
Louis Pickering
Judith A Pickersgill
Bob & Betty Pickles
Bryan & Joyce Pickles
David Pickles
Ian Pickles
A J Le Gresley Picot
Margaret E Pigott
Veronica Pikett
M D Pilkington
David Pinkney
R Pinkney
John W Plumb
William A Plumridge
David Pollard
Mrs M G Pollard
Mrs S M Porritt
Jean Poskitt
Harry Potter
David W Powell
Bill Powrie
Kenneth Barry Pratt
Mavis Prentis
Mr Arthur Preston
James Anthony Preston
Keith Preston

Daniel Rawson Price
Jane Price
J G Priestman
Mrs Eileen Pritchard
Gill Probert
Eileen Puddephatt
E A Pulleyn
John Leyland Quarmby
Norman Quarmby
Colin J Quickfall Esq.
Stanley Quinlan
Alan Rae
Margaret Ramsdale
Mrs L Ramsden
Philip W Ramsden
Stuart P Ramsden
Carole Ramsey
Mr G A Ratcliffe
Colleen & Tzeitel Rawlinson
Douglas Rawson
Mr Peter H Rayment
Allan Read
David Charles Reep
Mr Brian Reeve
Luke & William Charters Reid
Stephen Andrew Reid
Kenneth Relton
Susan Remmer
Christopher Renard
Sylvia Render
I Reynolds O B E
John Reynolds
P Reynolds
Alan Rhodes
Brian Rhodes
Doris Rhodes
John & Pauline Rhodes
Trevor Rhodes
John Lyndon Richards
Dennis & Katie Richardson
Ellen Richardson
Michael Simpson Richardson
Mrs Joyce D Richmond
Ken Richmond
Gerald L Ricketts
Philip Rickinson
Mr D & Mrs J Riddington
Ian G Ridley
Trevor Ridsdale
James Arthur Rigby
John Rigby
Stella A Rigby
Mr T A Rigg
Ian W Riley
Michael Riley
Richard S Riley
Peter Ripley
J P C Roach
Alison & Leslie Roberts
Angela Roberts
Colin Roberts
Howard Roberts
Mr & Mrs P Roberts
William Roberts
Mr K Robertshaw
W S Robertshaw
Kate E Robertson
Albert Robinson
B Robinson

Colin Robinson
David Robinson
Edward Robinson
Irene Robinson
Judy Robinson
Michael Robinson
M P Robinson
Phyllis M Robinson
Stan Robinson
James Robson
Pearl J Roe
Vernon Rogerson
Mr & Mrs J H Rollinson
Jack Rook
Mr J S Root
Frank Roper (Brighouse)
Leslie Barry Rothera
Jean Rounding
Audrey Rowland
D R Rowland
Eric Rowland
Gordon & Jean Rowling
Margaret I Rowling
Barbara Ruane
Katharine Rudd
Mrs I Rule
Derek Russell
Averille Ryan
A Saaliste
Stephen J Sadler
Janet Salmon
Mr Keith Salt
Mr G Salter
Mrs S Salter
Frederick Saltfleet
Mr J Samuel
Ruth Sanderson
Stephen C Sanderson
A M Saunders
Audrey Saunders
Mr Ken Sawyers
Gerald A Sayer
Mr & Mrs M J Sayles
Brian Scaife
Ian Scarr
Jack Schofield
Patricia Schofield
Mr Trevor Schofield
Michael Scholes
Stuart Scholey
Gerald Scorah
Roger Scorah
F Scott
John Scott
Winifred Scown
Mrs Gladys Scrimshaw
Mrs J Scrowston
Mrs Vera Scuffham
Brian Charles Seals
Duncan Patrick Seaman
Mr & Mrs W J G Seddon
Christine Sedgwick
Mr W F Seed
Jane Seels
Mrs C Seipp
David Sellars
Anne M Sellers
I D Sellers
M J W Sellers

N S Sellers
Richard Anthony Sellers
Doreen Senior
J P Senior
Mr K Senior
Joan Sephton
Colin Seymour
Jean & Barry Seymour
John Edward Shackleton
Phil Shand
John L Sharp
Neville D Sharp
Raymond Sharpe
Gemma Shaw
Jack Shaw
Mr John Kenneth Shaw
Mary & Brian Shaw
Roger Ian Copley Shaw Esq.
Mr Harry Sheard
John M Sheard
Keith Sheard
Pamela B Shearstone
Gordon Sheffield
Howard A Sheldon
Paul Sheldon
Ray & Audrey Sheldon
Mark Sheridan
K M Shipley
Trevor Shipston
B A Shuttleworth
Michael Shuttleworth
Mr & Mrs D Sibson
John Sidebottom
Anthony Silson
Michael Silversides
Maria Ann Simmonds
Monica Simmons
Charles Michael Simms
Alison K Simpson
Brian Simpson
Mrs B A Simpson
Eric P Simpson
Frank Simpson
Marie Simpson
Rowena Singleton
Mrs I L Skelton
Diane Skinner
L E Slack
William M Slater
Gordon Sleightholm
Mr J Sleightholm
Christine Elizabeth Slingsby
Francis Gerald Smailes
Rob & Vicky Small
A Eric Smith
Barrie Smith
C P Smith
Donald Smith
Mrs Enid Smith
G A Smith
Geoffrey Smith
Helen M Smith
I A Smith
Jean M Smith
Joan Smith
John & Brenda Smith
John Herbert Smith
John Robert Shelton Smith
Kathleen Margaret Smith

Maisie Smith
Dr Martyn Smith
May Smith
Nora Smith
Peter H Smith
Philip Robert Smith
Rosemary Smith
Sue Smith
Terry & Jean Smith
Valerie Mary Smith
Andrew J Snashall
Mrs D Snowden and Family
Mr & Mrs J Snowden
Graham R Snowdon
Frances Solman
Mrs Fern Solty
Ian David Somers
D V Southwell
Howard Sowerby
Steve Sowden
Mr B M Speight
Mrs S K Spence
Antony & Kate Spencer
Eillen Spencer
N Spencer
Richard G R Spencer
Martin G Spiers
Audrey Spink
Henry Spruce
Florence Spurdens
Stuart S Spurr
Mr Robert Martin Squire
Andrew Squires
Helen M Stainsby
Mrs June Stainthorpe
P H Stainthorpe
R G Staniforth
G & M Stanley
W Stark
The Statham Family
Mrs Janet Stather
Arthur Stead
Colin Stead
Jill Steele
Philip W Steele
Rickamond Harry Steel
Simon Stembridge (Yorkshire
Post Features 1968-1996)
Mr Stanley Stephens
Eddy Stephenson
James Stephenson
Miss N E Stephenson
Pauline Stephenson
June M Stevenson
R W Stevenson
Joanna Steventon
F R A Stirk
Ronald A Stokes
Frank Storey
Ms Violet Storey
B K Stott
Mr Geoffrey Stott
Pam Stott
Peter St Paul
A M Straker
Carl Gareth Ellis Straker
Alan Street
John Street
Helen Stringer

Mrs Margaret Stringfellow
John P W Strudwick
G D Strutt
Mr Allan Stubbs
Evelyn Stubbs
David Sturdy
J Sturdy
Patricia M Styan 23/7/04
Tony Styan
Patricia Sugden
Ronald Sugden
Douglas Summers
Theo Sumners
Margaret Sunderland
Doreen Sutcliffe
Mrs P Sutcliffe
Betty & John Sutton
Adam Swallow
Mrs Mary W Sweeney
Mrs Margaret Swiers
Jean H Swift
Ann & Roger Sykes
David Sykes
Derek Sykes
Edward Carl Sykes
George Sykes
J D (Bill) Sykes
Maurice E F Sykes
Reuben Sykes
Roger Sykes, Amberley, New
Zealand
Mr S Sykes
Timothy Alan Sykes
John & Doreen Sylvester
Catherine Sylvester
John L Sylvester
Andrew C Sylvester
Malcolm & Margery Symonds
Mr Ross Taggart
Susan & Fred Tasker
Arthur Alan Taylor
Charles Taylor
G Alec Taylor
Geoffrey Taylor
Harry W Taylor
Joan Taylor
Leonard Sydney Taylor
Marian Taylor
Patricia Taylor
Mr R C S Taylor
Mr Richard Taylor
Stephanie Taylor
William F Taylor
Edgar Tebbs
Geoffrey Tee
Mr N Tennant
Terry Thake
Barbara Maurren Theakston
Dorothy Thickitt
Mr & Mrs J Thomas & Family
Marjorie Thomas (nee
Frankland)
Richard T Thomas
Mr V R Thomas
A C Thompson
Darwin C Thompson
Derek Thompson
Miss Emma Rachel Thompson
Henry Thompson

H L Thompson
Marcus Alan Thompson
Max Thompson
Sheila Thompson
Arthur Thornton
B & L A Thornton
Gerald Thornton
Mrs Kathleen Thornton
Mr Paul Thornton
Peter Thornton
Dr R & Mrs Thornton
R S V Thornton
Trevor Thornton
B Thorp
Alan Thorpe
Trevor Thorpe
Derek Thwaites
Edith D Tidman
G & L Tidswell
Conrad John Tindall
Donald Todd
Mrs J A C Todd
Malcolm L Toes
Jenny Tole
Keith Tomlinson
Trevor Tomlinson
Harold Toothill
Mr Alfred W Towers
Robin Towler
Miss M Audrey Town
Mrs N E Townend
Ann Townsend
D & C Tracey
Diane Trant
Maureen Treacy
Lynton M Tremayne
Bob & Joyce Treweek
John Triffitt
Barry Trotter
Mr Martin Tuer
Chris Tully
Jack Tunnicliffe
James Turley
G Nicholas Turner
Grace Honey Turner
Jack Turner
J M Turner
Mr & Mrs Peter Turner
Stella Margaret Turner
T Havelock Turner
Mrs Winifred Turner
Colin Tushingham
Sally & Andrew Tuxworth
Michael J R Twiddle
Reg Twigge
Mary Tyler
R G Tyson
Mark A Underwood
Thomas Michael Uren
Mr R F Usher
Joan Valentine
Mrs Doreen Vallance
Rachel Vallow
D & J Vane
Barbara Varley
Mr & Mrs Derek Vaux
Derek Waddilove
Graham & Mary Waddington
John K B Waddington

Robert Waddington
Christopher Steven Wade
Gary Wade
Norma & Trevor Wade
Kenneth Edwin Wadsworth
Mrs G R Wagstaff
John Raymond Wagstaff
Brenda Mary Waite
Richard Waite
A Wake
Revd. David Wakefield
Mr J & Mrs A Walder
Anthony J Walker
Betty M Walker
Carol Walker
Chris Walker
Christopher Walker
Edward Walker
Eric D Walker
G Edward Walker
Ian D Walker
Ian David Walker
J Keith Walker
Mrs Joan Walker
John M Walker
John P Walker
Maralyn Walker
Peter D Walker
Rex Walker
Mr S Glen Walker
Violet Walker
Winnie Walker
A V Walkley
Bryan & Madeline Wall
George Waller
Grace Waller
Linda Waller
Geoffrey Wallis
Heather Wallis
Mona Walls
Adrian Walmsley
Mr & Mrs J L Walmsley
N G Walmsley
Ellen Walsh
Miss I P Walsh
Jim Walsh
John Bell David Walsh
Brian Walshaw
Joan Colleen Walshe
Anne Walton
Mr & Mrs D A Walton
John (Jack) Walton
Leonard Walton
John David Warburton
Peter Warburton
Audrey Ward
David Ward
Eric Ward
Ian J Ward (Thorner)
Trever John Ward
Olive Ware
Margaret E Warren
Michael Warren
Michael Andrew Wass
Audrey Waterhouse
Audrey & Peter Waterhouse
Elizabeth & Timothy
Waterhouse
Alan S Watkinson

Stephen Watling
Mrs Audrey P Watson
Barrie Watson
Bob Watson
Dennis Watson
Edith Lucie Watson
Frederick George Watson
Geoffrey H Watson
Mr P Watson
Mrs Pat Watson
Robert M Watson
Mrs Thelma Watson
Valerie Watson
Anthony Graham Watts
Cynthia Watts
J Waudby
Mr P H Waugh
Robert Waugh
Mrs Mary Way
K Weatherall
B & J Weatherhead
Raymond Weatherhogg
John Weatherstone
J R Weatherstone
Mrs S A Weatherup
T & P Webb
Ian Webber
Mr & Mrs P Webster
W T Grenfell Webster
Mr J M Wedgwood
Bob Weightman
Mary E Welbourn
Clifford W Welburn
Di & Charles Welburn
Andrew and Vanessa Wellock
John Wells
Michael Welsh
Malcolm West
Stanley Westmoreland
Ken Wharton
Miss Melissa Wharton
R G & D B Wheeldon
Ron Wheldrick
Brian Whitaker
Doreen Whitaker
Brenda & Reg White
Clive White
David & Maria White
Michael White
Pamela H White
Rachel Mary White
Mrs G Whitehead
Iris Whitehead
Mollie Whitehead
Peter Whiteoak
H E Whitewick
Jean Whitfield
Michael S Whitham
Sandra Whitson
J P V Whittaker
P T Whittaker
Peter Whittell
In memory of Thomas Alan
Whittington
Brian Whittle
Sam & Betty Whitworth
Alan Widdop
Mrs M Wigglesworth
Matt & Debs Wightman

Mr F R Wilcock
Miss J Wilcock
Harry Wilcock
Ron Wilcock
Mrs K Wilcox
Charles G Wild
S A Wild
Sheila Wild
Simon Wilde
John Anthony Wilding
Dorothy Wilkins
Mr Colin M R Wilkinson
David Wilkinson
Keith Wilkinson
Miss M Wilkinson
Margaret Wilkinson
(nee Crossley)
Mr & Mrs M S Wilkinson
S Wilkinson
Derrick N Willey
Jackie Williams
John Williams
Arnold Williamson
Barrie Williamson
George Williamson
Joyce Williamson
Mary Williamson
James Derek Willis
Nathaniel Willmer
G M Willmott
Harry Wilman

Mrs A Wilson
Charles Arthur Wilson
David G Wilson
Desmond G Wilson
Dorothy Wilson
Jack Wilson
Mrs J D Wilson
Mrs Joan Wilson
John Wilson
Mr K Wilson
Kellie Jay Wilson
Mavis Amy Wilson
Mrs M L Wilson
Nigel Wilson
Sheila Wilson
Trevor Wilson
Winburn Glass Norfolk
Mr Trevor Windsor
Ann Winduss
Ian & Sheila Winduss
Edward A Winpenny
Philip Winter
John Winterburn
Sue Wishart
C M Womersley
A S Wood
D Wood
David P Wood
Gerald Wood
Mrs Grace Anne Wood
Helen Wood

James R Wood
Mr J R Wood
Mrs M Y Wood
Nelly Wood
Mrs Edna Woodbridge
N T Woodcock
Jeffrey Woodward
Nancy Wooler
Andrew James Woolfoot
Derek Wooller
Barbara M Woolley
James Woolley
Jim Wormald
Mrs J M Wormald
Roger Worsdall
Elaine Worsley
Raymond Worsnop
Kathryn Worthington
Mr T M Wragg
Mr Michael Wren
Andrew S Wright
C G Wright
Colin R Wright
Daphne Wright
David Wright
David V Wright
Edward Wright
Eric Francis Noel Wright
Mrs G Wright
Garrick Wright
Jean and Ian Wright

Mr John Winston Wright
Joyce Wright
Lesley Wright
Mike Wright
Rachael Wright
Simon Aubrey Wright
Thomas G R Wright
Ernest Wriglesworth
Mrs Betty Wrigley
Jack & Doreen Wuest
Fred Wyatt
Liz Yates
Mrs Margaret Erica Yates
Mr & Mrs M G Yeadon
City of York Libraries
Gillian Youdan
Mrs V H Youell
Anne Young (nee Spooner)
Barbara Young
Miss E A Young
Malcolm Young
M W I Yule
Betty
David & Victoria
Grandma Norma & Grandad
Ken
Sue & Paul
Winnie